Red Hat® Linux® 7.2 Weekend Crash Course™

Naba Barkakati

Kurt Wall

Hungry Minds™

Best-Selling Books • Digital Downloads • e-Books • Answer Networks • e-Newsletters • Branded Web Sites • e-Learning

Cleveland, OH • Indianapolis, IN • New York, NY

Red Hat® Linux® 7.2 Weekend Crash Course™

Published by
Hungry Minds, Inc.
909 Third Avenue
New York, NY 10022
www.hungryminds.com

Library of Congress Control Number: 2001092935

ISBN: 0-7645-3642-7

Printed in the United States of America

10 9 8 7 6 5 4 3 2 1

1B/RU/RR/QR/IN

Distributed in the United States by Hungry Minds, Inc.

Distributed by CDG Books Canada Inc. for Canada; by Transworld Publishers Limited in the United Kingdom; by IDG Norge Books for Norway; by IDG Sweden Books for Sweden; by IDG Books Australia Publishing Corporation Pty. Ltd. for Australia and New Zealand; by TransQuest Publishers Pte Ltd. for Singapore, Malaysia, Thailand, Indonesia, and Hong Kong; by Gotop Information Inc. for Taiwan; by ICG Muse, Inc. for Japan; by Intersoft for South Africa; by Eyrolles for France; by International Thomson Publishing for Germany, Austria, and Switzerland; by Distribuidora Cuspide for Argentina; by LR International for Brazil; by Galileo Libros for Chile; by Ediciones ZETA S.C.R. Ltda. for Peru; by WS Computer Publishing Corporation, Inc., for the Philippines; by Contemporanea de Ediciones for Venezuela; by Express Computer Distributors for the Caribbean and West Indies; by Micronesia Media Distributor, Inc. for Micronesia; by Chips Computadoras S.A. de C.V. for Mexico; by Editorial Norma de Panama S.A. for Panama; by American Bookshops for Finland.

For general information on Hungry Minds' products and services please contact our Customer Care department within the U.S. at 800-762-2974, outside the U.S. at 317-572-3993 or fax 317-572-4002.

For sales inquiries and reseller information, including discounts, premium and bulk quantity sales, and foreign-language translations, please contact our Customer Care department at 800-434-3422, fax 317-572-4002 or write to Hungry Minds, Inc., Attn: Customer Care Department, 10475 Crosspoint Boulevard, Indianapolis, IN 46256.

For information on licensing foreign or domestic rights, please contact our Sub-Rights Customer Care department at 212-884-5000.

For information on using Hungry Minds' products and services in the classroom or for ordering examination copies, please contact our Educational Sales department at 800-434-2086 or fax 317-572-4005.

For press review copies, author interviews, or other publicity information, please contact our Public Relations department at 317-572-3168 or fax 317-572-4168.

For authorization to photocopy items for corporate, personal, or educational use, please contact Copyright Clearance Center, 222 Rosewood Drive, Danvers, MA 01923, or fax 978-750-4470.

Credits

Acquisitions Editor
Terri Varveris

Project Editor
Valerie Haynes Perry

Technical Editor
Joseph Traub

Copy Editor
Valerie Haynes Perry

Project Coordinator
Nancee Reeves

Graphics and Production Specialists
Joyce Haughey, Kristin Pickett,
Betty Schulte, Brian Torwelle

Permissions Editor
Laura Moss

Proofreading and Indexing
TECHBOOKS Production Services

About the Authors

Naba Barkakati is an expert programmer and successful computer-book author who has experience in a wide variety of systems, ranging from MS-DOS and Windows to UNIX and the X Window System. Over the past 12 years, Naba has written 25 computer books on a number of topics ranging from C++ programming to Linux. He has authored several best-selling titles, such as *The Waite Group's Turbo C++ Bible*, *Object-Oriented Programming in C++*, *X Window System Programming*, *Visual C++ Developer's Guide*, and *Borland C++ 4 Developer's Guide*. Naba's most recent book is the best-selling *Red Hat Linux 7.1 Secrets*, also published by Hungry Minds.

Naba lives in North Potomac, Maryland, with his wife Leha and their children Ivy, Emily, and Ashley.

Kurt Wall has been using and programming Linux and UNIX since 1993. Kurt is the author of two editions of Linux Programming Unleashed and Linux Programming by Example. Additionally, he has contributed chapters to The Informix Handbook, The Linux Bible, and forthcoming titles on Linux clustering, Linux performance tuning and capacity planning, and Microsoft Access database development. Kurt is does the technical editor for a wide variety of Linux titles.

Naba Barkakati
This book is dedicated to my wife Leha and
daughters Ivy, Emily, and Ashley.

Kurt Wall
I humbly dedicate this book to the light
of my life, Her Royal Highness M.M.J.

Acknowledgments

Naba Barkakati

I am grateful to Terri Varveris for giving me the opportunity to write the *Red Hat Linux Weekend Crash Course* — a guide that teaches Red Hat Linux over a weekend.

Thanks to everyone at Hungry Minds, Inc. for transforming the raw manuscript into this well-edited and beautifully packaged book.

Of course, there would be no reason for this book if it were not for Linux. For this, I have Linus Torvalds and the legions of Linux developers around the world to thank. Thanks also to Red Hat for providing a copy of Red Hat Linux for this book.

Finally, and as always, my greatest thanks go to my wife, Leha, and our daughters, Ivy, Emily, and Ashley — it is their love and support that keeps me going. Thanks for being there!

Kurt Wall

Like Naba, I appreciate Terri Varveris' confidence in my ability to write this book. Thanks to Valerie Haynes Perry, the whole thing ran smoothly. The entire team at Hungry Minds, Inc. deserves thanks — turning a marked-up manuscript into a real book with text, graphics, an index, and covers is no small task.

I share Naba's gratitude to Linus Torvalds and the development community around him. Linux is a remarkable phenomenon, and I am proud to be associated with it.

I am honored to have worked with Naba. I learned C++ from him, or rather, from one of his books because it was the course textbook. What a privilege and how satisfying it is to work with someone from whom I have learned! Thanks, Naba!

She will be embarrassed to be mentioned here, but someone entered my life while I worked on this book and unknowingly kept me going. M.M.J., I will spend the rest of my life showing you how much I love you.

Neither Naba nor I would be able to do this were if not for readers. Thanks to you all!

Finally, and above all, I thank God for giving me the desire and the ability to write and the opportunity to do so.

Contents at a Glance

Contents

Introduction

Because of Linux's increasing popularity, many computer users want to learn it quickly. Red Hat Linux is the dominant Linux distribution used in businesses large and small. If you work for an organization that is interested in Red Hat Linux, you need to get up to speed on how to install, configure, use, and manage Red Hat Linux systems. The best way to do so is to install Red Hat Linux and interactively learn its commands and applications. What potential Linux aficionados — beginners to advanced ones alike — need is a well-organized set of sessions that teach them Red Hat Linux over a weekend.

This *Red Hat Linux 7.2 Weekend Crash Course* is such a teaching guide. It provides 30 easy-to-use sessions, each a half an hour long, that gradually build up your Linux skills. These sessions are designed for you to complete over a weekend. They start with Red Hat Linux installation on Friday evening and end with several system administration topics on Sunday afternoon.

The crash course's pace is fast. Each session starts with a "Session Checklist," which is a short list of topics that you learn within the session through hands-on exercises. Each session ends with a "Quiz Yourself" section that enables you to test your new skills by answering some questions. Each major part corresponds with a time during the weekend, and the book includes Part Review questions that cover what was taught in the sessions within that part. You can try answering the Part Review questions and check your answers in Appendix A.

This book includes CD-ROMs with the latest version of Red Hat Linux. You can install Red Hat Linux by following the instructions in Sessions 1 through 3, and then you can use the program throughout the rest of the book.

What You Need to Get Started

To start the sessions, you need a PC on which you can install Red Hat Linux. The minimum system requirements for the PC are Intel 486 or Pentium-compatible processor, 32 MB RAM, 1 GB of disk space, 3.5-inch floppy drive, and a CD-ROM drive. For some of the other sessions, you need an Ethernet networking card, a modem, and Internet access. You also need a free weekend to go through all the sessions.

Organization of the Book

Red Hat Linux 7.2 Crash Course has 30 sessions, organized into six parts. It also has two appendixes.

Part I: Friday Evening guides you through the steps needed to install Red Hat Linux from this book's companion CD-ROMs and gets you through the first login to the newly installed system. Assuming that the installation program recognizes most of the hardware, you should be able to finish the installation in an hour or so.

Part II: Saturday Morning focuses on trying out Red Hat Linux quickly, customizing the GNOME and KDE graphical environments, exploring files and directories, learning some Linux commands and text editors, and performing some basic system administration tasks

Part III: Saturday Afternoon shows you how to set up networking (assuming the PC has an Ethernet card) and connect the Linux PC to the Internet (dial-up PPP, but briefly discusses xDSL and cable modem as well). Some of the lessons show how to use the Linux system in a networked environment as an Internet server (Web, e-mail) or as a Windows file server that uses Samba.

Part IV: Saturday Evening teaches you how to use the GNOME and KDE desktops as well as some of the applications that come bundled with Red Hat Linux.

Part V: Sunday Morning introduces you to various system administration tasks, such as configuring X, learning the Linux boot sequence, installing new software packages from RPM and tar files, building a new kernel, scheduling jobs to run at specific times, and performing system backups.

Part VI: Sunday Afternoon focuses on skills that a Linux system administrator should have. The afternoon starts with a lesson on how to use the programming tools to compile and build a new software package. Then it covers system performance monitoring, security, and obtaining further help.

Appendix A: Answers to Part Reviews provides answers to the Part Review Questions that appear after each of the six parts.

Appendix B: What's on the CD-ROM? describes the contents of the accompanying CD-ROMs.

If you are a new user, you should start with Part I, which covers the installation of Red Hat Linux from the CD-ROM. Then you can continue sequentially through the sessions. If you already installed Red Hat Linux, skip to Part II on Saturday morning.

Conventions Used in This Book

Red Hat Linux 7.2 Weekend Crash Course uses a simple notational style. All listings, filenames, function names, variable names, keywords, and Web addresses are typeset in a `monospace` font for ease of reading. The first occurrences of new terms and concepts are in *italics*. Text that you are directed to enter is in **bold** and `monospace` type combined.

Sidebars

Occasionally, we use sidebars to highlight interesting (but not critical) information. Sidebars explain concepts you may not have encountered before or give a little insight into a related topic. If you're in a hurry, you can safely skip the sidebars. On the other hand, if you find yourself flipping through the book looking for interesting information, we encourage you to read the sidebars.

The following icons help you quickly pinpoint useful information:

 The Note icon marks a general, interesting fact — something that we thought you'd like to know.

 The Tip icon marks shortcuts or methods that you can follow to make your job easier.

 The Never icon highlights potential pitfalls. With this icon, we are telling you: "Watch out! This could hurt your system!"

 The Cross-Reference icon points out other sessions in the book that discuss a specific topic — or to specific programs available on the CD-ROMs.

Each session also contains four time-oriented icons that let you know how you are progressing:

30 Min.   **20 Min.**   **10 Min.**   **Done!**
To Go   **To Go**   **To Go**

Reach Out

The publisher and authors would like your feedback. After you have had a chance to use this book, please take a moment to register this book on the http://my2cents. idgbooks.com Web site.

Also, feel free to contact us directly at:

naba@ieee.org
kwall@kurtwerks.com

Red Hat® Linux® 7.2
Weekend Crash Course™

☑ **Friday**

☐ Saturday

☐ Sunday

PART

I

*Friday
Evening*

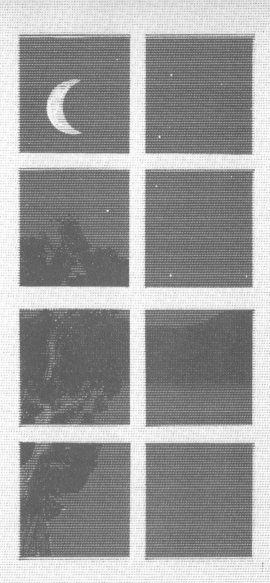

Installing Red Hat Linux

Session Checklist

✔ Taking stock of your PC's components

✔ Creating a Red Hat boot disk

✔ Installing Red Hat Linux

**30 Min.
To Go**

This evening's sessions guide you through installing Red Hat Linux using this book's companion CD-ROMs; troubleshooting a few common installation problems; and taking a first Red Hat Linux test drive. Assuming that the installation program recognizes most of your PC's hardware, you should finish the installation in an hour or so. By the end of the third session, you will have Red Hat Linux installed on your PC and will have begun to familiarize yourself with the GNOME and KDE desktops.

This session highlights key points and concepts of the standard Red Hat installation procedure to help you get started. For detailed, step-by-step installation procedures, we defer to the authoritative guide on the subject, *The Official Red Hat Linux Installation Guide*, available online at http://www.redhat.com/support/manuals/.

Checking If Red Hat Linux Supports Your PC Hardware

Before starting the installation, make sure Red Hat Linux supports your PC's hardware. At a minimum, you must have a Linux-compatible CPU, bus type, disk drive, video card, monitor, keyboard, mouse, and CD-ROM drive to install Red Hat Linux from the companion CD-ROMs. If you want to run the X Window System and graphical desktops such as GNOME or KDE, you also must ensure that XFree86 (the X Window System for Linux) supports your mouse, video card, and monitor. Perform the following steps to confirm that Red Hat Linux supports your PC's hardware:

1. Gather the make, model, and other technical details of all hardware installed on your PC. This is your hardware inventory. If you use Windows 95/98, double-click the System icon in the Control Panel, and then select the Device Manager tab to gather some of this information.

2. With your hardware inventory in hand, visit Red Hat's Web site at http://www. redhat.com/hardware. This Web site contains a list of hardware that the latest version of Red Hat Linux supports. Check your PC's hardware against that list and make sure that Red Hat Linux supports the key hardware components.

If you have a network card and your Linux PC is or will be part of a local area network (LAN), you should also gather the following information needed to configure the network:

- The PC's host name and the network's domain name
- Internet Protocol (IP) address of the PC; or, if the IP address is provided by a Dynamic Host Configuration Protocol (DHCP) server, the server's address
- The gateway, broadcast, and netmask addresses
- The addresses of the network's name servers

If you plan to use Linux on a stand-alone PC at home, you can use Point-to-Point Protocol (PPP) to connect to the Internet over a dial-up connection through an Internet Service Provider (ISP).

Creating the Red Hat Boot Disk

**20 Min.
To Go**

Assuming you have compatible hardware, the next step is to create a Red Hat boot disk if your PC does not support bootable CD-ROMs. The Red Hat Linux installation CD is bootable, so if your PC can boot from a CD-ROM, skip ahead to the next section, "Repartitioning Your Hard Drive with FIPS." Otherwise, read on. After installing Red Hat Linux, you no longer need the Red Hat boot disk.

You do not need a boot disk if you can start your PC under MS-DOS. Access the CD-ROM from the DOS command prompt.

Creating the Red Hat boot disk involves using a utility program called RAWRITE.EXE to copy a special file called the Red Hat Linux boot image to a disk.

To create the Red Hat boot disk under Windows, follow these steps:

1. Open an MS-DOS window (select Start ➪ Programs ➪ MS-DOS Prompt).
2. In the MS-DOS window, enter the following commands at the MS-DOS prompt. Replace d: with the drive letter of you CD-ROM. Your input is in bold text:

   ```
   d:
   cd \dosutils
   rawrite
   ```

```
Enter disk image source file name: \images\boot.img
Enter target diskette drive: a
Please insert a formatted diskette into drive A: and press -ENTER- :
```

3. As instructed, you should put a formatted disk into your PC's A: drive and then press Enter. RAWRITE.EXE copies the boot-image file to the disk.

After you see the DOS prompt again, you can take the Red Hat boot disk out of the A: drive and (if you haven't done so already) label it appropriately.

Repartitioning Your Hard Drive with FIPS

Once you have a Red Hat boot disk, if necessary, your next task is to make room on your hard disk for Red Hat Linux by partitioning your hard disk. There are two ways to repartition your hard disk:

- Destroy the existing partition and create two smaller, new partitions — one for Windows and the other for Red Hat Linux. This requires you to back up and restore the existing Windows files. This is the hard way to repartition a hard disk.
- Use the *FIPS (First Nondestructive Interactive Partition Splitting)* utility program (included on the companion CD-ROMs) to resize the existing partition and free up space for a second partition in which you can install Red Hat Linux without destroying your existing data. You can also use a commercial disk partitioning software such as PartitionMagic from PowerQuest (http://www.powerquest.com/partition-magic/index.html).

No matter which approach you take to repartition your hard disk, do not perform this step before you back up the current contents of your hard disk.

In this section, I show you how to repartition your hard disk using FIPS to create room for the Linux partition. During Red Hat Linux installation, you have to further divide the partition meant for Linux into at least two parts: one for the Linux root file system and the other for swap space.

The Linux directory tree is also known as the *file system*.

The FIPS.EXE program and related files are located in the \DOSUTIL subdirectory of the companion CD-ROMs. To use FIPS, follow these steps:

1. Use SCANDISK.EXE or another disk repair tool to make sure there are no errors on the disk.
2. Defragment the disk. How you defragment the hard disk depends on your current operating system. For example, in Windows 95/98, select Start ⇨ Programs ⇨ Accessories ⇨ System Tools ⇨ Disk Defragmenter.

3. In MS-DOS 6.0 or later, create a bootable disk using the command FORMAT A: /S. In Windows 95/98, create a startup disk by using the Add/Remove Programs option in the Control Panel and then following the instructions in the Startup Disk tab.

4. Copy the following files from the CD-ROM to the formatted disk. (The following example assumes that D: is the CD-ROM drive.)

    ```
    COPY D:\DOSUTILS\FIPS.EXE A:
    COPY D:\DOSUTILS\RESTORRB.EXE A:
    COPY D:\DOSUTILS\FIPSDOCS\ERRORS.TXT A:
    ```

    FIPS.EXE is the program that splits partitions. ERRORS.TXT is a list of FIPS error messages. You consult this list for an explanation of any error messages displayed by FIPS. RESTORRB.EXE, which is a program that enables you to restore certain important parts of your hard disk from a backup of those areas created by FIPS.

5. Leave the bootable disk in the A: drive, and restart the PC. The PC boots from A: and displays the A\> prompt.

6. Type FIPS. The FIPS program runs and shows you information about your hard disk. FIPS gives you an opportunity to save a backup copy of important disk areas before proceeding. After that, FIPS displays the first free cylinder where the new partition can start (as well as the size of the partition in megabytes).

7. Use the left- and right-arrow keys to adjust the starting cylinder of the new partition (the one that results from splitting the existing partition) to change the partition size. Press the right arrow to increase the starting cylinder number. This leaves more room in the existing partition and reduces the size of the new partition you create. Try to create a new partition that is 1GB or larger.

8. When you are satisfied with the size of the new partition, press Enter. FIPS displays the modified partition table and prompts you to enter **C** to continue or **R** to reedit the partition table.

9. Press **C** to continue. FIPS displays some information about the disk and asks whether you want to write the new partition information to the disk.

10. Press **Y**. FIPS writes the new partition table to the hard disk and then exits.

11. Remove the disk from the A: drive and reboot the PC.

When the system comes up, everything in your hard disk should be intact — but the C: drive will be smaller. You have created a new, unformatted partition from the unused parts of the old C: drive. During the Red Hat Linux installation, you will format it and set it up for use with Linux.

Starting the Red Hat Linux Installation

To start the Red Hat Linux installation, put the first CD-ROM into the caddy, the Red Hat boot disk in the A: drive if you need it, and restart the computer. When it restarts, your PC loads Red Hat Linux from the boot disk and starts the Red Hat installation program, called Anaconda.

If the CD-ROM is not in the drive when you reboot, the installer will start in text mode and prompt you for the CD-ROM. Only then will it start the X Window System and switch to a graphical installation screen.

After a few moments, the screen displays a Welcome message and ends with a boot: prompt. The Welcome message tells you that more information is available by pressing one of the function keys from F1 through F5. To start installing Red Hat Linux immediately, press Enter.

Installing Red Hat Linux from the companion CD-ROMs on a fast (200MHz or better) Pentium PC should take less than an hour, even if you install nearly all of the packages. For example, on a 266MHz Pentium PC with 128MB of RAM and a 2GB-disk partition devoted to Red Hat Linux, the installation takes about 45 minutes. On older PCs or PCs with less RAM or larger Linux partitions, the installation process will take somewhat longer. These time estimates also do not include checking for bad blocks on the installation disks, which will increase the duration of the installation process considerably.

Partitioning the Hard Disk for Red Hat Linux

Before you can install any software, you must prepare the empty partition you created using FIPS for Red Hat Linux. This involves subdividing the empty partition into at least two parts and formatting one of the parts for the Linux file system, called ext2. You can let the installer do this automatically, or you can perform the task manually using Disk Druid — a utility program that enables you to partition the disk and, at the same time, specify which parts of the Linux file system you want to load on which partition. Our example uses the simplest configuration: one small swap partition (see "Understanding swap partitions," later in this session for more information) and a large partition that contains all the files.

Before you begin to use Disk Druid to partition your disk, you need to know how to refer to the disk drives and partitions in Linux. Also, you should understand the terms *mount points* and *swap partition*. In the next three sections, you learn these terms and concepts and then proceed to use Disk Druid.

Naming disks and devices

The first step in partitioning the hard disk is to understand how Red Hat Linux refers to the various disks. Linux treats all devices as files and has actual files that represent each device. In Red Hat Linux, these *device files* are located in the /dev directory. Because Linux treats a device as a file in the /dev directory, the hard disk names start with /dev. Table 1-1 lists the hard disk and floppy drive names that you may have to use.

Table 1-1
Hard Disk and Floppy Drive Names

Name	Description
/dev/hda	First Integrated Drive Electronics (IDE) hard drive (the C: drive in DOS and Windows)

(continued)

Table 1-1 *Continued*

Name	Description
/dev/hdb	Second IDE hard drive (the D: drive in DOS and Windows)
/dev/sda	First Small Computer System Interface (SCSI) drive
/dev/sdb	Second SCSI drive
/dev/fd0	First floppy drive (the A: drive in DOS)
/dev/fd1	Second floppy drive (the B: drive in DOS)

When Disk Druid displays the list of partitions, the partition names take the form hda1, hda2, and so on. Linux constructs each partition name by appending to the disk's name the partition number — 1 through 4 for the four primary partitions on a hard disk. Therefore, if your PC's single IDE hard drive has two partitions, notice that the installation program uses hda1 and hda2 as the names of these partitions.

Mounting a file system on a device

In Red Hat Linux, you use a physical disk partition by associating it with a specific part of the file system. This is a hierarchical arrangement of directories known as a *directory tree*. If you have more than one disk partition (you may have a second disk with a Linux partition), you can use all of them in Red Hat Linux under a single directory tree. All you have to do is decide which part of the Linux directory tree should be located on each partition — a process known in Linux as *mounting a file system on a device*. (The disk partition is a device.)

A *mount point* is the directory associated with a disk partition.

Suppose that you have two disks on your PC, and you have created Linux partitions on both disks. Figure 1-1 illustrates how you can mount different parts of the Linux directory tree (the file system) on these two partitions.

For simplicity's sake, our installation example uses one partition, a configuration that is not ideal, as you will learn in Session 5.

Understanding swap partitions

Linux uses a *virtual memory* system, meaning it can use part of your system's hard disk as an extension of the physical memory (RAM). When Linux runs out of physical memory, it can move (or *swap out*) currently unneeded parts of RAM to make room for a program that needs more memory. If Linux needs to access anything in the swapped-out data, it finds something else to swap out and then swaps in the required data from the disk. This process of swapping data back and forth between the RAM and the disk is also known as *paging*.

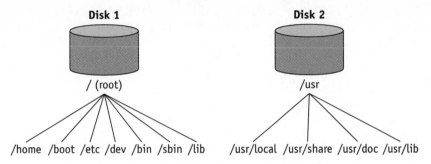

A Linux Filesystem Distributed Across 2 Disk Drives

Figure 1-1   *An example of mounting the Red Hat Linux file system on two disk partitions*

During the Red Hat Linux installation process, you will create a swap partition using Disk Druid. Follow the onscreen prompts, mark a partition type as a swap device, and Disk Druid will perform the necessary tasks.

Preparing disk partitions for Red Hat Linux

When the installer prompts you for the method you want to use to partition the disk, select Disk Druid and click the Next button. You should then see the Disk Druid screen (shown in Figure 1-2).

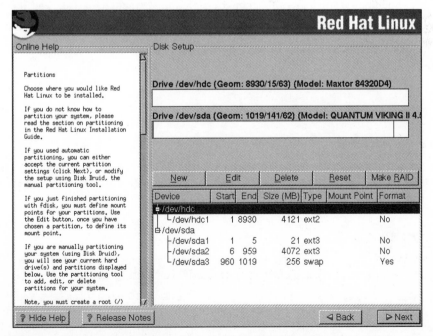

Figure 1-2   *Disk Druid screen from Red Hat Linux installation program*

Disk Druid's interface is a little intimidating at first, but it has ample context-sensitive help and prevents you from making silly mistakes that might destroy all the data on your disk. Create a swap partition up to twice the size of the amount of installed RAM, then use the remaining free space as the Linux root partition.

After you finish specifying the partitions in Disk Druid, the Red Hat installation program displays a screen listing the partitions that you may have to format for use in Linux. The list only shows Linux partitions; you do not format the swap partition.

To format a partition, click the button next to the partition's name. You should also click the button next to the item marked Check for bad blocks while formatting so that the formatting process marks any areas of the disk that may be defective physically. If you do enable checking for bad blocks, the installation will take considerably longer than the estimates given earlier in the session.

Configuring Red Hat Linux

*10 Min.
To Go*

With partitioning and formatting out of the way, you are *almost* ready to start installing software. First, the installer prompts you to set a few key system parameters: where to install the boot loader, providing network information (if applicable), defining your time zone, and setting authentication (login) information.

Install LILO

LILO, which stands for *Linux Loader,* is a *boot loader,* a program that starts operating systems after the PC hardware has booted. LILO can load Windows 95/98, if it is installed. For systems with Windows 95/98 and Red Hat Linux residing on a single hard disk, Red Hat recommends installing LILO on the master boot record.

Session 24 covers LILO in more detail.

Configure the network

Assuming the Linux kernel detected a network card, the Red Hat installation program displays the Network Configuration screen that enables you to configure the LAN parameters for your Linux system. This step is *not* for configuring dial-up networking.

Set the time zone

After completing the network configuration, select your time zone, making sure to check the box near the bottom of the screen that says your PC clock uses local time.

Set the root password and add user accounts

The next screen you will see is the Account Configuration screen. You must select a password for the root user and add at least one normal user account. The root user is the *super user* in Linux and can do almost anything on the system. Assign a password that you can remember — but that others cannot guess easily. The password should be at least eight characters long, include a mix of upper- and lowercase letters and numbers, and at least one special characters such as + or *. Passwords are case sensitive.

To add a user account, fill in the Account Name, Password, and Full Name fields, and then click the Add button. The new account information then appears in the table underneath the Add button. You do not have to add all the user accounts at this time.

Session 10 explains how to add user accounts.

Configure password authentication

The installation program displays a screen from which you can configure the password authentication options. There are several options that you can enable or disable. You should use the default settings for increased system security. Click the Next button to proceed to the next configuration step.

Selecting the Package Groups to Install

After you complete the key configuration steps, the installation program displays a screen from which you can select the Red Hat Linux package groups that you want to install. After you select the package groups, take a coffee break while Anaconda installs Red Hat Linux. You may have to insert the second CD-ROM, so check back occasionally.

Completing the Installation

After all the software is installed, some final configuration tasks are taken care of, and an emergency boot disk is created, the installer will prompt you to reboot the system. After clicking the OK button, remove the CD-ROM and the floppy disk from their drives.

Done!

REVIEW

This session covered verifying your hardware's compatibility with Red Hat Linux, creating a boot disk, partitioning your hard disk, and briefly explained how Linux uses disk partitions. Finally, the session described the major milestones of the actual Red Hat Linux installation.

QUIZ YOURSELF

1. Where can you find a list of hardware that Red Hat Linux supports? (See "Checking If Red Hat Linux Supports Your PC Hardware.")

2. If your PC has a network card, what parameters do you need to configure the network? (See "Checking If Red Hat Linux Supports Your PC Hardware.")

3. What do you do with the Red Hat boot disk? (See "Creating the Red Hat Boot Disk.")

4. What is FIPS and what can you do with it? (See "Repartitioning Your Hard Drive with FIPS.")

5. What is Disk Druid and what are you supposed to do with it? (See "Partitioning the Hard Disk for Red Hat Linux.")

Troubleshooting the Red Hat Linux Installation

Session Checklist

✔ Installing Red Hat Linux in text mode

✔ Installing Red Hat Linux in expert mode

✔ Configuring the X Window System

✔ Configuring printers

✔ Getting help with the Red Hat Linux installation

**30 Min.
To Go**

This session discusses methods for solving the most common installation and configuration problems. In most cases, the Red Hat Linux installation program, Anaconda, works just fine, correctly detecting and configuring key hardware components, such as SCSI controllers and network cards. However, if Anaconda cannot detect or configure a component properly, it skips that step. For example, if Anaconda fails to detect the network card correctly, it skips the network configuration step. The installation program also tries to simplify the installation by skipping some system configuration steps such as setting up a printer. You can recover from most of the installation and configuration problems because there are other ways to perform these tasks. This session also lists some of the resources available if you encounter installation problems you cannot solve.

Installing Red Hat Linux in Text Mode

The Red Hat installation program attempts to use a minimal X Window System to display the graphical user installation screens. If the program fails to detect a video card, X does not start. If, for any reason, X fails to start, you can always fall back on the older text mode installation program to configure the video card manually. You can also use the text mode installation if you are comfortable with the older installation program.

To use text mode installation, type **text** at the boot: prompt after booting the Red Hat Linux installation CD. From then on, the basic installation procedure resembles the graphical installation described in Session 1, but small details differ. In particular, you cannot use the mouse and you will need to enter some configuration values manually that Anaconda handles automatically during a graphical installation. If you collected the hardware information described in the section "Checking if Red Hat Linux Supports Your PC Hardware" in Session 1, you should have no trouble responding to the prompts and performing the installation.

In text mode, when the installation program fails to detect the video card, it displays a list of video cards. Select one video card from the list. Because of your help in selecting the video card, X may work when you install in text mode. If it does not, you can configure X using the information in "Configuring the X Window System," later in this session.

In some cases, using the text mode installation will allow you to install Red Hat Linux on systems containing hardware not specifically mentioned in Red Hat's hardware compatibility lists. Sometimes, selecting similar hardware options for unsupported hardware may even work. These are not supported or recommended options, however, nor do they always work.

To see how the Red Hat installation program detects certain devices, you can also look at the messages the installer's kernel displays while it boots. To view these boot messages, press Ctrl+Alt+F4 to switch to a text-mode virtual console where the messages appear. A *virtual console* is a screen of text or graphical information stored in memory that you can view on the physical screen by pressing the appropriate key sequence (Shift+PageUp to scroll up and Shift+PageDown to scroll down). Look for messages that relate to the device in question. If all else fails, you can specify certain devices manually by running the installation in expert mode, discussed next.

Installing Red Hat Linux in Expert Mode

The *expert mode* installation enables you to control almost the entire installation process. Other installation modes hide some of the installation steps and use autodetection, and default values for hardware configuration.

To run the installation in expert mode, follow these steps:

1. Type **expert** at the boot: prompt in the initial text screen that appears during the Red Hat Linux installation. The installation program then displays another text screen that asks for a driver disk, if you have one.

2. Your hardware vendor may provide a floppy disk containing Linux drivers. If you have one, press Enter and a dialog box prompts you to insert the disk into the A: drive. After you do so, press Enter, and the installation program loads the driver and guides you through the steps necessary to install the driver.

3. If you do not have a driver disk, select Cancel. The installation program then goes through two more screens in which you select the language and the keyboard layout. Then the installation program prompts for the media containing the packages to be installed.

4. Next, the installation program displays a dialog box that gives you another opportunity to add devices. Press Tab to highlight the Add Device button, and then

press Enter. The installation program then displays a dialog box that prompts for the type of device (SCSI or Network.

5. If you have any SCSI device, such as a SCSI hard drive, select SCSI and press Enter. Then, the installation program displays a list of SCSI controllers from which you should select the one on your system and press Enter. The installation program then loads that driver module.

   The SCSI driver automatically probes and determines the SCSI controller's settings, such as interrupt request (IRQ) and I/O port address. If the driver has problems detecting the SCSI controller's settings, you can specify these parameters manually. To do so, select the checkbox labeled Specify module parameters and press Enter. The installation program then prompts you for the module parameters.

6. You can then enter a line such as `aha152x=0x340,11,7` to specify the parameters for the driver module. (See the sidebar "Specifying SCSI Controller Settings," later in this session, for more information on these settings.)

7. After you add any SCSI controllers, you return to the dialog box that enables you to select a device type. You can add network cards from this dialog box as well. In the dialog box, select Network from the list and press Enter. The installation program then displays a list of network cards from which you can select your network card.

   When you press Enter, the installation program loads the driver module for the selected network card. That driver probes and determines the network card settings.

8. Once you return to the screen from which you select a SCSI or network device, select Back and press Enter. This takes you to the dialog box that asks you about adding devices. Select Done and press Enter. The installation program then switches to graphics mode and guides you through the rest of the installation, as explained in Session 1.

Specifying SCSI Controller Settings

If you have a SCSI controller in your system, the Red Hat installation program loads a SCSI driver module for that controller. You have to identify the type of SCSI controller (such as Adaptec 1542 or Adaptec 2940). The installation program can attempt to determine the controller settings, such as IRQ and I/O port address, by probing various I/O port addresses. However, if the installation program fails to determine the SCSI controller settings, you have to specify these parameters — IRQ and I/O address — as options for the driver module. The exact formats of these options vary from one module to another. For example, the driver for an Adaptec AHA 152x card accepts the options in the following format:

```
aha152x=IOPORT,IRQ,SCSI_ID[,Reconnect,Parity]
```

where *IOPORT* is the I/O port address, *IRQ* is the interrupt request number, and *SCSI_ID* is the SCSI ID of the SCSI controller. The last two items are optional. A typical module option for the aha152x module might be:

```
aha152x=0x340,11,7
```

Configuring the X Window System

**20 Min.
To Go**

If the installation program cannot detect your video card during the X configuration step, you can skip that step and configure X after completing the rest of the installation. Use the following procedure to configure X after the installation finishes:

1. After the installation is complete and you reboot the PC, you get a text login screen. Log in as root and type **Xconfigurator** to run a utility program with that name. The Xconfigurator utility enables you to create a configuration file that the X server needs.

2. The Xconfigurator program starts with a Welcome dialog box that displays a message about the X configuration file. After reading the message, press Enter to continue with the configuration process.

Xconfigurator automatically detects the chipset used by your video card and displays a summary message, as shown in Figure 2-1.

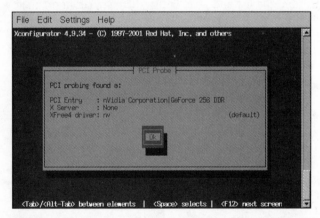

Figure 2-1   *The message that results from the Xconfigurator's probing of the video card*

In this case, Xconfigurator found a video card based on the nVidia GeForce 256 DDR chipset and recommends the nv XFree4 driver. The dialog box in Figure 2-1 is only an example, so the dialog box you see will likely be different. Make sure the Xconfigurator identifies the proper card, and then press Enter to continue with the rest of the configuration. The next dialog box you see enables you to select your monitor from a list.

Press the up- and down-arrow keys to browse through the list. If you find your monitor model listed, position the cursor on that monitor and then press Enter. Otherwise, select Custom and press Enter. If you choose Custom, Xconfigurator displays another dialog box in which you have to provide two critical parameters for your monitor:

- *Horizontal synchronization frequency* is the number of times per second that the monitor draws a horizontal line, in kilohertz (kHz).

- *Vertical synchronization rate* or vertical refresh rate is how many times per second the monitor draws the entire screen.

You can find the parameters for the frequencies in your monitor's manual or, in many cases, on the manufacturer's Web site. Press Enter to continue. Xconfigurator displays a list of predefined horizontal synchronization ranges.

 The values for the monitor synchronization rates should match your monitor's specifications. Do not guess! If you specify a rate that exceeds your monitor's actual capabilities, you may damage it.

For example, if your monitor's manual says that it is capable of displaying 1,280 by 1,024 resolution at 60Hz, then you should pick the item that matches this specification. After selecting the horizontal synchronization capabilities, press Enter.

Xconfigurator next prompts you for the vertical synchronization rate of your monitor. Pick the vertical synchronization range that is nearest to your monitor's specifications and press Enter.

If Xconfigurator is unable to detect the amount of video memory on your video card, it displays a dialog box that prompts you to select the amount of video memory from a list. Select the amount closest to your video card's memory and press Enter.

Xconfigurator prompts you to identify the clock chip — a timing device on the video card. You can safely press Enter to accept the default selection labeled No Clockchip Setting (recommended).

Xconfigurator then displays a Select Video Mode dialog box containing a list of video modes, combinations of pixel resolutions, such as 800 × 600 pixels or 1,280 × 1,024, and color depths, such as 16 or 24 bits per pixel, as shown in Figure 2-2. Your card or monitor will support only certain video modes, so refer again to your monitor manual if necessary.

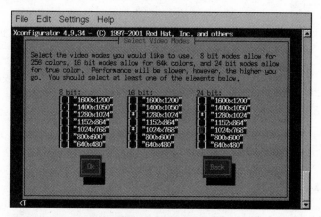

Figure 2-2 *Selecting one or more video modes*

Press Tab to move the cursor to a video mode and press the spacebar to select that mode. You can choose as many modes as you want. Then press Tab to select the OK button and press Enter.

Next, Xconfigurator gives you the option of starting X to test your configuration. You should press Enter. A graphical X screen appears and Xconfigurator shows a dialog box that asks if you can read the text. Click with the mouse to close the dialog box.

Finally, Xconfigurator writes the XF86Config-4 file in the /etc/X11 directory and exits. This completes the X configuration. The next time you reboot the PC, X should start and you should get a graphical login screen.

Configuring Printers

10 Min.
To Go

The Red Hat installation program does not include a printer configuration step. However, as long as the Linux kernel can detect your PC's parallel port, you can configure a printer from an X utility program. To see if Red Hat Linux detects the parallel port, type dmesg | grep par in a terminal window. Here is a typical output from that command:

```
dmesg | grep par
parport0: PC-style at 0x378 [SPP,PS2]
parport0: no IEEE-1284 device present.
lp0: using parport0 (polling)
```

The first line starts with parport0, indicating that Linux detected the parallel port. The text parport0 is "Linuxspeak" for parallel port zero, the first parallel port (LPT1 under DOS and Windows).

To set up printers, you must be running X. From the graphical login screen, log in as root and select Programs ⇨ System ⇨ Printer Configuration from the GNOME desktop. The printer configuration tool is named printconf-gui. Figure 2-3 illustrates its main window.

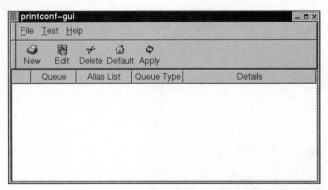

Figure 2-3   *printconf-gui enables you to manage printers.*

Click the New button to configure a new printer, which starts Red Hat's new printer configuration wizard. Click the Next button to start configuring the printer, which begins by selecting the type of printer and giving it a name, as shown in Figure 2-4. If the printer is attached to your PC, click Local Printer, and then click Next to continue.

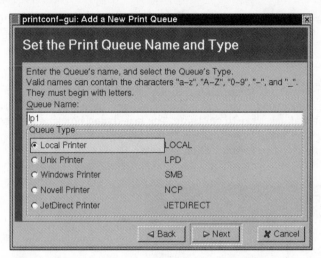

Figure 2-4   *Configuring a printer in printconf-gui*

In Figure 2-4, the local printer has been selected and the *queue,* the printer's name, has been set to lp1. The next step is specifying how you access the printer (see Figure 2-5).

 The lp1 **stands for Line Printer 1. Linux uses named** *printer queues* **to distinguish printers. Queues also serve as temporary holding areas for print jobs and the associated files that are sent to a specific printer.**

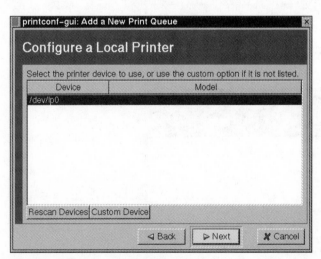

Figure 2-5   *Associating a printer name to a printer device in printconf-gui*

For this discussion, we assume that the printer is connected to your PC's parallel port. Select the device that corresponds to the parallel port to which your printer is attached — in most cases, this will be /dev/lp0, the Linux equivalent of the DOS/Windows LPT1 printer port. Click Next to continue.

Session 10 explains the Linux printing model and how to customize Red Hat Linux to get the best results from your printer.

In the next dialog box, Select a Print Driver, shown in Figure 2-6, scroll down the list until you find the manufacturer of your printer, click the name, and then select your printer and the corresponding driver file. Click Next to continue. The last dialog box summarizes the printer configuration you have made (see Figure 2-7). Review it to make sure it is correct, and then Finish to complete the configuration process.

Figure 2-6   *printconf-gui lists a large variety of printers from which to choose.*

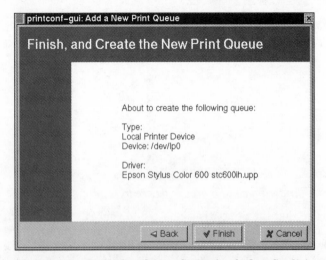

Figure 2-7   *Reviewing the configuration before finalizing it*

If everything has worked properly, you should see your printer listed in printconf-gui's display, as shown in Figure 2-8.

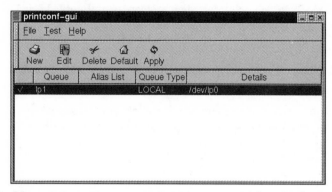

Figure 2-8   *The newly-configured printer appears in printconf-gui's main dialog box.*

The last step is to print a test page to confirm that the printer is properly configured. First, from the menu bar, select Test ⇨ Print ASCII Test Page to make sure that simple text prints properly, and then select Test ⇨ Print Postscript Test Page to confirm that images and other graphical elements print properly.

Getting Help with the Red Hat Linux Installation

Red Hat Linux installs on most PCs with supported hardware without incident. But, if you run into difficulties that neither a text mode nor an expert mode installation solve, experienced help is just a few clicks away. In fact, even if your installation runs flawlessly, you may find some of the following links and resources valuable and informative.

Red Hat makes their complete set of manuals available on the Web. For installation and initial configuration problems not addressed in these first two sessions, be sure to look at one or both of the following links:

The Official Red Hat Linux x86 Installation Guide: http://www.redhat.com/support/manuals/RHL-7.1-Manual/install-guide/

The Official Red Hat Linux Getting Started Guide: http://www.redhat.com/support/manuals/RHL-7.1-Manual/getting-started-guide/

These two guides are the authoritative references for installing Red Hat Linux and making basic customizations.

The Red Hat Knowledgebase at http://www.redhat.com/apps/support/ is another rich source of information. If you have had the problem, someone else probably has, too, so search for a solution using the Knowledgebase.

A third likely source of information is the product errrata and updates, available at http://www.redhat.com/apps/support/updates.html.

Finally, other Red Hat Linux users are sometimes the best source of information. The archives of Red Hat's mailing lists have a lot of useful information (and some not so useful information, too). Search the archives at `http://www.redhat.com/apps/support/` `updates.html` or, better still, subscribe to one of the mailing lists, yourself. A complete list and description are available at the previous URL.

In short, in the unlikely event you do encounter some problem installing Red Hat Linux, you can find out how to solve it in just a few clicks by taking advantage of the ample information available.

Done!

REVIEW

This session showed you how to overcome some common installation problems by running the installation in different modes. You learned how to use the text mode installation and how to use expert mode to install devices that the installation program does not detect. Finally, you learned how to configure X and printers.

QUIZ YOURSELF

1. How do you start the installation in text mode? (See "Installing Red Hat Linux in Text Mode.")
2. What do you do if the Red Hat installation program does not detect your network card? (See "Installing Red Hat Linux in Expert Mode.")
3. When would you configure the X Window System manually? (See "Configuring the X Window System.")
4. How do you start the utility program that enables you to configure printers? (See "Configuring Printers.")
5. What does it mean to "fix stair-stepping text"? (See "Configuring Printers.")

Test-Driving Red Hat Linux

Session Checklist

✔ Starting Red Hat Linux for the first time

✔ Logging in

✔ Logging out

✔ Understanding window managers

✔ Exploring GNOME

✔ Exploring KDE

✔ Shutting down Red Hat Linux

✔ Troubleshooting

**30 Min.
To Go**

Now that you have installed Red Hat Linux from this book's companion CD-ROMs, you are ready to explore and learn it. In this session, you first learn how to log in and log out. You take quick tours of the GNOME and KDE *graphical user interfaces (GUIs* — pronounced "goo-ease"), learn how to shut down a running Red Hat Linux system, and find out how to solve common startup and login problems.

Starting Red Hat Linux for the First Time

After the installation is complete, the Red Hat Linux installation program automatically reboots the system. The PC goes through its normal power-up sequence, loads LILO from the C: drive, and a screen appears with the names of the partitions that LILO can boot. If you do nothing, LILO proceeds to boot from the partition that was designated as the default when you configured LILO in Session 1. If you press Ctrl+X, the following prompt appears:

```
LILO boot:
```

Booting from Another Partition

If you want to boot from another partition (such as Windows), press the Tab key. LILO displays the names of the available bootable partitions. For example, a typical display might be:

```
linux dos
```

You can then type the name of the partition you want to boot (linux or dos, in this case) or press Enter to boot from the first partition, also referred to as the default partition.

When you install LILO, if you specify the Linux partition as the default, you can simply wait; after a few seconds, LILO boots Linux.

After LILO boots Linux, you should see a long list of opening messages — including the names of the devices that Linux detects. At the end of all the messages, you see a graphical login screen like the one in Figure 3-1.

Figure 3-1 *Graphical login screen in Red Hat Linux*

The window in the middle of the screen displays a welcome message with your system's host name — the name you assign to your system when you configure the network. If the network is not configured, localhost.localdomain is used as the host name. Now you can log into your new Red Hat login system for the first time.

Logging In

You can log in using any of the accounts, including root, which you define during the installation. For example, to log in as the user bubba, type bubba (move the mouse over the login window before you begin typing) in the text field and press Enter. Then type bubba's password, which you provided during installation (if you added accounts in addition to the root account), and you eventually see a screen resembling that shown in Figure 3-2).

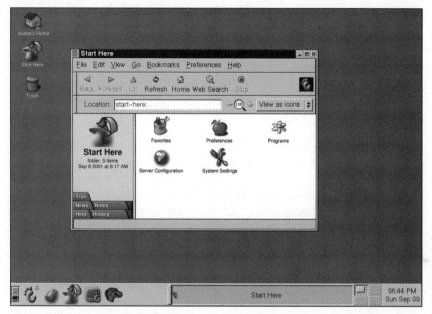

Figure 3-2   *Initial GNOME desktop after logging in as a normal (non-root) user*

You will explore the GNOME desktop in a few minutes. For now, I want to show you how to log out and shut down your Linux system.

Logging Out

Before you explore the GNOME GUI, you should learn how to log out. To do so, select Main menu — the stylized foot icon at the left edge of the GNOME Panel in the GNOME desktop (see Figure 3-2) — and then select Log Out from the menu. (The GNOME Panel is discussed later in this session under "Exploring GNOME.") The screen grays out and a dialog box prompts to see if you really want to log out and also to give you the option to halt or reboot the PC. Click the Yes button to log out. After a few moments, the graphical login screen (Figure 3-1) appears so that another user (or you again) can log in and use the system.

Understanding Window Managers

X Window, unlike other OS GUIs, such as OS/2 or Windows, relies on window managers to decorate windows. That is, X handles the mechanics of drawing windows and communicating between an X client (an application that runs in X) and the X server or another X client. X does nothing to decorate a window with pretty title bars, scrollbars, interpret mouse movement, keystrokes, and the like. All X does is provide a *protocol*, which consists of the rules or general framework that window managers must follow. Accordingly, a *window manager*, following the basic X protocol, creates title bars, scrollbars, menus, and so on, on the unadorned windows that X creates.

Why separate the functionality this way? One benefit is that doing so allows X to be device-, OS-, and network-protocol independent. Another advantage is that one particular part of the system, say, the window manager, can be modified simply by replacing the relevant component, without destabilizing or otherwise affecting the rest of the system.

Exploring GNOME

**20 Min.
To Go**

Now that you know how to log in and log out, log back in. You should again see the GNOME desktop because it is the default. In this section, you spend a few minutes exploring the GNOME desktop.

The exact appearance of the GNOME display depends on the current session. A *session* is nothing more than a set of applications (including a window manager) and the state of these applications. GNOME stores the session information in a file named session **in the** .gnome **subdirectory of your home directory. This is a text file; if you are curious, you can browse the file with the command** more ~/.gnome/session.

Don't worry about the syntax of the session **file right now. You'll learn more about Linux commands in Sessions 6, 7, and 8.**

The initial GNOME desktop (see Figure 3-2) produced by the default session description is very similar to the Windows 95/98/NT/2000 desktop. It includes the GNOME Panel, or simply the *panel* (similar to a Windows taskbar) and the Sawfish window manager, resulting in a desktop similar to the one shown in Figure 3-2.

What Is GNOME?

GNOME stands for *GNU Network Object Model Environment*. *GNU* stands for *GNU's Not UNIX*. GNOME is a graphical user interface (GUI) and a programming environment. From the user's perspective, GNOME is like the motif-based *Common Desktop Environment (CDE)* or Microsoft Windows. Behind the scenes, GNOME has many features that enable programmers to write graphical applications that can work together well. In this session, we point out some key features of the GNOME GUI and leave the details to you to explore on your own.

You can always find out the latest information about GNOME by visiting the GNOME home page at http://www.gnome.org.

The GNOME Panel is a key feature of the GNOME desktop The panel is a separate GNOME application. As Figure 3-3 shows, it provides a display area for menus and small panel applets. Each panel applet is a small program designed to work inside the panel. For example, the clock applet on the panel's far right displays the current time.

Figure 3-3 *The GNOME Panel*

As you can see from the icons appearing on the left side of the GNOME desktop (refer to Figure 3-2), GNOME enables you to place folders and applications directly on the desktop. This is similar to the way you can place icons directly on the Windows 95/98/NT/2000 desktop.

You can move and resize the windows just the way you do in Microsoft Windows. Also, as in the window frames in Microsoft Windows 95/98/NT/2000, the right-hand corner of the title bar includes three buttons. The leftmost button reduces the window to an icon, the middle button maximizes the window to fill up the entire screen, and the right-most button closes the window.

Notice the two outward-pointing arrows at the left and right ends of the panel. Click the arrow and see that the panel slides away, reducing its display area down to a small sliver along the edge of the screen. This frees up more desktop area for windows. Click the arrow again and the panel reappears.

The panel includes several other applets:

- **The GNOME pager applet:** This provides a virtual desktop that is larger than the physical dimensions of your system's screen. In Figure 3-3, the pager displays four pages in a small display area. Each page represents an area equal to the size of the X display screen. To go to a specific page, click that page in the pager window. The GNOME pager applet also displays buttons for each window that appears in the current virtual page.

- **Launcher applets:** These are the buttons to the right of the foot icon. Each applet displays a button with the icon of the application that the button starts. Clicking a button starts (launches) that application. Try clicking each of these buttons to see what happens. The question mark (?) button launches the GNOME Help Browser; the toolbox button launches the GNOME Control Center; the terminal icon launches a terminal window; and the earth icon launches Netscape Communicator. The lock icon starts the screen saver and requires you to enter the password to get back to the desktop.

- **Main Menu button:** The GNOME Panel also displays the Main Menu button that behaves like the Windows Start menu. This is the button at the left-hand side of the panel (see Figure 3-3) with the image of a stylized foot (the GNOME logo). That foot is the Main Menu button. As with the Start button in Windows 95/98/NT/2000, you can launch applications from the menu that pops up when you click the left mouse button on the foot. Typically, this pop-up menu lists items that start an application. Some of the menu items have an arrow. Another pop-up menu appears when you place the mouse pointer on an item with an arrow.

When time permits, you should explore all the items in the Main menu to see all the tasks that you can perform from it. At this point, select Main menu (foot) ⊏⟩ Log Out so you can begin a KDE session.

Exploring KDE

To try the KDE GUI, you must have installed the KDE package as part of the Red Hat Linux during Session 1. Typically, the installation program makes GNOME your default GUI. For now, you can change the GUI for the next session by selecting Session ⊏⟩ KDE from the graphical login window.

Don't confuse the term session as used in the login window, which refers to the period of time you are logged in, and the term session as used in this book, which refers to the 30 lessons or chapters.

In Session 17, you learn how to change the default GUI from GNOME to KDE and vice versa.

When you log in, you should get the KDE desktop for the current session. The next time you log in, the system reverts to GNOME (assuming that is your default GUI).

After you select KDE as the GUI for the session and log in, you see an initial KDE desktop similar to the one shown in Figure 3-4.

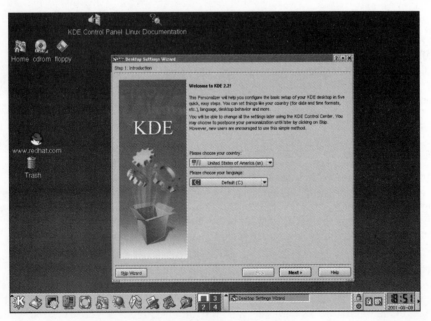

Figure 3-4   *The initial KDE desktop for a typical user*

What Is KDE?

KDE stands for the *K Desktop Environment*. The KDE project started in October 1996 with the intent to develop a common GUI for UNIX systems that use the X Window System. The first beta version of KDE was released a year later in October 1997, and KDE version 1.0 was released in July 1998.

From the user's perspective, KDE provides a graphical desktop environment that includes a window manager (kwm), a file manager (kfm), a panel (kpanel) for starting applications, a help system, configuration tools, and many applications, including an image viewer, PostScript viewer, as well as mail and news programs.

From the developer's perspective, KDE has class libraries and object models for easy application development in C++. KDE itself is a large development project.

You can always find out the latest information about KDE by visiting the KDE home page at `http://www.kde.org/`.

KDE is easy to use and shares many similarities with the Windows 95/98/NT/2000 GUI. You can start applications from a menu that is similar to the Start menu in Windows. KDE also enables you to place folders and applications directly on the desktop.

The KDE Panel appearing along the bottom edge of the screen starts applications. The left and right ends of the Panel show outward-pointing arrows. You can click these arrows to hide the Panel and make more room on the desktop for applications. When the Panel is hidden, it still shows a small bar with an arrow. To view the entire Panel again, click that arrow and the Panel slides out.

The following is a list of the most important buttons on the KDE Panel. If you don't know what a button does, simply move the mouse over the button and a small pop-up window displays a brief message about that button.

Sessions 4, 17, and 19 cover additional features of the KDE desktop, including customizing its appearance and using some of the KDE applets.

- **Start button/Main menu:** The most important component of the Panel is the K button on the left-hand side of the Panel. That button is like the Start button in Windows 95/98/NT/2000. When you click the K button, a pop-up menu appears. From this menu, you can get to other menus by moving the mouse over items with a rightward pointing arrow. You can start applications from this menu. That's why the KDE documentation calls the K button the *Application Starter*.

- **Show Desktop:** Minimizes all windows and shows only the desktop.

- **Terminal Emulation:** The KDE Panel also includes a button with the icon of a terminal covered by a shell. Click this button to run a terminal emulation program and get a terminal window. You can type Linux commands at the shell prompt in the terminal window.

- **KDE Control Center:** Click on the button with an icon of a terminal covered by a circuit board to start the KDE Control Center. The Control Center enables you to configure various aspects of the KDE desktop.
- **Online Help:** To read the online help on KDE, click the button with an icon of a book.
- **File Manager:** To view the contents of your home directory, click the button with the icon of a folder and a home.
- **Virtual Desktop:** KDE supports a virtual desktop. By default, you get four virtual desktops. You can click one of the buttons labeled 1, 2, 3, or 4 to switch to a specific desktop. You can use the desktops to organize your application windows. You do not need to clutter up a single desktop with many open windows. When a desktop gets crowded, simply switch to another desktop and open the applications there.

To log out of KDE, select K ➪ Logout and click the Logout button on the resulting dialog box. The next section shows you how to shut down Red Hat Linux and power off your PC.

Shutting Down Red Hat Linux

10 Min.
To Go

When you are ready to shut down Red Hat Linux, you must do so in an orderly manner. Even if you are the sole user of a Linux system, several other programs are usually running in the background. Also, operating systems such as Linux try to optimize the way that they write data to the disk. Because disk access is relatively slow (compared to the time needed to access memory locations), data generally is held in memory and written to the disk in large chunks. Therefore, if you simply turn off the power, you run the risk of some files not updating properly.

Any user (you do not have to be logged in) can shut down the system from the desktop or the graphical login screen. The System menu in the Login dialog box provides menu options for rebooting or halting the system. To shut down the system, simply select System ➪ Halt in the graphical login screen of Figure 3-1.

Another dialog box asks you to confirm if you really want to halt the system. Click the Yes button. The system then shuts down in an orderly manner.

As the system shuts down, you see messages about processes being shut down. You may be surprised at how many processes there are, even though no one is explicitly running any programs on the system. If your system does not automatically power off on shut down, you can manually turn off the power.

Troubleshooting

One of the most common problems when installing Red Hat Linux is not being able to log in after the post-installation reboot. If you did not create a user account during the installation, you must log in as root and create a user account as described in Session 10. Similarly, if you forget the user account password you created during installation, login as the root user, then use the techniques described in Session 10 to change the password for that user account.

If you forget the root password, reboot and follow these steps:

1. At the LILO boot: prompt, type linux single and press Enter.
2. At the # prompt, type passwd root, and follow the prompts to reset root's password.
3. Finally, type shutdown -r now and the system will reboot and recognize the new password.

Sometimes, your sound card may not work after installation. If this happens, run the sound configuration utility. Log in as root and type sndconfig in a terminal window. Follow the prompts to configure your sound card.

Done!

REVIEW

You began this session by logging into your Linux system. You learned how to log out and shut down the system. After learning a little bit about different X Window window managers, you logged in again and explored the key features of the GNOME desktop. Next, you learned how to select KDE as your GUI for a session and explored the key features of KDE. For both GUIs, you discovered how to start applications. Finally, you learned the proper method of shutting down a Red Hat Linux system.

QUIZ YOURSELF

1. How do you log in to Red Hat Linux after it boots and presents the graphical login prompt? (See "Logging In.")
2. What is the "foot" in GNOME? (See "Exploring GNOME.")
3. How do you switch your GUI to KDE? (See "Exploring KDE.")
4. How do you open a terminal window in KDE? (See "Exploring KDE.")
5. Why must you shut down a Linux system in an orderly manner? (See "Shutting Down Red Hat Linux.")

Customizing the GNOME and KDE Desktops

Session Checklist

✔ Customizing the GNOME desktop

✔ Changing the default desktop

✔ Customizing the KDE desktop

**30 Min.
To Go**

This evening's last session focuses on using the GNOME and KDE graphical desktops and some of the applications and utilities that come bundled with Red Hat Linux. It also shows you how to customize the GNOME and KDE desktops, and teaches you how to switch your default desktop from GNOME to KDE, and vice versa.

Customizing the GNOME Desktop

As Session 3 explained, the default look and feel of the GNOME graphical desktop is similar to that of Windows 95/98/NT/2000, so you do not really have to customize anything to begin using Red Hat Linux. However, if you want, you can customize the GNOME desktop just as you can customize Windows 95/98/NT/2000. For example, you can select a different background, change the appearance of the window borders, or select and configure a screen saver.

To try your hand at customizing the GNOME desktop, log in from the graphical login screen. I assume that GNOME is your default desktop environment because that's what you usually get when you install Red Hat Linux

If GNOME is not your default desktop, select Session ➪ GNOME from the Login window before entering your user name and password.

Tip

You can configure most aspects of the GNOME desktop's look and feel — the appearance and behavior selecting Main Menu ⇨ Programs ⇨ Settings ⇨ Desktop or Main Menu ⇨ Programs ⇨ Settings ⇨ Sawfish window manager and then selecting one of the items from that submenu, such as Appearance or Sound. Each one of these configuration items, known as *capplets*, short for configuration *applets*, allow you to configure one aspect or another of the desktop's look and feel. The user interface is typically a dialog box with settings that you can change. In the next sections, you will try out a few customizations.

Changing the background

To try a simple customization, select Desktop ⇨ Background from the tree to run the background properties capplet that, in turn, displays a dialog box in the workspace (as shown in Figure 4-1).

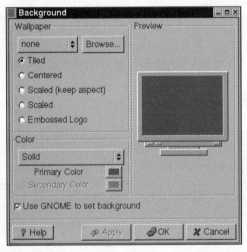

Figure 4-1   *Customizing GNOME desktop's background*

As you can see, this dialog box looks similar to the Display Properties dialog box in Windows 95/98/NT. It enables you to select a solid color or color gradient background or to pick the *wallpaper* (an image used as the background). A *color gradient* refers to a two-color background that starts with one color and gradually changes to another color. The gradient can start in the vertical direction (top to bottom) or horizontal (left to right).

Go ahead and click the Color drop down box, select Vertical Gradient, and then click the Primary Color and Secondary Color buttons to select the colors for the gradient. You get to preview the changes in the image of a monitor that appears in the dialog box.

If you want to use an image as the wallpaper, click the Browse button in the Wallpaper section of the dialog box. A Wallpaper selection dialog box displays the contents of the /usr/share/nautilus directory, so browse the /usr/share/pixmaps/backgrounds directory for more background images. For example, try the /usr/share/pixmaps/backgrounds/space directory that has a collection of images of the earth as seen from space. You can select any Joint Photographic Experts Group (JPEG) or Portable Network Graphics (PNG) format image file as the wallpaper.

To try out any of these changes on the desktop, click the Apply button. You can revert to the original setting by clicking the Cancel button. When you are finished making the changes, click the OK button to close the dialog box and apply the changes.

Selecting a theme

Another more exciting customization is to select a new theme for the entire user interface. A *theme* refers to a collection of user interface components, such as buttons, checkboxes, scrollbars, and so on, that are similar in both look and feel. In some cases, the total effect of a theme can be quite stunning. To try out some new themes, select Desktop ⇨ Theme Selector from the tree menu. From the theme selector dialog box, you can try out different themes and select one that you like. When you select a theme, you can see its appearance in the preview area. For example, select the MockMack theme from the list of available themes, and then click the Try button. It causes the look and feel of the GNOME desktop, including the Control Center window, to resemble that of the Apple Macintosh.

If you like a theme, click the OK button to use that theme. Otherwise, click the Revert button to return to the default theme.

Customizing the window manager

20 Min.
To Go

GNOME does not depend on any one window manager. The default window manager is called Sawfish, but you can select another window manager if you want. To choose a window manager, select Desktop ⇨ Window Manager from the Control Center tree menu. You should see a list of window managers available on your system, as shown in Figure 4-2.

Figure 4-2 *Selecting or customizing a window manager*

In this case, the list shows two window managers: Sawfish and twm. As you can see, the parenthetical note shows that Sawfish is the current window manager. If you want, you can try out the twm window manager by selecting it and then clicking the Try button. Later on, click Revert to return to the Sawfish window manager.

Like any window manager, Sawfish controls title bars, frames, and other decorations around each window. These features enable users to click and drag a window to change its location or adjust its size. (Think for a moment; if there were no frame or title bar, you could not move or resize the window.)

Sawfish includes a configuration tool for changing the look and feel of the window frames and title bars. You can activate the configuration tool by clicking the button labeled Run Configuration Tool for Sawfish (refer to Figure 4-2). This brings up the Sawfish configurator, which provides a tree menu of configuration options. Through this menu, the Sawfish configurator enables you to change how the Sawfish window manager decorates windows, adds special visual effects and sounds, and behaves in response to mouse clicks and keystrokes. You can try out some of the configuration items in the Sawfish configurator.

10 Min.
To Go

Changing the Default Desktop

GNOME and KDE are both capable graphical desktop environments. Red Hat Linux comes with both of these GUIs, but GNOME is the default desktop. Just before you log in at the graphical login screen, you can always select a specific desktop from the Session menu of the login window. However, Red Hat also includes a Desktop Switcher utility that enables you to switch the default desktop from GNOME to KDE, and vice versa. To switch from GNOME to KDE, follow these steps:

1. From your GNOME desktop, select the Main Menu ⇨ Programs ⇨ System ⇨ Desktop Switching Tool. The Desktop Switcher dialog box appears, as shown in Figure 4-3.

Figure 4-3 *Desktop Switcher changes your default desktop environment.*

2. In the Desktop Switcher dialog box, click the KDE radio button to select it. Then click the OK button. A confirmation dialog box, also named Desktop Switcher, appears.

3. A message in the new dialog box informs you that the desktop configuration has been changed, but you must restart X. Click the OK button to dismiss the dialog box.

   Although the message in Step 3 says you must restart X, all you need to do is log out of the session and log back in. To log out, select Main Menu ⇨ Log out. When you log in again, you should get the KDE desktop.

To switch the default desktop from KDE back to GNOME, log in and select K ⇨ System ⇨ Desktop Switching Tool from the KDE desktop. In the Desktop Switcher dialog box, select GNOME as the desktop. After you log out of KDE and log back in, you should get GNOME as your desktop.

Customizing the KDE Desktop

Now that you know how to change your desktop from GNOME to KDE and vice versa, select the KDE desktop and log in as a user. Like GNOME, KDE also includes a graphical application called the KDE Control Center that you can use to customize various aspects of KDE, including the desktop background, icons, and font. To start the KDE Control Center, select K ⇨ Control Center; or on the Panel, click the button with the icon of a circuit board and a monitor.

When the KDE Control Center starts, it displays the main window with a tree menu on the left and some summary information about your system in the workspace to the right (see Figure 4-4).

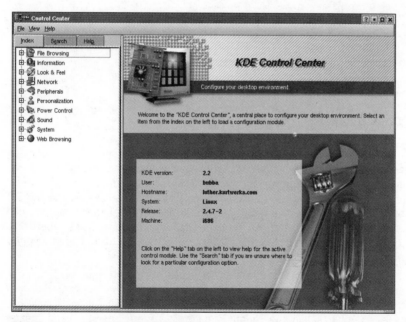

Figure 4-4   *The KDE Control Center*

The KDE Control Center's tree menu shows the items that you can control with this tool. The tree menu is organized into eight categories that include Applications, Desktop, Information, Input Devices, Keyboard Shortcuts, Network, Sound, and Window Behavior. Click the plus sign (+) to the left of an item to view the subcategories for that item. To change an item, go through the tree menu to locate the item and then click it. That item's configuration options then appear in a tabbed dialog box on the right side of the window.

Changing the background and theme

To customize the desktop background, select Look & Feel ⇨ Background from the tree menu. The Background tab appears (see Figure 4-5) with options for customizing the desktop's background.

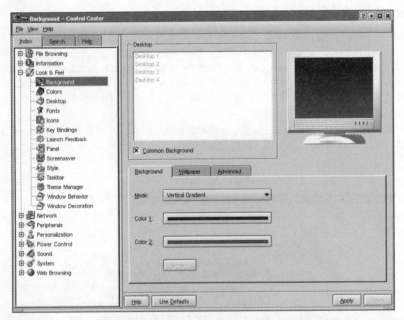

Figure 4-5 *Customizing the desktop background with the KDE Control Center*

You can select either a one or two color background or wallpaper. For example, if you want to use wallpaper as your background, click the Wallpaper tab, and then click the Browse button on the Wallpaper tab. This brings up an Open dialog box showing the JPEG files in the /usr/share/wallpapers directory. You can select one of these images and click OK. Then click the Apply button in the KDE Control Center to apply this wallpaper to the desktop. If you like the appearance, click OK. Otherwise, click Default and then Apply again to revert to the original background.

As you can see from the menu items in the Look & Feel category (Figure 4-5), you can customize a number of aspects of the background from borders and colors to language for menus. I won't go through all the items here, but you should experiment with some of these customizations. For example, select the Theme Manager to try out one of several themes, much like the themes offered in the GNOME Control Center. Figure 4-6 shows the result of selecting and previewing a theme.

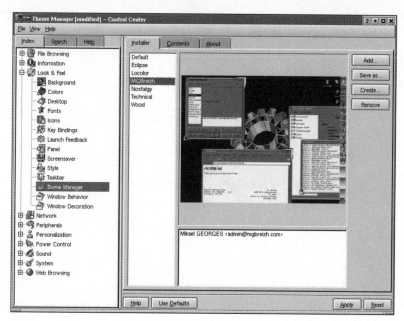

Figure 4-6   *Selecting and previewing a theme in the KDE Control Center*

Selecting a color scheme

If you want to pick a color scheme for the desktop colors, much like the color schemes in Windows 95/98/NT/2000, select Look & Feel ⇨ Colors in the KDE Control Center's tree menu. The Colors tab appears. You can then scroll down the list of color schemes and select one to preview. When you select a color scheme, the preview area in the tab shows how that color scheme looks. To apply a color scheme to the desktop, click the Apply button. If you don't like the scheme, click Use Defaults and then Apply again to revert to the default color scheme.

Performing other tasks

In addition to desktop customization, the Information item in the KDE Control Center enables you to perform many more tasks, including associating sound files with *events* (such as opening or closing a window), defining keyboard shortcuts, and viewing information about your system. You should take the remaining time in this session to explore the other items in the tree menu of the KDE Control Center.

Done!

REVIEW

This session showed you how to customize the GNOME graphical desktop's appearance (look) and behavior (feel). You used the GNOME Control Center to change various aspects of the desktop's look and feel. You learned how to change the default desktop from GNOME to the KDE graphical desktop and vice versa. Finally, you also used the KDE Control Center to customize the look and feel of KDE.

Quiz Yourself

1. What graphical application do you use to customize the GNOME desktop? (See "Customizing the GNOME Desktop.")

2. How do you customize the Sawfish window manager? (See "Customizing the window manager.")

3. How do you change your default desktop from GNOME to KDE and vice versa? (See "Changing the Default Desktop.")

4. What tool do you use to customize the KDE desktop? (See "Customizing the KDE Desktop.")

5. How do you select a color scheme for the KDE desktop? (See "Customizing the KDE Desktop.")

PART

I

Friday Evening

1. Why is it important to review the Red Hat Linux hardware compatibility lists?

2. Is it always necessary to create and use a Red Hat Linux boot floppy?

3. Why must you partition a hard disk before installing Red Hat Linux?

4. What does the Linux fdisk utility do?

5. What is the purpose of a swap partition?

6. How do you add user accounts during the Red Hat Linux installation?

7. What is a package group?

8. Name two other installation options and describe the situations in which you might use them.

9. What is the name of the X Window configuration utility described in Session 2?

10. What are the two most important monitor configuration parameters, and why are they important?

11. How can you tell whether or not the Red Hat Linux kernel has detected the parallel port on your computer?

12. What sources of information are available for troubleshooting the Red Hat Linux installation?

13. What are the key differences between Red Hat Linux windows managers and the GUI systems of other operating systems?

14. How do you log out of a GNOME session? Of a KDE session?

15. If you forget the root password, can you change it? If so, how?

16. What is the name of the capplet that switches between GNOME and KDE?

17. When using the GNOME Control Center, how do you cancel a change?

18. What is a desktop theme?

19. Name and describe at least five features of the KDE desktop that you can configure using the KDE Control Center.

20. Name and describe at least five features of the GNOME desktop that you can configure using the GNOME Control Center.

☑ Friday

☑ **Saturday**

☐ Sunday

PART

II

Saturday
Morning

Exploring Linux Files and Directories

**30 Min.
To Go**

I n Friday night's sessions, you installed Red Hat Linux, learned how to log in, log out, how to shut down your Red Hat Linux system, and how to perform basic desktop customizations. This morning's sessions push deeper into Linux, starting with an introduction to the Linux file system followed by an explanation of how to use the Nautilus file manager. This session also teaches you several Linux commands that work with files and directories.

Understanding the Linux File System

Like other operating systems, Linux organizes information in files that are contained in directories. In Linux, a *directory* is just a special file that can contain other files and directories, resulting in a hierarchical structure. This hierarchical organization of files is called the *file system*.

The Linux file system provides a unified model of all storage in the system. The file system has a single root directory, indicated by a forward slash (/). A hierarchy of files and directories grows from the root directory. Parts of the file system can reside in different physical media such as a hard disk, a floppy disk, and a CD-ROM. Figure 5-1 illustrates the concept of the Linux file system and how it spans multiple physical devices.

Note

Unix has no concept of drive letters, in contrast to MS-DOS and Windows 95/98/ME/NT/2000. Also note that Linux filenames are not restricted to a strict 8.3 name-extension format. The term *8.3 filename* comes from MS-DOS's use of an eight-character name and three-character extension.

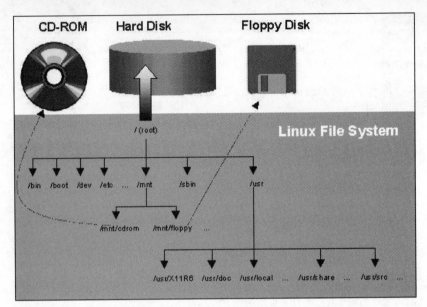

Figure 5-1 *The Linux file system provides a unified view of storage that may span multiple drives.*

In Linux, you can have long filenames (up to 256 characters) and filenames are case-sensitive. Often, UNIX filenames have multiple extensions such as `sample.tar.Z`. Here are some examples of UNIX filenames: `index.html`, `Makefile`, `kernel-2.2.15-2.5.0.i686.rpm`, `.bash_profile`, and `httpd_src.tar.gz`.

To locate a file, you need more than just the file's name; you also need information about the directory hierarchy. The term *pathname* refers to the complete specification necessary to locate a file — the complete hierarchy of directories leading to the file — which includes the filename. Figure 5-2 shows a typical Linux pathname for a file.

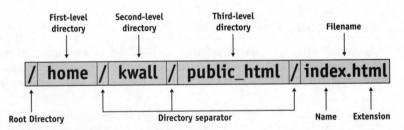

Figure 5-2 *A typical Linux pathname*

As you can see from Figure 5-2, a complete Linux pathname consists of the following parts:

- The root directory, indicated by a forward slash (/) character.
- The directory hierarchy, with each directory name separated from the previous one by a forward slash (/) character. A / appears after the last directory name.
- The filename, with a name and one or more optional extensions.

Now that you know the basics of the Linux file system, you can access the files and directories in two ways:

- Use a graphical file manager in the GNOME or KDE desktop.
- Type appropriate Linux commands in a terminal window or text console.

Graphical file managers resemble Windows Explorer and are easy to use. Because the file managers for GNOME and KDE are very similar, we will only cover the former in this session.

Using the Nautilus File Manager

After you log into your Red Hat Linux system from the graphical login screen, you can view your home directory with the Nautilus file manager by double-clicking on the house icon on the desktop. Figure 5-3 shows the initial display of a sample home directory. Your home directory should look similar.

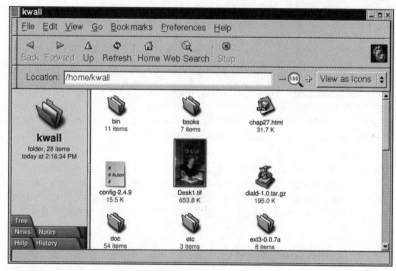

Figure 5-3   *A sample home directory, as it appears in the Nautilus file manager*

Viewing files with Nautilus file manager

The right side of the Nautilus file manager's window shows the files and directories in the currently selected directory as icons. As you can see in Figure 5-3, Nautilus shows the contents of the /home/kwall directory. The Location bar shows the name of the currently selected directory. To see a tree view of the entire file system, click the Tree tab in the small pane on the left-hand side of Nautilus' window. The result display should resemble Figure 5-4.

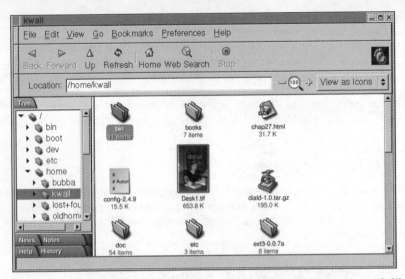

Figure 5-4   *Nautilus shows a tree view of the entire file system, much like Windows Explorer.*

If you have used Windows Explorer, you will find the Nautilus file manager familiar. To view the contents of another directory, first locate the directory in the tree view. For example, to view the /etc/X11 directory, click the arrow next to the etc directory. This causes Nautilus to display the subdirectories in etc and change that plus sign to a minus sign. Then click the X11 directory. The right-hand side of the window now shows the contents of the /etc/X11 directory. Different files have different icons. Ordinary files appear as a sheet of paper. Directories appear as folders.

The Nautilus file manager window has the usual menu bar and a toolbar. Notice that, in Figure 5-3, the toolbar drop down labeled View As Icons is pressed. That means the directory contents are displayed using large icons. You can select the View As List option from this drop down box to cause Nautilus to display the contents using smaller icons in a list format.

Performing tasks with Nautilus file manager

**20 Min.
To Go**

In addition to moving around the file system and viewing contents of directories, you can use the file manager to perform tasks such as relocating a file from one directory to another and deleting a file. We don't show you each and every step, but you can take a few moments to try the following tasks.

- **Moving a file to a different directory:** Left-click on its icon and then drag-and-drop it on the directory where you want the file.

- **Copying a file to a new location:** Select the file's icon and then choose File ⇨ Copy. You may also right-click the mouse on the file's icon and select Copy from the pop-up menu. A dialog box prompts you for the name of the directory to which the file should be copied.

- **Deleting a file or directory:** Right-click the icon and select Delete from the pop-up menu. A dialog box asks you to confirm if you really want to delete the file or directory. You can click Yes to delete the selected item or click No to cancel the operation.

- **Renaming a file or a directory:** Click the name in the Icon view (refer to Figure 5-3). Then you can type the new name or edit the name.

- **Creating a new directory:** Right-click in an empty area of the right-hand window and select New Directory from the pop-up menu. A dialog box prompts you for the name of the new directory.

- **Finding files:** Select Commands ⇨ Find Files from the menu bar. A dialog box prompts you for what you want to find and where to start the search. After you enter this information, click OK to start the search. The results of the search appear in a new window.

Navigating and Manipulating Files and Directories with Linux Commands

Although the graphical file managers are easy to use, you can employ them only if X Window is running. Sometimes you may not have a graphical environment in which to run a graphical file manager. For example, you might be logged in through a text terminal or X might not work on your system. In these situations, you have to rely on Linux commands to work with files and directories. The nice part is that you can always use Linux commands — even in the graphical environment. All you have to do is open a terminal window and type the Linux commands. Click the terminal icon in the GNOME panel to start a terminal emulation program that displays a terminal window.

Directory navigation

In Linux, your home directory is /root when you log in as root. For other users, the home directory is usually in the /home directory. The sample home directory (when the user logs in as kwall) is /home/kwall. This information is stored in the /etc/passwd file. By default, besides the super user, you are the only user with permission to save files in your home directory and to create subdirectories in your home directory to further organize your files.

 Never log in as the root user unless you are performing system administration work. Because the super user has complete access to the entire system, a careless mouse click or command could severely damage the system.

Linux supports the concept of a *current directory*, which is where all file and directory commands operate. For example, after you log in, your current directory is the home directory. To see the current directory from the terminal window, type the pwd command.

To change the current directory, use the cd command. To change the current directory to /usr/share/doc, type the following:

```
cd /usr/share/doc
```

Then, to change the directory to the bash-2.04 subdirectory in /usr/share/doc, type this command:

    cd bash-2.04

Now, if you use the pwd command it shows /usr/share/doc/bash-2.04 as the current directory. Therefore, you can refer to a directory's name in two ways:

- *Absolute pathname* (such as /usr/share/doc), which specifies the exact directory in the directory tree.
- *Relative directory* name (such as bash-2.04), which represents the bash-2.04 sub-directory of the current directory.

If you type cd bash-2.04 in /usr/share/doc, the current directory changes to /usr/share/doc/bash-2.04. However, the same command in /home/naba tries to change the current directory to /home/naba/bash-2.04, which probably does not exist. Incidentally, typing the cd command without any arguments changes the current directory to your home directory.

 You can use a shortcut to refer to any user's home directory. Prefix a user's login name with a tilde (~) to refer to that user's home directory. Therefore, ~kwall refers to the home directory of the user kwall and ~root refers to the home directory of the root user. If your system has a user with the login name emily, you can type cd ~emily to change to Emily's home directory.

The directory names . and .. have special meanings. A single period (.) refers to the current directory, whereas two periods (..) refer to the parent directory. If the current directory is /usr/share/doc, for example, you can change the current directory to /usr/share by typing this command:

    cd ..

This command takes you up one level in the directory hierarchy.

Directory listings and permissions

As you move around the Linux directories, you may want to know their contents. You can get a directory listing by using the ls command. By default, the ls command — without any options — displays the contents of the current directory in a compact, multicolumn format. For example, type the following commands to see the contents of the /etc/X11 directory. (Type the commands shown in bold text; the command prompts are not included in the listing.)

    cd /etc/X11
    ls

    applnk   lbxproxy   rstart   xdm   XftConfig   Xmodmap
    fs   prefdm   twm   XF86Config   xinit   xserver
    gdm   proxymngr X   XF86Config-4 xkb   xsm

From this listing, you cannot tell really whether an entry is a file or a directory. To distinguish the directories from the files, use the -F option with ls as follows:

```
ls -F
applnk/    lbxproxy/    rstart/    xdm/            XftConfig    Xmodmap
fs/        prefdm*      twm/       XF86Config      xinit/       xserver/
gdm/       proxymngr/   X@         XF86Config-4    xkb@         xsm/
```

The -F option causes ls to append a character to the end of certain files that indicates their type. For example, directory names have a slash (/) appended to them. Plain filenames appear as is. An at sign (@) indicates that a file, such as xkb in the listing, is actually a link to another file.

A *link* is a filename that refers to another file. It's like a shortcut in Windows.

An asterisk (*) is appended to executable files (for example, the prefdm file in the listing).

The exact files you see may vary slightly depending on the kind of installation you performed during Friday night's session.

You can see even more detailed information about the files and directories with the -l option:

```
ls -l
```

For the /etc/X11 directory, a typical output from ls -l looks like the following:

```
total 76
lrwxrwxrwx   1 root    root       24 Jul 31 20:32 X -> /usr/X11R6/bin/XF86_SVGA
-rw-r--r--   1 root    root    14549 Jul 31 20:59 XF86Config
-rw-r--r--   1 root    root     1545 Jul 31 20:32 XF86Config-4
-rw-r--r--   1 root    root      491 Jul 14 14:46 Xmodmap
drwxr-xr-x   9 root    root     4096 Jul 31 15:29 applnk
```

This listing shows considerable information about each directory entry, which can be a file or another directory. Looking at a line from the right column to the left, you see that the rightmost column shows the name of the directory entry. The date and time before the name shows its MTime, when it was last modified. The file size, in bytes, appears before the MTime.

The file's group and owner appear to the left of the file size column. The next number to the left indicates the number of links to the file or, if the entry is a directory, the number of files it contains (including . and ..). Finally, the leftmost column shows the file's *permission settings*, which control who can read, write, or execute the file. The very first letter of the permission setting has one of the following special meanings:

- If the first letter is l, the file is a symbolic link to another file.
- If the first letter is d, the file is a directory.

- If the first letter is a dash (-), the file is a normal file.
- If the first letter is b, the file represents a block device such as a disk drive.
- If the first letter is c, the file represents a character device such as a serial port or a terminal.

After that first letter, the leftmost column shows a sequence of nine characters that appears as rwxrwxrwx when each letter is present. Each letter indicates a specific permission: read (r), write (w), and execute (x). A hyphen (-) in place of a letter indicates no permission for a specific operation on the file. Thus, the string rw- means that the owner has read and write permission, but no execute permission. Think of these nine letters as three groups of three letters (rwx), interpreted as follows:

- The leftmost group of rwx controls the read, write, and execute permission of the file's owner.
- The middle three rwx letters control the read, write, and execute permission of any user belonging to that file's group.
- The rightmost group of rwx letters controls the read, write, and execute permission of all other users (collectively referred to as the *world*).

Thus, a file with the permission setting rwx------ is accessible only to the file's owner. Meanwhile, the permission setting rwxr--r-- makes the file readable by the world.

Typically, executable programs (including shell programs) have execute permission. However, for directories, the execute permission is equivalent to a use permission — a user must have execute permission on a directory to list its contents.

An interesting feature of the ls command is the fact that it does not list any file whose name begins with a period. Such files are called *hidden files* or *dot files* because their names begin with a dot (.). To see these files, you must use the ls command with the -a option as follows:

```
ls -a
```

10 Min. To Go

File manipulation

You might want to copy files from one directory to another. To do so, use the cp command to perform this task. The cp command makes a new copy of a file, leaving the original intact. To copy the file /usr/X11R6/lib/X11/xinit/Xclients to the Xclients.sample file in the current directory (such as your home directory), type the following:

```
cp /usr/X11R6/lib/X11/xinit/Xclients Xclients.sample
```

If you want to copy a file to the current directory and retain the same name, use a period (.) as the second argument of the cp command. Thus, the following command copies the XF86Config file from the /etc/X11 directory to the current directory (denoted by a single period):

```
cp /etc/X11/XF86Config .
```

Another Linux command, mv, moves a file to a new location. The original copy is gone, and a new copy appears at the specified destination. You can use mv to rename a file. If you want to change the name of today.list to old.list, use the mv command as follows:

```
mv today.list old.list
```

On the other hand, you can move the today.list file to a subdirectory named saved with this command:

```
mv today.list saved
```

Another common file operation is deleting a file. Use the rm command to delete a file named old.list, for example, by typing the following command:

```
rm old.list
```

 Be careful with the rm command, particularly when you log in as root. Inadvertently deleting important files with rm is very easy.

In addition to copying, renaming, and deleting files, you may want to view a file's contents. Use the more command to look at a text file one page at a time. To view the file /etc/X11/XF86Config-4, for example, use this command:

```
more /etc/X11/XF86Config-4
```

The more command pauses after each page, so you have to press the spacebar to move to the next page. Press Enter to move forward one line at a time in the file. To move to the previous page, press b.

Another useful Linux command for file viewing is less. The name is a play on words because less does more than more, that is, less has a richer set of features for viewing files than does more.

Directory manipulation

To organize files in your home directory, you have to create new directories or subdirectories. Use the mkdir command to create a directory. For example, to create a directory named images in the current directory, type the following:

```
mkdir images
```

After you create the directory, you can use the cd images command to change to that directory.

When you no longer need a directory, use the rmdir command to delete it. You can delete a directory only when the directory is empty.

 To delete a directory and its file simultaneously, use the rm command's recursive option, -r. So, to delete the images directory and all of its files with a single command, type rm -r images.

File and directory finder

Finally, you should know about the find command because it's very useful for locating files (and directories) that meet specified search criteria. The Linux version of the find command comes from GNU, and it has more extensive options than the standard UNIX version. However, we show the syntax for the standard UNIX find command because that syntax works in Linux and you can use the same format on other UNIX systems.

Suppose that you want to find any file or directory with a name that starts with gnome. You can use find to perform this search, as follows:

```
find / -name "gnome*" -print
```

This command tells find to start at the root directory (/), look for filenames that match gnome*, and display the full pathname of any matching files.

You can use variations of this simple form of find to locate a file in any directory (as well as subdirectories contained in the directory). If you forget where in your home directory you stored all files that start with the string report*, you can search for the files using the following command:

```
find ~ -name "report*" -print
```

When you become comfortable with the syntax of find, you can use its other options. For example, to find only specific types of files (such as directories), use the -type option. The following command displays all top-level directory names in your Linux system:

```
find / -type d -maxdepth 1 -print
```

The preceding example uses the simple form of the find command. You probably do not have to use the complex forms of find in a typical Linux system, but you can look up the rest of the find options by using this command:

```
man find
```

Troubleshooting

If you cannot move, rename, or delete a file, use the ls -l command to verify that you have permissions to do so.

If you receive an error message resembling rmdir: `*dirname*': directory not empty when using rmdir to delete a directory, either delete the files in the directory before retrying the rmdir command or use rm -r to delete the directory and its contents. For example,

```
$ rmdir images
rmdir: `images': directory not empty
$ rm -r images
```

A common question is how to delete a file whose name begins with a minus (-). Suppose, for example, a file in your home directory is named -foo. The command rm -foo fails and generates the following error:

```
$ rm -foo
corm: invalid option -- o
```

This problem occurs because most Linux commands interpret a minus sign followed by a letter as a command option, and anything following that as an argument to the command. So, the argument to the rm command, -foo, looks like invalid syntax, not a filename. The solution is to use two minus signs (- -) between rm and -foo. Most Linux commands interpret two minus signs standing alone as the end of all options; everything afterward is interpreted as an argument. So, to remove that file named -foo, try rm -- -foo, as follows:

```
$ rm -- -foo
```

Done!

REVIEW

This session began with a brief introduction to the Linux file system and discussed how files are named. It then showed you how to use the Nautilus file manager to navigate the file system and look at different views of directories. You also performed some basic operations such as copying files, deleting files, and creating new directories. Next, you learned a number of Linux commands for navigating the file system and manipulating files and directories. Finally, you learned a few troubleshooting tips.

QUIZ YOURSELF

1. What is a *pathname*? (See "Understanding the Linux File System.")
2. In the Nautilus file manager, how do you sort the list of files and directories alphabetically by name? (See "Using the Nautilus File Manager.")
3. What Linux command do you use to change quickly from the current directory to your home directory? (See "Directory navigation.")
4. What option can you use with the ls command to view all files and see the directory names listed with a / suffix? (See "Directory listings and permissions.")
5. Which Linux command finds all files named COPYING starting in the /usr/doc directory? (See "File and directory finder.")

Understanding the Shell

Session Checklist

✔ Getting started with the Bash shell

✔ Using the Bash shell

30 Min.
To Go

As discussed in Session 5, unfortunately you can't do everything from a graphical environment such as GNOME or KDE. In such cases, you have to use Linux commands to accomplish specific tasks. Session 5 introduced you to some of the Linux commands that you can use from a text terminal to manipulate files and directories. This session introduces you to the *Bash shell* — the default command interpreter in Linux. Here, you learn some important features of how the shell executes commands.

Getting Started with the Bash Shell

If you have used MS-DOS, you may be familiar with the DOS command interpreter. That program (named COMMAND.COM) displays the infamous C:\> prompt. In Windows, you can see this prompt in an MS-DOS command window. Linux provides a command interpreter, referred to as a *shell*, which resembles the MS-DOS command interpreter. However, as you might expect, the shell has a lot more capabilities than the MS-DOS command interpreter.

Although this session covers the Bash shell, Red Hat Linux allows you to use other shells, too. They include ash, a small but capable shell, and tcsh, a full-featured shell with a syntax similar to the C programming language.

The default Linux shell is called Bash, and its program is named /bin/bash (found in the /bin directory). When you open a terminal window from the GNOME or KDE desktop, or log in at a text console, the Bash shell prompts you for commands. When you type a command, the shell executes it.

To see all of the shells available on your Red Hat Linux system, type the command chsh -l **in a terminal window.**

In addition to the standard Linux commands, Bash can launch any program stored in an executable file. Bash can also execute a *shell script*, which is a text file that contains one or more commands.

During this session, you will try out various features of the Bash shell ranging from the general command syntax to the basics of shell programming. If you haven't already done so, open a terminal window so you can use the shell.

Using the Bash Shell

Because a shell interprets what you type, it is important to know how the shell *interprets*, or processes, the text that you enter. Most shell commands have this general format:

```
command option1 option2 ... optionN
```

A single line of commands is commonly referred to as a *command line*. On a command line, you enter a command followed by one or more options known as *command-line options*. The options control how the command operates or behaves. In addition, the command itself and the command-line options may take one or more arguments, both or either of which are (somewhat confusingly) referred to as *command-line arguments*. Whereas command-line options control the command's behavior, command-line arguments provide additional information either for the option or for the command, such as the name of a file on which to operate. For example, consider the following command line:

```
grep -A 1 -i naba /etc/passwd
```

In this case, grep is the command, -A and -i are options, the numeral 1 is an argument to the -A option, and naba and /etc/passwd are arguments to the grep.

One basic rule is that you have to use a space or a tab to separate the command from the options. You also must separate options with a space or a tab. If you want to use an option that contains embedded spaces, you have to put that option inside quotation marks (""). For example, to search for the name, *Kurt*, in the password file, enter the following grep command (grep searches for text in files):

```
grep "Kurt Wall" /etc/passwd
```

When grep prints the line with the name, *Kurt*, it looks like this:

```
kwall:x:500:500:Kurt Wall:/home/kwall:/bin/bash
```

If you created a user account in your name, go ahead and type the grep command with your name as the first argument.

In the output from the grep **command, you can see the name of the shell (**/bin/bash**) following the last colon (**:**).**

The number and the format of the command-line options, of course, depend on the actual command. As you learn more commands, you will see that most of the command-line options take the form *-X* in which *X* is a single character.

 Because various GNU tools and utilities implement most Linux commands, you should know that GNU command support includes so-called *long options*. These are command-line options that begin with two dashes followed by one or more descriptive words. Thus, the GNU options take the form --xxxx in which xxxx is a word denoting the option. For example, the GNU ls --all command shows all directory entries including those that begin with a period (.). This is the same as the ls -a command in all UNIX systems.

If a command is too long to fit on a single line, you can press the backslash (\) key, followed by Enter. Then, continue entering the command on the next line. For example, type the following command (press Enter after each line):

```
cat \
/etc/passwd
```

The cat command then displays the contents of the /etc/passwd file.

You can concatenate several shorter commands on a single line; just use the semicolon (;) as a separator (also called a command *terminator*) between each command. For example, the following command

```
cd; ls -F
```

changes the current directory to your home directory and then lists the contents of that directory.

Getting help with Bash

Bash comes with many built-in commands, some of which mimic or duplicate the functionality of other programs on your Red Hat Linux system. To see the complete list of these Bash *built-ins*, as they are called, type help and press Enter at the Bash command prompt. To get help with a specific Bash built-in, type help command, where command is the Bash command about which you want to learn. For example, type the following command and then press Enter:

```
help pwd
```

The short help text shows the syntax of Bash's built-in command pwd, briefly describes what it does, and provides an explanation of pwd's command-line options:

```
pwd: pwd [-PL]
    Print the current working directory.  With the -P option,
    pwd prints the physical directory, without any symbolic
    links; the -L option makes pwd follow symbolic links.
```

The exact appearance on your system will be different because the output shown here has been edited to fit this book's formatting requirements.

Combining commands

Linux follows the UNIX philosophy of giving the user a toolbox of many simple commands that can be combined in a myriad of ways to create a more sophisticated command. Suppose you want to find out whether a device file named sbpcd resides in your system's /dev directory because some documentation tells you that for a Sound Blaster Pro CD-ROM drive you need that device file. You can use the command ls /dev to get a directory listing of the /dev directory and see whether anything that contains sbpcd appears in the listing. Unfortunately, the /dev directory has a great many entries and it may be difficult to locate any item that has sbpcd in its name. You can, however, combine the ls command with grep and come up with a command that does exactly what you want, as shown here:

```
ls /dev | grep sbpcd
```

The shell sends the output of the ls command (the directory listing) to the grep command, which searches for the string sbpcd. That vertical bar (|) is known as a *pipe* because it acts as a conduit between the two programs; the output of the first command becomes the input of the second one.

Most Linux commands are designed in a way that enables the output of one command to feed into the input of another. To do this, simply concatenate the commands and place pipes between them.

20 Min. To Go

Redirecting command input and output

Linux commands that are designed to work together have a common feature — they always read from the *standard input* (usually the keyboard) and write to the *standard output* (usually the screen). Error messages are sent to the *standard error* (usually the screen). These three devices often are referred to as *stdin*, *stdout*, and *stderr*, respectively.

If you want a command to read from a file, you can redirect stdin to come from that file. Similarly, to save a command's output in a file, redirect stdout to a file. These features of the shell are called *input* and *output redirection*, or, more generally, *I/O redirection*.

For example, type cd to change to your home directory and then type the following command:

```
grep typedef /usr/include/* > typedef.out
```

For the time being, ignore the messages resembling grep: /usr/include/org: is a directory; these are error messages from the grep command. This command searches through all files in the /usr/include directory for the occurrence of the string typedef and then saves the output in a file called typedef.out. As this command shows, the greater than sign (>) redirects stdout to a file.

This command also illustrates another feature of Bash. When you use an asterisk (*), Bash replaces the asterisk with a list of all the filenames in the specified directory. Thus, /usr/include/* means "display all the files in the /usr/include directory."

You can also redirect stdin so that a command reads from a file instead of the keyboard. For example, type the following command:

```
sort < /etc/passwd
```

This should display a sorted list of the lines in the /etc/passwd file. In this case, the less than sign (<) redirects stdin so the sort command reads its input from the /etc/passwd file.

Letting Bash complete your commands

Many commands take a filename as an argument. To browse through a file named /etc/X11/XF86Config, for example, type the following command:

```
more /etc/X11/XF86Config
```

This command displays the file /etc/X11/XF86Config one screen at a time. For the commands that take a filename as an argument, Bash includes a feature that enables you to type short filenames. All you have to type is the bare minimum — just the first few characters — to identify the file uniquely in its directory.

To see an example, type more /etc/X11/XF but don't press Enter; press Tab instead. Bash automatically completes the filename so that the command becomes more /etc/X11/XF86Config. Then press Enter to run the command.

Using wildcard characters

Another way to avoid typing too many filenames is to use *wildcards* — special characters, such as the asterisk (*) and question mark (?), to match characters in a string. If you are familiar with MS-DOS, you may have used commands such as COPY *.* A: to copy all files from the current directory to the A: drive. Bash accepts similar wildcards in filenames. In fact, Bash provides many more wildcard options than MS-DOS.

Bash supports three types of wildcards:

- Asterisk (*) character matches zero or more characters in a filename. Therefore, * denotes all files in a directory.
- Question mark (?) matches any single character.
- Set of characters in brackets matches any single character from that set. For example, the string [xX]*, matches any filename that starts with x or X.

Wildcards are handy when you want to perform a task on a group of files. For instance, to copy all the files from a directory named /mnt/cdrom to the current directory, type the following:

```
cp /mnt/cdrom/* .
```

Bash replaces the wildcard character * with the names of all the files in the /mnt/cdrom directory. The period at the end of the command represents the current directory.

You can use the asterisk with other parts of a filename to select a more specific group of files. Suppose you want to use the grep command to search for the string typedef struct in all files of the /usr/include directory that meet the following criteria:

- Filename starts with s.
- Filename ends with .h.

The wildcard specification s*.h denotes all filenames that meet these criteria. Thus, you can perform the search with the following command:

```
grep "typedef struct" /usr/include/s*.h
```

The string contains a space you want the grep command to find, so you have to enclose that string in quotation marks (""). This method ensures that Bash does not try to interpret each word in the string as a separate command-line argument.

Although the asterisk (*) matches any number of characters, the question mark (?) matches a single character. Suppose you have four files — image1.pcx, image2.pcx, image3.pcx, and image4.pcx — in the current directory. To copy these files to the /mnt/floppy directory, use the following command:

```
cp image?.pcx /mnt/floppy
```

Bash replaces the single question mark with any single character and copies the four files to /mnt.

The third wildcard format — [...] — matches a single character from a specific set. You may want to combine this format with other wildcards to narrow down the matching file-names to a smaller set. To see a list of all filenames in the /etc/X11/xdm directory that start with x or X, type the following command:

```
ls /etc/X11/xdm/[xX]*
```

 If Bash does not find any filenames matching the [...] wildcard format when expanding it, Bash leaves the wildcard specification intact.

Looking at the command history

To make it easy for you to repeat long commands, Bash stores up to 500 (the default) previously executed commands. This feature is called a *command history* (a list of old commands). To see the command history, type history. Bash displays a numbered list of the old commands, including those that you entered during previous logins. That list may resemble the following:

```
1   cd
2   ls -a
3   more /etc/X11/XF86Config
4   history
```

If the command list is too long, you may choose to see only the last few commands. To see the last 10 commands only, type this command:

```
history 10
```

To repeat a command from the list that the history command shows, simply type an exclamation point (!), followed by that command's number. To repeat command number 3, type !3.

You also can repeat an old command without knowing its command number. Suppose you typed more /usr/lib/X11/xdm/xdm-config a while ago, and now you want to look at that file again. To repeat the previous more command, type the following:

```
!more
```

Often, you may want to repeat the last command that you typed — perhaps with a slight change. For example, perhaps you displayed the contents of the directory by using the ls -l command. To repeat that command, type two exclamation points as follows:

```
!!
```

Sometimes, you may want to repeat the previous command but add extra arguments to it. Suppose that ls -l shows too many files. Simply repeat that command, but pipe the output through the more command as follows:

```
!! | more
```

Bash replaces the two exclamation points with the previous command and then appends | more to that command.

 An easy way to recall previous commands is to press the up arrow key, which causes Bash to go backward in the list of commands. To move forward in the command history, press the down arrow key.

Using aliases for commands

To see the benefit of aliases, type the following command:

```
alias goboot='cd /usr/src/linux/arch/i386/boot'
```

This defines goboot as an *alias* — another name — for the text that appears within the single quotes ("). That text is a command to change the current directory to /usr/src/linux/arch/i386/boot.

Now that you've defined the alias, type the following at the Bash prompt:

```
goboot
```

Type pwd to confirm that the current directory is indeed /usr/src/linux/arch/i386/boot.

As you can see, an alias is simply an alternative (and usually shorter) name for a lengthy command. Bash replaces the alias with its definition and performs the equivalent command.

If you no longer need an alias, use the unalias command to remove the alias. For example, if you no longer want to use the goboot alias, type

```
unalias goboot
```

After this step, typing goboot causes you to get an error message like this:

```
goboot

bash: goboot: command not found
```

Redefining Dangerous Commands

Another good use of an alias is to redefine a dangerous command, such as rm, to make it safer. By default, the rm command deletes one or more specified files. If you type rm * by mistake, rm deletes all files in your current directory. One user learned this the hard way one day when he wanted to delete all files that ended with .xwd. (These files contained old screen images that he no longer needed.) He intended to type rm *.xwd, but somehow he ended up typing rm * .xwd. He got the following message:

```
rm: .xwd: No such file or directory
```

Puzzled by the message, he typed ls to see the directory's contents again. When the listing showed nothing, he realized that he had an extra space between the * and .xwd. All the files in that directory, of course, were gone forever.

The rm command provides the -i option, which asks for confirmation before deleting a file. To make that option a default, add the following alias definition to the .bash_profile file in your home directory:

```
alias rm='rm -i'
```

From now on, when you use rm to delete a file, the command first asks for confirmation as follows:

```
rm .bash_profile
rm: remove `.bash_profile'? n
```

Press y to delete the file; otherwise, press n.

Many users take advantage of the alias feature to give more familiar names to common commands and to create shortcuts to frequently typed long commands. If you are a DOS user and you issue the md command to create a directory, you can simply define md as an alias for mkdir (the Linux command that creates a new directory). You do this as follows:

```
alias md='mkdir'
```

Now, you can type md *dirname* to create a new directory named *dirname*.

10 Min.
To Go

Running commands in the background

When you use MS-DOS, you have no choice but to wait for each command to complete before you enter the next one. You can type ahead a bit, but the MS-DOS system can hold only a few characters in its internal buffer. However, Linux can handle multiple tasks simultaneously. The only problem you may have is that the terminal or console is tied up until a command completes.

If you work in a terminal window and a command takes too long to complete, you can open another terminal window and continue to enter other commands. If you work in text mode, however, and a command seems to take too long, you need some other way to access your system.

Linux allows you to execute a long-running command *in the background*, which means that the shell starts the process corresponding to a command and immediately returns to accept more commands. The shell does not wait for the command to complete; the command runs as a distinct process in the background. To start a process in the background, you simply place an ampersand (&) at the end of a command line.

For example, when you want to search the entire file system for a file using the find command, you can run that command in the background and send the output to a file. To try out the find command in the background, type cd to change to your home directory and then type the following command:

```
find / -name "README*.*" -print > all.readme &
```

You should immediately get a Bash prompt. You can now go on with other commands. When the find command finishes, the search results should appear in the file all.readme in your home directory.

 If a command that you did not run in the background seems to be taking a long time, press Ctrl+Z to stop it. Then type bg to put that process in the background.

Using virtual consoles

Red Hat Linux comes with a number of *virtual consoles*. The combination of a monitor and a keyboard is called the *terminal* or *console*. Even though your Red Hat Linux system only has one physical terminal or console, it gives you the appearance of having multiple consoles. From the graphical X screen (the GNOME or KDE desktop), press Ctrl+Alt+F1 to get to the first virtual console, press Ctrl+Alt+F2 for the second one, and so on. Each of these virtual consoles is a text screen where you can log in and type Linux commands to perform various tasks.

Go ahead and press Alt+F2 to switch to the second virtual console. Then log in and try some Linux commands. You can log out by typing exit at the Bash prompt. To get back to the graphical X display, press Alt+F7 (or, possibly, Ctrl+Alt+F7).

Troubleshooting

If you pass an argument made up of multiple words to a command and get an error message stating, in part, No such file or directory, try enclosing the argument between weak quotes ("") and trying again. Remember that Bash uses spaces and tab characters to distinguish between commands, options, and arguments. For example, the following command grep Kurt Wall /etc/passwd generates an error message before showing its result:

```
grep: Wall: no such file or directory
/etc/passwd:kwall:x:500:500:Kurt Wall:/home/kwall:/bin/bash
```

Enclosing Kurt Wall within weak quotes solves the problem:

```
grep "Kurt Wall" /etc/passwd
/etc/passwd:kwall:x:500:500:Kurt Wall:/home/kwall:/bin/bash
```

If you use grep to search for certain characters, such as ;, \, $, ?, or *, the search will fail because Bash interprets these characters specially. To prevent this, use the \ character in front of these characters to suppress their special meaning. For example, the command grep ; /usr/include/zutil.h fails, generating the following error message:

```
Usage: grep [OPTION]... PATTERN [FILE]...
Try `grep --help' for more information.
bash: /usr/include/zutil.h: Permission denied
```

After adding \ in front of the ;, the command works just fine:

```
grep \; /usr/include/zutil.h
    extern int errno;
typedef unsigned char  uch;
typedef uch FAR uchf;
typedef unsigned short ush;
typedef ush FAR ushf;
```

Most of the output was deleted to preserve space.

Done!

REVIEW

In this session, you tried out many key features of the Bash shell — the Linux command interpreter. Among other things, you learned the syntax of commands, how you can combine commands, how to run commands in the background, and how to use aliases.

QUIZ YOURSELF

1. What is the shell and what does it do? (See "Using the Bash Shell.")
2. How would you continue a long command on multiple lines? (See "Combining commands.")
3. How do you save the output of a Linux command in a file? (See "Redirecting command input and output.")
4. What are aliases and why would you use them? (See "Using aliases for commands.")
5. What keys would you press to get the second virtual console? (See "Using virtual consoles.")

Learning Linux Commands

Session Checklist

✔ Reviewing commands you've learned so far

✔ Commands for managing processes

✔ Useful date and time commands

✔ Commands for working with text files

✔ File-system maintenance commands

**30 Min.
To Go**

I n this session, you'll review the commands you learned in previous sessions and be introduced to a few Linux commands from several categories. However, because of the large number of Linux commands, you cannot really explore each and every command in a half-hour session. You'll try out more commands in later sessions. To begin this session, log in at the graphical login screen and open a terminal window. You can then type the commands in that login screen.

Reviewing Commands You've Learned So Far

You've already tried quite a few Linux commands in previous sessions. Browse through Table 7-1 to refresh your memory about these commands. We organized them in categories for your convenience.

Table 7-1   *Linux Commands You've Learned in Previous Sessions*

Command Category and Name	Description
Getting Online Help	
help	Displays a list of Bash built-in commands. Type help at a Bash prompt.
help *command*	Displays help text for the Bash built-in command named *command*. Type help cd for help with Bash's built-in cd command.
man	Displays online help information. Type man ls for help with the ls command.
Making Commands Easier	
alias	Defines an abbreviation (shortcut) for a long command. Type alias alone to view all currently defined aliases. Type alias topdir='cd /' and then type topdir to change the directory to the root directory (/).
unalias	Deletes an abbreviation defined using alias. Type unalias topdir to undefine the topdir abbreviation.
Managing Files and Directories	
cd	Changes the current directory. Type cd /usr to change to the /usr directory.
chmod	Changes file permissions. Type chmod +x *filename* to make that file executable (replace *filename* with the name of an existing file).
cp	Copies files. Type cd to change the directory to your home directory. Then type cp /etc/X11/XF86Config . to copy a file to your home directory.
ls	Displays the contents of a directory. Type ls -F to see the contents of the current directory.
mkdir	Creates a directory. Type cd to change to your home directory and then type mkdir temp to create a directory named temp.
mv	Renames a file moves it from one directory to another. Type mv *filename1* *filename2* to change a file's name; use an existing file's name for *filename1*.
rm	Deletes files. The syntax is rm *filename*. (Use with caution because the file gets deleted.)

rmdir	Deletes directories. Type rmdir ~/temp to remove the directory named temp from your home directory (see the mkdir command earlier in this table).
pwd	Displays the current directory. Type pwd to see the current directory name.

Finding Files

find	Finds files based on specified criteria such as name, size, and so on. Type find /usr -name "README*" -print to try this command.

Processing Files

cat	Displays a file on standard output (can concatenate several files into one big file). Type cd to go to your home directory and then type cat .bash_profile to see the contents of that file.
grep	Searches for regular expressions within a text file. Type cd to go to your home directory and then type grep BASH .b* to see the result of searching for the string, BASH, in specified files.
more	Displays a text file one page at a time. Type more /etc/inittab to see the contents one page at a time. (Press the spacebar to advance or type q to quit.)

Managing Users

passwd	Changes the password. Type passwd and follow the prompts to change your password.
su	Becomes another user or root when invoked without any argument. Type su and enter the root password when prompted. Be careful what you do because now you are the super user. Type exit to return to normal user.

The following sections cover new commands, by category, that were not covered in the earlier sessions.

Commands for Managing Processes

20 Min. To Go

Every time the shell acts on a command that you type, it starts a *process*, a single instance of a running program. The shell itself is a process, as are any scripts or applications that it executes. You can use the ps command to see a list of processes. When you type ps x, for example, Bash shows you the current set of processes. Following is partial output from the command. I also included the --cols 132 option to ensure that you can see each command in its entirety:

```
ps x --cols 132
  PID TTY    STAT TIME COMMAND
    1 ?      S    0:05 init [5]
  325 ?      S    0:00 syslogd -m 0
```

```
  335 ?       S     0:00 klogd
  480 ?       S     0:00 crond
  511 ?       S     0:00 xinetd -reuse -pidfile /var/run/xinetd.pid
  580 ?       S     0:00 sendmail: accepting connections
  596 ?       S     0:00 gpm -t imps2
  849 ?       S     0:01 /usr/bin/gnome-session
  893 ?       S     0:00 gnome-smproxy --sm-client-id default0
  901 ?       S     0:02 sawfish --sm-client-id=default2
  967 ?       S     8:36 magicdev --sm-client-id=default12
  985 ?       S     0:00 gnome-name-service
  994 ?       S     0:01 panel --sm-client-id default7
 1001 ?       S     0:00 gmc --nowindows --sm-client-id default8
21437 ?       S     0:00 gnome-terminal --use-factory --start-factory-server
21443 ?       S     0:00 gnome-pty-helper
21444 pts/1   S     0:00 bash
21455 pts/0   R     0:00 ps x --cols 132
```

In the preceding output, the COMMAND column shows the commands that create the processes. This list shows the Bash shell and the ps command as processes. Other processes include all the programs that the shell starts when you log in at the graphical login screen and start a GNOME session. In particular, the list includes the sawfish (window manager) process and the gnome-terminal (terminal window) process. Note that ps even shows its own process as the last one in the list.

The default ps x command does not provide all the processes running on a Linux system. What ps x shows are the commands that you start either directly or indirectly through shell scripts that run automatically when you log in. To see the full complement of processes, use the a option of the ps command together with the x option as follows:

```
ps -ax
```

 If you study the output of the ps command, you find that the first column has the heading PID and that it shows a number for each process. *PID* stands for *process ID* (identification), which is a sequential number assigned by the Linux kernel. If you look through the output of the ps ax command, you should see that the init command is the first process; it has a PID or process number of 1. That's why init is referred to as the *mother of all processes*.

Date and Time Commands

You can use the date command to display the current date and time or set a new date and time. Type date at the shell prompt and you get a result similar to the following:

```
date
Wed Jun 13 19:46:31 MDT 2001
```

You can also format the way you want the date or time to appear. For example, to view the date alone (without the current time), try the following command:

```
date +"%A %B %d %Y"
Wednesday June 13 2001
```

The format specification is in the form of a text string containing single letters with the percentage sign (%) prefix. This is similar to the way in which formats are specified in the C and C++ programming languages. In this example, the format characters mean the following:

%A   displays the full name of the weekday.

%B displays the full name of the month.

%d displays the day of the month.

%Y displays the year using all four digits.

To set the date, log in as root and then use date -s followed by the date and time in any common date/time. For example, to set the date and time to December 31, 2002 at 10:30 p.m., type:

```
date -s "December 31, 2002 10:30 p.m."
```

Here is how this command worked on my system:

```
# date -s "December 31, 2002 10:30 p.m."
Tue Dec 31 22:30:00 MST 2002
# date
Tue Dec 31 22:30:00 MST 2002
```

After setting the time using date -s, a simple date command shows the new time.

To restore the system time to the proper value, execute the command hwclock --hctosys **as the root user.**

The other interesting date-related command is cal. If you type cal without any options, it prints a calendar for the current month. If you type cal followed by a number, cal treats the number as the year and prints the calendar for that year. To view the calendar for a specific month in a specific year, provide the month number (1 = January, 2 = February, and so on) followed by the year. Thus, to view the calendar for January 2001, type the following:

```
cal 1 2001
     January 2001
Su Mo Tu We Th Fr Sa
    1  2  3  4  5  6
 7  8  9 10 11 12 13
14 15 16 17 18 19 20
21 22 23 24 25 26 27
28 29 30 31
```

Commands for Processing Files

10 Min.
To Go

You already saw how to search through a text file with the grep command and how to view a text file one screen at a time with the more command. Red Hat Linux includes many more utilities that work on files — mostly on text files — but some commands also work on any file.

Counting characters, words, and lines in a text file

You can use the wc command to display the line, word, and character count of a text file. Try the following:

```
wc /etc/inittab
     57      244      1756 /etc/inittab
```

This causes wc to display the number of lines (57), words (244), and bytes (characters, in most cases) (1756) in the /etc/inittab file. If you simply want to see the number of lines in a file, use the -l option like this:

```
wc -l /etc/inittab
     57 /etc/inittab
```

In this case, wc simply displays the line count. Use the -c option to count characters only and type the -w option to count only words. The -w option defines a word as any consecutive sequence of characters or digits delimited by at least one space on each side or at the beginning or end of the a file.

If you don't specify a filename, the wc command expects input from the standard input. You can use the pipe(|) feature of the shell to feed the output of another command to wc. This is handy sometimes. For example, suppose you want a rough count of the processes running on your system. You can get a list of all processes with the ps ax command; but instead of manually counting the lines, just pipe the output of ps to wc to get a rough count as follows:

```
ps ax | wc -l
     61
```

This means the ps command produces 61 lines of output. Because the first line simply shows the headings for the tabular columns, you can estimate that there are about 60 processes running on your system.

Sorting text files

You can sort the lines in a text file using the sort command. To see how this command works, first type more /etc/passwd to see the current contents of the /etc/passwd file. Now type sort /etc/passwd to see the lines sorted alphabetically. If you want to sort a file and save the sorted version in another file, you have to use the Bash shell's output redirection feature like this:

```
sort /etc/passwd > ~/sorted.text
```

This command sorts the lines in the /etc/passwd file and saves the output in a file named sorted.text in your home directory.

By default, sort display all lines, even duplicate ones. Use sort's -u option to show only unique lines (that is, to suppress duplicates). Suppose, for example, you have a file named names.txt that contains the following four lines:

```
Kurt Wall
Naba Barkakati
Kurt Wall
Naba Barkakati
```

The sort names.txt command displays the following:

```
Kurt Wall
Kurt Wall
Naba Barkakati
Naba Barkakati
```

If you use sort -u names.txt, the output is more sensible:

```
sort -u names.txt
Kurt Wall
Naba Barkakati
```

The duplicate occurrences of Kurt Wall and Naba Barkakati did not appear.

Splitting any file into several smaller files

The split command is handy for those times when you want to copy a file to a floppy disk, but the file is too large to fit on a single floppy. You can then use the split command to break up the file into smaller files, each of which can fit on a floppy.

By default, split puts 1,000 lines into each file. The files are named by groups of letters such as aa, ab, ac, and so on. You can specify a prefix for the filenames. For example, to split a large file named hugefile.tar into smaller files that fit onto high-density 3.5-inch floppy disks, use split as follows:

```
split -b 1440k hugefile.tar part.
```

This command splits the hugefile.tar file into 1,440K chunks so that each can fit onto a floppy disk. The command creates files named part.aa, part.ab, part.ac, and so on.

To combine the split files back into a single file, use the cat command as follows:

```
cat part.?? > hugefile.tar
```

In this command line, each question mark (?) matches a single character. Thus, the Bash shell expands part.?? to filenames, such as part.aa, part.ab, part.ac, and so on.

Commands for Maintaining the File System

Suppose you want to access the files on this book's companion CD-ROMs. To do so, you have to first mount the CD-ROM drive's file system on a specific directory in the Red Hat Linux file system.

mount and unmount

To try the mount command, log in as root, insert a CD-ROM in the CD-ROM drive, and then type the following command:

```
mount /dev/cdrom /mnt/cdrom
mount: block device /dev/cdrom is write-protected, mounting read-only
```

This command mounts the file system on the device named /dev/cdrom (the CD-ROM) in the /mnt/cdrom directory (also called the *mount point*) in the Linux file system. The response from the mount command indicates that the CD-ROM is mounted as a read-only file system. After the mount command successfully completes its task, you can access the files in the CD-ROM by referring to the /mnt/cdrom directory as the top-level directory of the CD-ROM. In other words, to see the contents of the Red Hat directory in the CD-ROM, type:

```
ls -F /mnt/cdrom/RedHat
RPMS/   TRANS.TBL  base/
```

You can actually mount a device in any directory on the Linux file system. Essentially, the mount point does not have to be /mnt/cdrom; it can be any empty directory. For example, if you like to refer to the CD-ROM drive as /cd, first create the /cd directory with the mkdir /cd command and then use the following mount command:

```
mount /dev/cdrom /cd
```

Before you try this command, you have to "unmount" the CD-ROM with the following umount command:

```
umount /dev/cdrom
```

Only then can you mount the CD-ROM again on another directory in the Linux file system.

I have shown you the longer syntax for the mount command in which you explicitly specify the device name and the mount point, but Red Hat Linux contains a line in the /etc/fstab file that enables you to mount the CD-ROM through one of the following commands:

```
mount /mnt/cdrom
mount /dev/cdrom
```

It is customary to mount devices on directories in the /mnt directory. Red Hat Linux comes with two predefined directories: /mnt/cdrom for mounting the CD-ROM and /mnt/floppy for mounting the floppy.

df and du

In addition to mount and umount, you should know two more commands — df and du — that enable you to check the disk space usage. These commands are simple to use. The df command shows you a summary of disk space usage for all mounted devices, as shown in this example:

```
df
Filesystem          1k-blocks      Used Available Use% Mounted on
/dev/hda7            711508      218484    456880  33% /
/dev/hda1             15522        3485     11236  24% /boot
/dev/hda6           1011928      267804    692720  28% /home
/dev/hda5           3028080     1068372   1805888  38% /usr
```

The output is a table that shows the device, the total kilobytes of storage, how much is in use, how much is available, the percentage being used, and the mount point. For example, on a sample system, the /dev/hda7 device (a disk partition) is mounted on the Linux file system's root directory (/). It has about 695MB of space of which 214MB (or 33 percent) are used and 446MB are available. Similarly, you can see from the last line that the /usr file system on /dev/hda5 has about 1.1GB of storage in use.

If you want to see the space in more familiar units, such as megabytes and gigabtyes, use the -h (for human readable) with df:

```
df -h
Filesystem          Size  Used Avail Use% Mounted on
/dev/hda7           695M  214M  446M  33% /
/dev/hda1            15M  3.5M   10M  24% /boot
/dev/hda6           988M  262M  676M  28% /home
/dev/hda5           2.9G  1.1G  1.7G  38% /usr
```

The information is easier to read now. A suffix of M stands for megabytes, and a suffix of G stands for gigabytes.

The other command, du, is useful for finding out how much space a directory takes up. For example, type the following command to view the contents of all the directories in the /var/log directory (containing various error logs):

```
du /var/log
4        /var/log/httpd
4        /var/log/news/OLD
8        /var/log/news
4        /var/log/vbox
4        /var/log/samba
4        /var/log/sa
120      /var/log
```

A number precedes each directory name. That number denotes the number of kilobytes of disk space used by that directory. Thus, the /var/log directory as a whole uses 120K of disk space, whereas the /var/log/httpd subdirectory uses 4K. If you simply want the total disk space used by a directory (including all the files and subdirectories contained in that directory), use the -s option as follows:

```
du -s /var/log
120      /var/log
```

Notice that the -s option causes du to print just the summary information for the /var/log directory.

 The -h **option works with** du **as well as** df.

Troubleshooting

If a command does not work as you expect it to, it may be because the command executed is a Bash built-in command rather than a normal Linux program. For example, there are two pwd commands that you can use: Bash's pwd command and the program /bin/pwd. If you do not want to use the Bash built-in command, you have to type the full pathname of the command, for example, /bin/pwd. If the output of the ps command scrolls off the screen too fast to read it, you can either redirect its output to a file (ps ax > ps.out) or pipe its output through the more command (ps ax | more).

If the output of the df or du commands does not seem correct, try executing them as the root user. Some directories or the files they contain are not readable by normal users.

Done!

REVIEW

You began this session by reviewing the Linux commands that you encountered in previous sessions. Then you tried out a number of Linux commands in several important categories — managing processes, date and time, and file system maintenance.

QUIZ YOURSELF

1. How do you see a list of all currently defined aliases or shortcuts? (See "Reviewing Commands You've Learned So Far.")

2. How do you find out the process ID (PID) of a process? (See "Commands for Managing Processes.")

3. What command do you use to print the calendar for the month of August 2001? (See "Date and Time Commands.")

4. How do you find out how many processes are currently running on your Linux system? (See "Counting characters, words, and lines in a text file.")

5. What do you have to do to access the files on this book's companion CD-ROMs? (See "Commands for Maintaining the File System.")

SESSION

8

Editing Text Files in Red Hat Linux

Session Checklist

✔ Using the GUI text editors in GNOME and KDE

✔ Using the ed and vi text-mode text editors

30 Min. To Go

In this session, you learn to use the GUI editors and the ed and vi text-mode editors. Text editing is an important part of all operating systems, including Red Hat Linux, because many system configuration files are text files. In Red Hat Linux, you may have to create and edit a variety of text files, such as: system configuration files, including /etc/fstab, /etc/hosts, /etc/inittab, and /etc/X11/XF86Config; user files, including .newsrc and .bash_profile; mail messages and news articles; shell script files; Perl and Tcl/Tk scripts; and C or C++ programs.

Text Editing with GUI Text Editors

Both of the Linux graphical desktops — GNOME and KDE — come with *GUI text editors* (text editors that have graphical user interfaces). To try the GNOME text editor, gEdit, select Main Menu ⇨ Programs ⇨ Applications ⇨ gEdit from the GNOME desktop. You can open a file by clicking the Open button on the toolbar. This brings up the Open File dialog box. You can then change directories and select the file to edit by clicking the OK button.

The gEdit editor then loads the file in its window. You can open more than one file and move among them as you edit the files. Figure 8-1 shows a typical editing session with gEdit.

In this case, the editor has three files — fstab, hosts, and innittab (all from the /etc directory) — open for editing. The filenames appear as tabs between the toolbar and the editing window. You can switch among the files by clicking the tabs with the filenames.

The rest of the text-editing steps behave as you would expect. To enter new text, click to position the cursor and begin typing. You can select text, copy, cut, and paste using the buttons on the toolbar above the text-editing area.

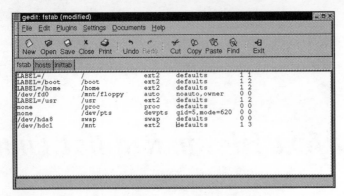

Figure 8-1   *Editing three text files with gEdit*

From the KDE desktop, you can start KWrite (a KDE text editor) by selecting K ➪ Editors ➪ Advanced Editor. To open a text file, select File ➪ Open from the menu. A dialog box appears. From this dialog box, you can go to the right directory, select the file to open, and click the OK button. The KDE text editor then opens the /etc/fstab file and displays its contents in the window. Figure 8-2 shows a KWrite editing the /etc/fstab file.

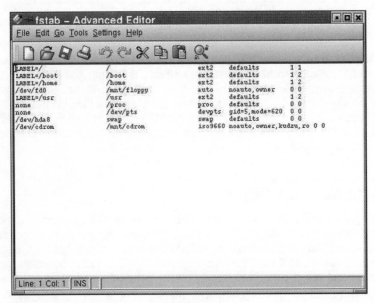

Figure 8-2   *Editing a text file with Kwrite*

Text Editing with ed and vi

All UNIX systems, including Linux, come with two text-mode text editors:

- ed, a line-oriented text editor
- vi, a full-screen text editor that supports the command set of an earlier editor named ex

Although the graphical text editors are easy to use, ed and vi may be more cryptic than other, more graphical, text editors. You should learn the basic editing commands of ed and vi because sometimes these two may be the only editors available. When you run into a system problem and Linux refuses to boot from the hard disk, for example, you may have to boot from a floppy. In this case, you have to edit system files with the ed editor because that editor is small enough to fit on the floppy. As the next two sections demonstrate, learning the basic text-editing commands of ed and vi isn't hard.

Using ed

The ed text editor works with a *buffer* — an in-memory storage area where the actual text resides until you explicitly save the text to a file. Typically, you have to use ed only when you boot a minimal version of Linux (for example, from a boot floppy) and the system does not support full-screen mode. In all other situations, you can use the vi editor that works in a text-mode full-screen.

As you will see in the following examples using the ed editor, you work in either command mode or text-input mode, which are defined as follows:

- *Command mode* is the default. In this mode, anything that you type is interpreted as a command. The ed text editor has a simple command set in which each command consists of one or more characters.
- *Text-input mode* enables you to enter text into the buffer. You can enter input mode with the commands a (append), c (change), or i (insert). After entering lines of text, you can leave input mode by entering a period (.) on a line by itself.

To practice editing a file, copy the /etc/fstab file to your home directory with the following commands:

```
cd
cp /etc/fstab .
```

Now you should have a file named fstab in your home directory. Type the following command to begin editing a file in ed:

```
ed -p: fstab
608
:
```

This example uses the -p (for *prompt*) option to set the prompt to the colon character (:) and then opens the fstab file for editing in the current directory, which should be your home directory. The ed editor opens the file, reports the number of characters in the file (690), displays the prompt (:), and then waits for a command.

When editing with ed, you may find it helpful to turn on a prompt character using the -p option. Without the prompt, it's difficult to tell whether ed is in input mode or command mode.

After ed opens a file for editing, the current line is the last line of the file. The *current line* is the line to which ed applies your command. To see the current line number use the .= command:

```
:.=
8
```

This output tells you that the fstab file has eight lines. (Your system's /etc/fstab file may have a different number of lines, in which case you will see a different number.)

You can use the 1,$p command to see all lines in a file, as the following example shows:

```
:1,$p
LABEL=/              /                    ext2     defaults        1 1
LABEL=/boot          /boot                ext2     defaults        1 2
LABEL=/home          /home                ext2     defaults        1 2
/dev/fd0             /mnt/floppy          auto     noauto,owner    0 0
LABEL=/usr           /usr                 ext2     defaults        1 2
none                 /proc                proc     defaults        0 0
none                 /dev/pts             devpts   gid=5,mode=620  0 0
/dev/hda8            swap                 swap     defaults        0 0
:
```

To go to a specific line, type the line number:

```
:5
LABEL=/usr           /usr                 ext2     defaults        1 2
:
```

The editor responds by displaying that line.

Suppose you want to delete the line that contains fd0. To search for a string, type a forward slash (/) followed by the string that you want to locate:

```
:/fd0
/dev/fd0             /mnt/floppy          auto     noauto,owner    0 0
:
```

The editor locates the line that contains the string and then displays it. That line becomes the current line.

To delete the current line, use the d command as follows:

```
:d
:
```

If you are skeptical about whether the line was deleted, reenter the 1,$p command to redisplay the file:

```
:1,$p
LABEL=/              /                    ext2     defaults        1 1
LABEL=/boot          /boot                ext2     defaults        1 2
LABEL=/home          /home                ext2     defaults        1 2
```

```
LABEL=/usr          /usr          ext2    defaults        1 2
none                /proc         proc    defaults        0 0
none                /dev/pts      devpts  gid=5,mode=620  0 0
/dev/hda8           swap          swap    defaults        0 0
```

The line containing fd0 (the current line after the search command) has been deleted from the buffer's copy of the file. Because you have not yet saved the file, the copy on disk has not been changed; only the copy in memory has been altered.

To replace one string with another one on the current line, use the s command. To replace fd0 with the string floppy, for example, use this command:

```
:s/fd0/floppy/
:
```

Until you become comfortable with ed, use 1.$p to confirm that ed actually performed the changes you requested.

To insert a line in front of the current line, use the i command:

```
:i
    (type the line you want to insert)
.   (type a single period to indicate you're done)
:
```

You can enter as many lines as you want. After the last line, enter a period (.) on a line by itself. That period marks the end of text-input mode, and the editor switches to command mode. In this case, you can tell that ed switched to command mode because you see the prompt (:).

When you are happy with the changes, you can write them to the file with the w command. If you want to save the changes and exit, type wq to perform both steps at the same time:

```
:wq
632
```

The ed editor saves the changes in the file, displays the number of saved characters, and exits. If you want to quit the editor without saving any changes, use the Q command.

This sample editing session gives you an idea of how to use ed commands to perform the basic tasks of editing a text file. Table 8-1 lists some of the commonly used ed commands.

Table 8-1   *Commonly Used ed Commands*

Command	Meaning
!*command*	Executes a shell command (for example, !pwd shows the current directory).
$	Goes to the last line in the buffer.
%	Applies the command that follows the % to all lines in the buffer (for example, %p prints all lines).
+	Goes to the next line.

Continued

Table 8-1 *Continued*

Command	Meaning
+*n*	Goes to *n*-th next line (*n* is a number).
,	Applies a command that follows the , to all lines in the buffer (for example, ,p prints all lines); similar to %.
-	Goes to the preceding line.
-*n*	Goes to *n*th previous line (*n* is a number).
.	Refers to the current line in the buffer.
/*text*/	Searches forward for the specified text.
;	Refers to a range of lines that is current through the last line in the buffer.
=	Prints the current line number.
?*text*?	Searches backward for the specified text.
^	Goes to the preceding line; also see the - command, earlier in this table.
^*n*	Goes to *n*th previous line (where *n* is a number); also see the -*n* command, earlier in this table.
A	Appends text after current line.
C	Changes specified lines.
D	Deletes specified lines.
I	Inserts text before the current line.
N	Goes to line number *n*.
Newline	Displays the next line and makes it current.
Q	Quits the editor.
Q	Quits the editor without saving changes.
r *file*	Reads and inserts contents of a file after the current line.
s/*old*/*new*/	Replaces an *old* string with a *new* one.
U	Undoes the last command.
W *file*	Appends the contents of the buffer to the end of the specified *file*.
w *file*	Saves the edit buffer in the specified *file*. If no file is named, saves the contents of the edit buffer in the default file — the file whose contents ed is currently editing.

Using vi

20 Min. To Go

The vi editor is a full-screen text editor that enables you to view a file several lines at a time. It is an extremely rare Linux or UNIX system that does not have vi or another editor that behaves like vi. Because vi is so ubiquitous, learning vi's basic features enables you to edit text files on almost any UNIX system.

Pronounce *vi* as "vee eye," not "vie."

Like the ed editor, vi works with a buffer. When vi edits a file, it reads the file into a *buffer*, which is a block of memory. All changes reside only in the buffer. Although vi uses temporary files during editing, the original file is not altered until you save the changes with a specific vi command.

Setting the terminal type

Before you start a full-screen text editor such as vi, you may have to set the TERM environment variable to the terminal type (such as vt100 or xterm). For example, type export TERM=vt100 to set the terminal type to VT100. The vi editor uses the terminal type to control the terminal in full-screen mode. This step is rarely necessary on a Red Hat Linux system.

When you run X and a graphical user interface such as GNOME or KDE, you can use vi in a terminal window. The terminal window's terminal type is xterm. To verify this, type echo $TERM at the command prompt. When you start the terminal window, it automatically sets the TERM environment variable to xterm. Therefore, you should be able to use vi in an xterm window without explicitly setting the TERM variable.

Starting the editor

To start the editor, use the vi command name followed by an optional filename. You can provide other arguments besides the filename. However, most of the time vi starts with a filename as the only argument, as shown here:

```
vi /etc/hosts
```

Another common way to start vi is to jump to a specific line number right at startup. To do so, add +n between the vi command and the filename, where *n* is the line number. For example, to begin editing at line 296 of the file /etc/X11/XF86Config, use this command:

```
vi +296 /etc/X11/XF86Config
```

This way of starting vi is useful when you edit a source file after the compiler reports an error at a specific line number.

When you edit a file with vi, the editor loads the file into a buffer, displays the first few lines of the file in a full-screen window, and positions the cursor on the first line. The last line shows information about the file, including the number of lines and the number of characters in the file, as Figure 8-3 illustrates.

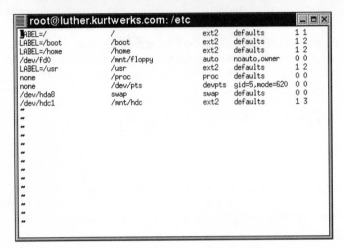

```
root@luther.kurtwerks.com: /etc                    _ □ ✕
LABEL=/           /              ext2    defaults      1 1
LABEL=/boot       /boot          ext2    defaults      1 2
LABEL=/home       /home          ext2    defaults      1 2
/dev/fd0          /mnt/floppy    auto    noauto,owner  0 0
LABEL=/usr        /usr           ext2    defaults      1 2
none              /proc          proc    defaults      0 0
none              /dev/pts       devpts  gid=5,mode=620 0 0
/dev/hda8         swap           swap    defaults      0 0
/dev/hdc1         /mnt/hdc       ext2    defaults      1 3
~
~
~
~
~
~
~
~
~
~
~
~
~
~
```

Figure 8-3   *The vi editor editing* /etc/fstab

Later, the bottom line functions as a command entry and status line. The rest of the lines display the file. If the file contains fewer lines than the window, vi displays the empty lines with a tilde (~) in the first column.

The current line is marked by the cursor, which appears as a small black rectangle. The cursor appears on top of a character.

vi modes

In vi, you work in one of three modes:

- *Visual command mode* is the default. In this mode, anything that you type is interpreted as a command that applies to the line containing the cursor. The vi commands are similar to ed commands.

- *Colon command mode* enables you to read or write files, set vi options, and quit the vi editing session. All colon commands start with a colon (:). When you enter the colon, vi positions the cursor at the last line and enables you to type a command. The command takes effect when you press Enter.

- *Text input mode* enables you to enter text into the buffer. You can enter input mode with the commands a (append after cursor), A (append at end of line), or i (insert after cursor). After entering lines of text, you have to press Esc to leave input mode and reenter visual command mode.

One problem with all these modes is that you cannot easily tell vi's current mode. It is frustrating to begin typing, only to realize that vi is not in input mode. The converse situation also occurs commonly — you may be typing text when you want to enter a command. If you want to make sure that vi is in command mode, just press Esc a few times. (Pressing Esc more than once doesn't hurt.)

To view online help in vi, type :help while in command mode. Type :q to exit the help screen and return to the file you are editing.

Moving the cursor

The vi editor initially positions the cursor on the first character. One of the first things that you need to learn is how to move the cursor around. Try the following commands. Just type the letter (in visual command mode) and vi responds.

b moves the cursor one word backward.

h moves the cursor one character to the left.

j moves the cursor one line down.

k moves the cursor one line up.

l moves the cursor one character to the right.

w moves the cursor one word forward.

Ctrl+D moves down half a screen.

Ctrl+U scrolls up half a screen.

Luckily, you can also move the cursor using the arrow keys. If you cannot remember the meaning of the hjkl **characters, just use the arrow keys to move around the file.**

You can go to a specific line number at any time. This is when a colon command comes in. To go to line 1, for example, type the following and then press Enter:

    :1

When you type the colon, vi displays the colon on the last line of the screen. From then on, vi uses the text that you type as a command. You have to press Enter to submit the command to vi. In colon command mode, vi accepts all the commands that the ed editor accepts — and then some.

Searching for strings

To search for a string, first type a slash (/). The vi editor displays the slash on the last line of the screen. Type the search string and then press Enter. The vi editor locates the string and positions the cursor at the beginning of that string. Thus, to locate the string cdrom in the file /etc/fstab, type:

    /cdrom

Deleting lines

To delete the line that contains the cursor, type dd (two lowercase *d*s). The vi editor deletes that line of text and makes the next line the current one.

Entering text before cursors

To begin entering text in front of the cursor, type i (a lowercase *i* all by itself). The vi editor switches to text input mode. Now you can enter text. When you finish entering text, press Esc to return to visual command mode.

10 Min.
To Go

Saving changes

After you finish editing the file, you can save the changes in the file with the :w command. To quit the editor without saving any changes, use the :q! command. If you want to save the changes and exit, you can type :wq to perform both steps at the same time. The vi editor saves the changes in the file and exits. You can also save the changes and exit the editor by pressing Shift+zz (hold down the Shift key and press z twice).

Commands

In addition to the few commands you have just learned, vi accepts a large number of commands. Table 8-2 lists some commonly used vi commands, organized by task.

Table 8-2 *Commonly Used vi Commands*

Task and Command	Meaning
Insert text	
a	Inserts text after the cursor.
A	Inserts text at the end of the current line.
I	Inserts text at the beginning of the current line.
I	Inserts text before the cursor.
o	Inserts a new line below the current line.
O	Inserts a new line above the current line.
Delete text	
D	Deletes up to the end of the current line.
dd	Deletes the current line.
dl	Deletes the character on which the cursor rests.
dh	Deletes the character preceding the cursor.
dw	Deletes from the cursor to the end of the following word.
x	Deletes the character on which the cursor rests.
Change text	
C	Changes up to the end of the current line.
cc	Changes the current line.

J	Joins the current line with the next one.
r*x*	Replaces the character under the cursor with *x* (*x* is any character).

Move cursor

h	Moves one character to the left.
j	Moves one line down.
k	Moves one line up.
L	Moves cursor to the end of the screen.
l	Moves one character to the right.
w	Moves to the beginning of the following word.

Scroll text

Ctrl-b	Scrolls backward by one full screen.
Ctrl-d	Scrolls forward by half a screen.
Ctrl-f	Scrolls forward by one full screen.
Ctrl-u	Scrolls backward by half a screen.

Cut and paste text

P	Puts a yanked (copied) line above the current line.
p	Puts a yanked line below the current line.
yy	Yanks the current line into an unnamed buffer.

Colon commands

:!*command*	Executes the shell *command*.
:q	Quits the editor.
:q!	Quits the editor without saving changes.
:r *filename*	Reads a file and inserts text after the current line.
:w *filename*	Writes a buffer to a file.
:wq	Saves changes and exits the editor.

Search text

/*string*	Searches forward for *string*, a series of one or more characters.
?*string*	Searches backward for *string*, a series of one or more characters.

Miscellaneous

u	Undoes the last command.
Esc	Ends input mode and enters visual command mode.
U	Undoes recent changes to the current line.

To try these commands, copy a file such as /etc/X11/XF86Config to your home directory and use vi to edit that file with the following commands:

```
cd
cp /etc/X11/XF86Config .
vi XF86Config
```

As you edit the file, try the commands shown in Table 8-2. Because good vi skills are useful in all UNIX systems, including Red Hat Linux, you should spend a few minutes familiarizing yourself with some of the commands from Table 8-2.

Troubleshooting

If you get an error message resembling TERM variable not set when starting vi, use the export command to set the TERM environment variable. For example,

```
export TERM=linux
```

Similarly, if your vi sessions scroll strangely or the bottom lines of the screen seem jumbled and the TERM environment variable is set, try setting TERM to vt100 (export TERM=vt100), which is a very generic, basic terminal type setting.

If you have trouble remembering what mode you are in (visual command mode, colon command mode, or insert mode) while using vi, execute the colon command :set showmode. This will cause the bottom line of the vi window to display the current mode constantly, unless you are executing a colon command or a search.

If you have totally fouled up a file and want to abandon all your changes, use the colon command, :q!, to exit without saving any changes.

Done!

REVIEW

This session showed you how to use the graphical text editors in GNOME and KDE to edit files. The graphical text editors are intuitive to use, but sometimes you may have to edit text files without the benefit of a graphical login. For those situations, you practiced editing text files with the text-mode editors: ed and vi.

QUIZ YOURSELF

1. How do you start the GNOME text editor? (See "Text Editing with GUI Text Editors.")
2. When editing with the ed editor, how do you view all lines of a file? (See "Using ed.")
3. When editing a file with the ed editor, what command do you use to locate a line containing the string monitor? (See "Using ed.")
4. What are the three modes of the vi editor? (See "Using vi.")
5. How do you exit the vi editor without saving any changes? (See "Using vi.")

Learning More Linux and Bash Commands

Session Checklist

✔ Changing the Bash prompt

✔ Formatting text files

✔ Changing text in files

✔ Compressing and uncompressing files

30 Min.
To Go

This session helps you to become more familiar with Linux and Bash commands. First, you learn how to customize the Bash prompt. Then, because many Linux activities involve text files, you will learn how to format them using a few simple commands, and how to make bulk changes to text files. This session's last topic teaches you how to work with compressed files.

Changing the Bash Prompt

One of the most enjoyable features of Red Hat Linux is the degree to which you can customize and personalize it. Bash is no different in this respect than the more visually dominant GNOME and KDE window managers. In this section, you will learn how to change the Bash command prompt to your liking.

Before proceeding, bear in mind that Bash maintains four levels of prompts, named PS1, PS2, PS3, and PS4. PS1 is the primary command prompt and the one you will learn how to change. PS2 is the prompt Bash displays when it needs more input to complete a command. PS3 and PS4 are infrequently used, so they are not discussed in this book.

Bash lets you use over 20 different tokens to define its command prompt, the most commonly used of which appear in Table 9-1. Each token is a single letter or symbol preceded by a backslash (\), which stands for a certain element of information. You can also use literal text, such as numbers and letters, in the prompt string. To see how the prompt is defined, type echo $PS1 and press Enter.

Table 9-1 *Common Bash Command Prompt Tokens*

Token	Description
\h	Hostname up to the first .
\H	Full hostname
\t	Current time in 24-hour HH:MM:SS format
\T	Current time in 12-hour HH:MM:SS format
\@	Current time in 12-hour a.m./p.m. format
\u	Username of the current user
\w	Current working directory
\W	Basename of the current working directory
\!	History number of the current command
\#	Command number of the current command

For example, Bash's default command prompt in Red Hat Linux is [\u@\h \W]\$. As you can see from Table 9-1, this corresponds to a prompt of the form [*username@hostname currentdir*]$. On a sample system, this looks like [kwall@luther kwall]$ when he is in his home directory.

Bash replaces the token $ with a literal $ for normal users. The literal # for the root user indicates when you are working as the root user.

Suppose you do not want to see your user name or your host name. Instead, you want to see the current time in a.m./p.m. format. To change your Bash prompt to show the time this way, type export PS1='\@' and press Enter. The change takes effect immediately, as shown in the following example:

```
[kwall@luther kwall]$ export PS1='\@ \$ '
05:59pm $
```

The time displayed in the prompt will update each time you press Enter.

In Session 6, you learned how to use Bash's command history. Table 9-1 listed two tokens, \! and \#, that display history information in the prompt. The \! Token shows the cumulative history number of the current command. The \# token shows the command number of the current command for the current session only. (*Cumulative* refers to all commands that are stored in the Bash history file plus all commands executed during the current session.) To illustrate the difference between these two tokens, the following command sets the prompt to show the history number:

```
[kwall@hoser kwall]$ export PS1='\! \$ '
1019 $
```

The number to the left of **$** indicates that the next command typed will be the 1019th command. However, by setting the prompt to show the command number, the displayed value will be much smaller because it only counts the commands executed during the current session:

```
1019 $ export PS1='\# \$ '
21 $
```

In this case, the number to the left of the **$** shows that the next command executed will be the twenty-first command *in this session*. The command values you can set in the prompt make it much easier to use and manipulate Bash's command history features. You can try other prompt forms until you settle on one that you like best.

Formatting Text Files

Recall that many Linux activities involve working with text files. As Linux and Unix have evolved, many programs and utilities have been developed to process and manipulate text files. You will learn how to use two of these in this session: cut and fmt. These two commands reduce or eliminate much of the tedium and repetition of manipulating and reformatting text files.

Selecting text with cut

The cut command selects user-specified parts of each line in a file and writes those parts to stdout. The general format of the cut command is:

```
cut option file
```

option tells cut what information to select, and *file* tells cut the file to use. Table 9-2 lists the most common options.

Table 9-2 *Common* cut *Options*

Option	Description
-c *columns*	Displays the columns specified by *columns*.
-f *fields*	Selects the field number(s) specified by *fields*.
-d *delim*	Uses the character *delim* as the field separator (the tab character is the default).

You can use the -c option to select specific columns (or characters) from each line. The fields are specified by number, starting with 1. By default, fields are tab-separated, but the -d option lets you declare a different field *delimiter*, or separator.

Suppose you have a file named phnlist.txt that consists of the names and telephone numbers of your friends, such as the following:

```
Kurt Wall       801-555-1212
Naba Barkakati  301-666-2323
Bubba Tippetts  212-777-3434
```

A tab separates the names from the telephone numbers. Suppose you want to display only the names in the file. Because tab characters separate the names and telephone numbers, use cut's -f with the numeral 1 to tell cut to display only the first field. Executing the command cut -f 1 phnlist.txt will show only the names in the file (you type the following bold text):

```
cut -f1 phnlist.txt
Kurt Wall
Naba Barkakati
Bubba Tippetts
```

If, on the other hand, you only want to see your friends' first names, combine the -f option with the -d option to define the space character as the field delimiter:

```
cut -f1 -d" " phnlist.txt
Kurt
Naba
Bubba
```

Notice that the space character had to be embedded between double quotes ("") to make the command work properly. If you only want to see the prefix of each telephone number, you could use the command cut -f2 -d- phnlist.txt.

To display one or more columns, use cut's -c option, followed by a list of the columns to show. Use the comma character (,) to list non-contiguous characters and the minus sign (-) to identify a range of contiguous characters. For example, the command, cut -c1,5 phnlist.txt, will show the first and fifth characters in each line, while the command, cut -c6-8 phnlist.txt, will show columns 6, 7, and 8 from each line.

Reformatting paragraphs with fmt

**20 Min.
To Go**

The fmt command makes short work of reformatting paragraphs. It is especially useful for breaking long lines of text into shorter lines and removing superfluous spaces. For example, suppose you have a text file named formatme.txt that looks like the following:

```
`fmt' prefers breaking lines at the end of a sentence, and tries to avoid line  breaks
after the first word of a sentence or before the last word of a sentence.    A "sentence
break" is defined as either the end of a paragraph or a word ending in either a period
(.), a question mark (?), or an exclamation point (!), followed by two spaces or the end
of a line, ignoring any intervening parentheses or quotes.
```

Although you cannot see it in the printed text, there are no embedded new lines or carriage returns in the text, so if you viewed this file in the vi editor, it would look like Figure 9-1.

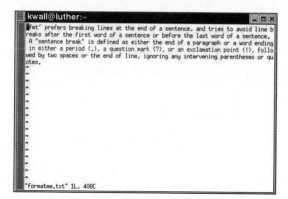

Figure 9-1 *An awkwardly formatted text file viewed in the vi editor*

The fmt command will reformat this text, adding a new line at the word break closest to the seventy-fifth column. Type fmt formatme.txt and press Enter, as shown in the following example, to see how the fmt command reformats the text file:

```
fmt formatme.txt
`fmt' prefers breaking lines at the end of a sentence, and tries to avoid
line breaks after the first word of a sentence or before the last word
of a sentence.  A "sentence break" is defined as either the end of a
paragraph or a word ending in either a period (.), a question mark (?),
or an exclamation point (!), followed by two spaces or the end of line,
ignoring any intervening parentheses or quotes.
```

Notice how fmt inserted new line characters without breaking words in half. You can specify a different width using fmt's -w option followed by the width in characters. For example, the command fmt -w 50 formatme.txt would break each line at the word break closest to the fiftieth column.

E-mail messages in HTML format often have extra spaces between words, making them hard to read. To reduce the clutter in such messages, use fmt's **-u option, which puts one space between words and two spaces after the end of a sentence.**

Changing Text in Files

Another useful Linux command is the tr (for *translate*) command, which you can use to change one character to another or to delete certain characters without editing the file using an editor like vi or gEdit.

Deleting text

Suppose you want to replace the tab characters in the phnlist.txt file with a single space. To do so, execute the command, tr "\t" " " < phnlist.txt. This command instructs tr to replace each tab character it encounters, denoted by "\t", with a single space character, denoted by " ". Using the phnlist.txt file shown in the section "Selecting text with cut," the output should resemble the following:

```
Kurt Wall 801-555-1212
Naba Barkakati 301-666-2323
Bubba Tippetts 212-777-3434
```

Notice that the command used < to redirect stdin to a file. This is because tr reads stdin by default. The "\t" represents the tab character.

To save tr's output, redirect output to another file using >.

Changing text

Another handy trick uses a special notation that refers to sets of characters. To convert all the lowercase characters in phnlist.txt to uppercase, use [:lower:] and [:upper:] in place of "\t" and " ". Here is what the command and its results looks like:

```
tr [:lower:] [:upper:] < phnlist.txt
KURT WALL        801-555-1212
NABA BARKAKATI   301-666-2323
BUBBA TIPPETTS   212-777-3434
```

As you can see from the output, [:lower:] refers to all lowercase characters and [:upper:] to all uppercase characters. Table 9-3 lists some of the special symbols, in addition to [:lower:] and [:upper:], that you can use to refer to specific sets of characters when using the tr command.

Table 9-3 tr *Character Set Symbols*

Symbol	Description
[:alnum:]	All letters and digits
[:alpha:]	All letters
[:blank:]	Any whitespace (spaces and tabs)
[:digit:]	All numerals (0-9)
[:punct:]	All punctuation characters

You can use the tr command to make bulk edits to files with a single command rather than making them manually using a standard text editor.

Compressing and Uncompressing Files

A common task when using Linux is compressing and uncompressing files. The last few minutes of this session show you how to use the gzip and ungzip commands to compress and decompress files. Compressing files reduces the amount of disk space they use on your

10 Min.
To Go

system. Compression also makes sending files over the Internet via e-mail, or by using the FTP or HTTP protocols, much faster.

Compressing files

To compress a file, use the command gzip *filename*, where *filename* is the name of the file you want to compress. The gzip command will compress the file and replace it with one that has a .gz extension, indicating it has been compressed using gzip (This is commonly called a *gzipped* file.)

For example, suppose you want to compress a large file named important.txt that you want to e-mail to a friend. To do so, execute the command, gzip important.txt. The following commands show the file's size before being compressed, the gzip command to compress it, and the file's size after compressing it:

```
ls -l important.txt
-rw-rw-r--    1 kwall    kwall      2514780 Jun 17 21:21 important.txt
gzip important.txt
ls -l important.txt.gz
-rw-rw-r--    1 kwall    kwall       204228 Jun 17 21:22 important.txt.gz
```

Notice that the gzipped file is less than 10 percent of its original size. Depending on the type of file, the reduction in file size will vary. As you can see from the example, gzip is an easy command to use.

If you want to see what a gzipped file contains, use the -l option with gzip. The -t option tests a gzip file for possible corruption. Because large files can take a long time to compress, you can use the -1 option to instruct gzip to operate quickly, but the compression will be less complete than normal. Conversely, to obtain the best possible compression, use the -9 option, but it will take noticeably longer to compress the file. The results of using the -1 and -9 options are shown in the following example:

```
gzip -1 important.txt
ls -l important.txt.gz
-rw-rw-r--    1 kwall    kwall       304827 Jun 17 21:29 important.txt.gz
```

Notice that the compressed file after using the -1 option is not as small as it was using gzip without the -1 option:

```
gzip -9 important.txt
ls -l important.txt.gz
-rw-rw-r--    1 kwall    kwall       191489 Jun 17 21:32 important.txt.gz
```

Using gzip's -9 option, the resulting file was somewhat smaller than ordinary, but not dramatically so.

Uncompressing files

To uncompress a gzipped file, the command to use is gunzip *filename*, where *filename* is the name of the file you want to decompress. The gunzip command will uncompress the file and replace it with one that has the .gz extension removed. So, to decompress important.txt.gz, use the command gunzip important.txt.gz.

The command `gzip -d` **also decompresses a** `gzipped` **file.**

Troubleshooting

If you are having trouble setting the Bash command prompt, make sure you are enclosing the prompt within apostrophes (') or double quotes (") and that each token is preceded by a backslash (\).

To restore the Bash prompt to its default value for Red Hat Linux, execute the command `export PS1="[\u@\h \W]\$ "`.

If the `tr` command complains that you are using too many arguments, make sure that you are using < to redirect `stdin` from a file. Remember, `tr` reads `stdin`, not disk files, by default.

If `gunzip` fails to uncompress a file, use the command `gzip -t` to test the `gzipped` file for possible corruption. If the file is corrupted, you will have to obtain a fresh copy of it.

Done!

REVIEW

This session showed you how to change the Bash command prompt by using special tokens to set the PS1 variable that defines the prompt's appearance. Next, you learned how to use the `cut`, `fmt`, and `tr` commands to edit text files without using an editor. Finally, you learned how to use the `gzip` and `gunzip` commands to compress and uncompress files.

QUIZ YOURSELF

1. What is the token to insert the current date in the Bash command prompt? (See "Changing the Bash Prompt.")
2. What is the option for selecting the second field from a line when using the cut command? (See "Selecting text with cut.")
3. What command option should you use with `fmt` to change the width of lines in a paragraph? (See "Reformatting Paragraphs with fmt.")
4. What option does the `tr` command use to remove characters from a file? (See "Deleting text.")
5. How do you list the contents of a file compressed with gzip? (See "Compressing files.")

Performing Basic System Administration Tasks

Session Checklist

✔ Understanding Linux system-and-network administration

✔ Adding user accounts with Linuxconf

✔ Exploring other Linuxconf features

**30 Min.
To Go**

This final Saturday morning session introduces you to Linux system and network administration. Then you learn to perform some system administration tasks using *Linuxconf*, a graphical system administration tool that comes with Red Hat Linux. Specifically, you learn how to add user accounts and then you explore other tasks that Linuxconf enables you to perform. This overview of Linuxconf should help you execute other system administration tasks as the need arises.

Understanding Linux System and Network Administration

System administration refers to tasks that you must perform to keep a computer system up and running properly. Now that almost all computers are networked, another set of tasks is needed to keep the network up and running. These tasks are collectively called *network administration*. A site with many computers probably has a full-time *system administrator* who takes care of all system- and network-administration tasks. Very large sites may have separate system-administration and network-administration personnel. If you run Red Hat Linux on a home PC or on a few systems in a small company, you probably perform the duties of both the system administrator and the network administrator.

As the following descriptions of system and network administration tasks demonstrate, you can perform these tasks using the Linuxconf tool — an X Window application that enables you to perform most system and network administration tasks without having to edit configuration files manually or type cryptic commands. After the overview of system and network administration, you learn to use Linuxconf.

System administration tasks

A system administrator's typical tasks include the following:

- *Installing, configuring, and upgrading the operating system and various utilities.* You learned how to install Red Hat Linux in Session 1. This session shows you how to configure various features or Red Hat Linux, and Sessions 23 and 27 will show you how to upgrade applications using the Red Hat Package manager.
- *Adding and removing users.* Later in this session, you learn to use Red Hat's graphical Linuxconf tool to add a new user account. If a user forgets the password, you can also change the password using Linuxconf.
- *Installing new software.* For the typical Linux software, which you get in source-code form, this task involves using tools such as gunzip (to uncompress the software), tar (to unpack the archive), and make (to build the executable programs). For software distributed by Red Hat in Red Hat Package Manager (RPM) files, you have to use the rpm command to install the software.

Session 23 shows you how to install RPM packages. In Session 27, you learn how to use tools, such as tar **and** make, **to build software packages.**

- *Making backups.* You can use the tar or cpio program to archive one or more directories and to copy the archive to a floppy disk (if the archive is small enough) or to a tape (if you have a tape drive).

In Session 26, you learn how to back up and restore files.

- *Mounting and unmounting file systems.* When you want to access the files on a CD-ROM, for example, you have to mount that CD-ROM's file system on one of the directories of the Linux file system. You have to use the mount command to accomplish this task. You can also use Linuxconf to mount a file system. (An example appears later in this session.)

Mounting is covered in Session 7.

- *Monitoring the system's performance.* You have to use a few utilities, such as top (to see where the processor spends most of its time) and free (to see the amount of free and used memory in the system).

You learn to use utilities to monitor system performance in Session 28.

- *Starting and shutting down the system.* You must always shut down your Linux system properly using the shutdown command to stop all programs before turning off your PC's power switch.

Network administration tasks

Typical network-administration tasks that you can perform with Linuxconf include the following:

- *Editing the network configuration files.* In Linux (as well as in other UNIX systems), the TCP/IP network is configured through several text files that you may have to edit in order to make networking work. Linuxconf enables you to configure the network.

You learn about the TCP/IP configuration files in Sessions 12 and 13.

- *Setting up PPP and SLIP.* You can use Linuxconf to set up Point-to-Point Protocol (PPP) and Serial Line Internet Protocol (SLIP) connections.

You learn about using a modem to connect to the Internet in Session 13.

- *Monitoring network status.* You have to use tools such as netstat (to view information about active network connections), /sbin/ifconfig (to check the status of various network interfaces), and ping (to make sure that a connection is working).

Adding User Accounts with Linuxconf

**20 Min.
To Go**

When you installed Red Hat Linux on Friday night, one of the steps gave you the opportunity to set up other user accounts besides root. If you did not add other user accounts during installation, you can do so now. You also must perform this step if you want to enable other users to access and use the system.

It is a good idea to create other user accounts besides root. Even if you are the only user of the system, logging in as a less-privileged user is good practice; that way, you cannot damage any important system files inadvertently. When necessary, you can log in as root and perform any system-administration tasks.

To start Linuxconf from the GNOME Main Menu in Red Hat Linux, select Main Menu (Foot) ⇨ Programs ⇨ System ⇨ LinuxConf.

The initial Linuxconf window shows three tabs — Config, Control, and Status (see Figure 10-1). Each tab includes tree lists that you can expand to perform various system and network administration tasks with Linuxconf. When you select a particular list item, it expands to show additional options. You can continue selecting list items this way until you reach the item corresponding to the configuration task you wish to perform.

Figure 10-1 *Initial Linuxconf window*

To add a new user, follow these steps:

1. Select the Users Accounts item, and then select the User accounts item in the Normal tab. This causes Linuxconf to display the Users Accounts dialog box, as shown in Figure 10-2.

2. Click the Add button in the Users Accounts dialog box of Figure 10-2. This brings up the User Account Creation dialog box.

3. Fill in the requested information. In particular, you must enter the login name and the home directory. For example, create an account with a login name of gnuuser with /home/gnuuser as the home directory. After filling in all of the fields, click the Accept button. If the /home/gnuuser directory does not exist, Linuxconf creates the directory.

4. The Linuxconf tool displays the Changing Password dialog box, in which you enter the password for the new account. Enter the password, click the Accept button, and then retype the password for confirmation. Notice that Linuxconf warns you if the password is a combination of words that you can find in the dictionary. After entering the password, click the Dismiss button in the Users Accounts dialog box.

5. To quit Linuxconf, click the File ⇨ Quit from the menu in the main window. The Linuxconf tool displays the Status of the System dialog box that asks you if you want to activate the changes. Click the Do It button to finish the task and exit Linuxconf.

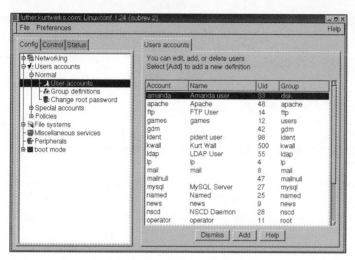

Figure 10-2   *The Users Accounts dialog box in Linuxconf*

Exploring Other Linuxconf Features

Here, you explore the tabs and buttons for the kinds of tasks that Linuxconf can perform. This session's coverage of Linuxconf, however, is far from complete. It would take many more pages to cover Linuxconf's features thoroughly and explain each of the tasks it can perform.

Linuxconf has its own home page on the Web at
`http://www.solucorp.qc.ca/linuxconf/`. **Visit the home page to learn the latest news about Linuxconf and read online documentation.**

Help button

Linuxconf includes a Help button in the main Linuxconf window. This Help button provides an overview of Linuxconf. A Help window appears when you click the Help button.

Most Linuxconf windows also include Help buttons that provide *context-sensitive help* — information that relates to the task you are performing. Press the nearest Help button to read some relevant information about the task at hand. In a few cases, Linuxconf might display a message saying that the help file for that item is not written yet.

Config, Control, and Status buttons

10 Min.
To Go

In the initial Linuxconf window (refer to Figure 10-1), you should note that there are three tabs: Config, Control, and Status. The Config tab enables you to configure various system services, and the Control tab allows you to start and stop services and control various Linuxconf features. The Status tab enables you to view various message logs such as the messages displayed by the Linux kernel as your Red Hat Linux system boots.

To explore the Config, Control, and Status options, click each tab and then drill down into each of the available options to see what they do. You should spend a few minutes exploring all three tabs in Linuxconf to get a feel for the types of system and network administration tasks that you can perform with this tool.

Troubleshooting

If Linuxconf is not listed in the System menu as described at the beginning of this session, make sure you are logged in as the root user. Normal users do not have Linuxconf on their GNOME or KDE menus.

If you *are* logged in as root and Linuxconf is not available in the menu, you can start it in a terminal window by typing linuxconf at the command prompt and pressing Enter.

If Linuxconf does not start, make sure the following three RPMs are installed, installing any that are missing:

- gnome-linuxconf
- linuxconf
- linuxconf-devel

Done!

REVIEW

This session began with an overview of Linux system-administration and network-administration tasks. Then you used Linuxconf to add one or more user accounts. Finally, you explored the tabs in Linuxconf to learn the types of system-administration and network-administration tasks that you can perform using Linuxconf.

QUIZ YOURSELF

1. What are some of the typical Linux system-administration tasks? (See "Understanding Linux System and Network Administration.")

2. In Linuxconf, which button do you click to add a new user account? (See "Adding User Accounts with Linuxconf.")

3. Where can you get the latest information about Linuxconf? (See "Exploring Other Linuxconf Features.")

4. What are the three tabs in Linuxconf's main window? (See "Exploring Other Linuxconf Features.")

5. Can you view message logs from Linuxconf and, if so, which tab enables you to perform this task? (See "Exploring Other Linuxconf Features.")

PART

II

Saturday Morning
Part Review

1. What is the Linux file system? Can you put different parts of the file system on different disks or disk partitions?

2. If your current directory, /tmp, lists three commands that change your current directory to your home directory, for example, /home/naba.

3. What is the command that gives a detailed listing of the files in the current directory in order of last modification?

4. What is the command to switch the most recent working directory?

5. Name two commands for find files in the file system and give an example of using one of them to find a file named book.txt.

6. How do you type several Linux commands on a single line? What is the syntax for continuing a command on multiple lines?

7. Show an example that uses the output of one command as the input to another.

8. What is the "I/O redirection" feature of the shell?

9. Show the Linux command line you would use to find all processes with gnome in their names.

10. You want to kill the gpm process. Explain the steps you follow to perform this task.

11. Show the command to sort an input file based on the value of the third field and display only unique results.

12. Give an example of the command that displays the amount of used disk space in an easily understood format, such as in megabytes or gigabytes.

13. Explain how you would edit the /etc/inittab file with the vi editor. What keys would you press to go to line number 16 and enter a new line of text? How would you save the file and exit?

14. Write a shell function that takes two arguments, swaps their values, and displays both the original and swapped values.

15. Show a command that finds the literal character "*" in a text file named myfile.txt and displays the number of lines containing it.

16. Write an example command that swaps the case of letters and converts any sequence of two or more spaces to a single space. The source file should be named swapme.txt.

17. Show three different ways to use the same command name to uncompress a compressed file named unpackme.gz.

18. Name two commands that let you work with the contents of compressed files without first needing to uncompress the files.

19. List three common system administration tasks and the command names to perform them.

20. List three common network administration tasks and the command names to perform them.

21. What information do you have to provide when you add a new user account in Linuxconf? Does Linuxconf check the password for words that are easily guessed?

22. Show how to edit the /etc/passwd file to disable a user login account.

PART

III

Saturday Afternoon

Using Modems in Red Hat Linux

✔ Connecting a modem to your PC

✔ Dialing out with Minicom

**30 Min.
To Go**

This afternoon's sessions focus on data communications using a modem or an Ethernet local area network (LAN). This first session covers the fundamentals: using a modem and a serial port to make a dial-up connection to another system. If you are using Red Hat Linux at home or in your office, you probably want to use a modem for one or more of the following reasons: to use dial-up networking with Point-to-Point Protocol (PPP) to connect to the Internet through an Internet Service Provider (ISP); to dial out to another computer (such as a bulletin-board system) or another UNIX system; or to enable other people to dial in and use your Linux system.

Session 13 covers dial-up networking with PPP.

Connecting a Modem to Your PC

When you install Red Hat Linux from this book's companion CD-ROMs, you automatically install some tools that you can use to dial out from your Linux system with a modem. Before you can dial out, however, you have to make sure that you have a modem properly connected to one of the serial ports of your PC and that the Linux devices for the serial ports are set up correctly. Make sure that your modem is properly connected to the power supply and that the modem is also connected to the telephone line.

If you have an external modem, buy the right type of cable to connect the modem to the PC. You need a straight-through serial cable to connect the modem to the PC. The connectors at the ends of the cable depend on the type of serial connector on your PC. The modem end of the cable needs a male 25-pin connector. The PC end of the cable often is a female 9-pin connector. You can buy modem cables at most computer stores. The 9-pin female and 25-pin male modem cables are often sold under the label "AT Modem Cable."

If your PC has an internal modem, all you have to do is connect the phone line to a phone jack at the back of the internal modem card.

Learning the serial port device names

The PC typically has two serial ports, called COM1 and COM2 in MS-DOS parlance. Many new PCs with a Universal Serial Bus (USB) have only one serial port. The PC also can support two more serial ports: COM3 and COM4. Because of these port names, the serial ports are often referred to as *COM ports*.

Like other devices, the serial ports need interrupt request (IRQ) numbers and I/O port addresses. Two IRQs — 3 and 4 — are shared among the four COM ports. Table 11-1 lists the IRQs and I/O port addresses assigned to the four serial ports. Like other devices in Linux, device files in the /dev directory represent the serial port devices. Table 11-1 shows the serial device names corresponding to the PC's COM ports.

Table 11-1 *Device Names for Serial Ports*

COM Port	Device Name	IRQ	I/O Address
COM1	/dev/ttyS0	4	0x3f8
COM2	/dev/ttyS1	3	0x2f8
COM3	/dev/ttyS2	4	0x3e8
COM4	/dev/ttyS3	3	0x2e8

If you install Red Hat Linux from this book's companion CD-ROMs, all these devices should already be in your system. If you check the /dev directory, you should find the /dev/ttyS* devices in which * is 0, 1, 2, and 3. From a terminal window, type ls -l /dev/ttyS* to see a listing of these device files.

Checking if Red Hat Linux detects the serial devices

When you install Red Hat Linux from this book's CD-ROMs, following the directions in Sessions 1 through 3, the necessary Linux serial devices are automatically created for you. You should have the /dev/ttyS* devices for dialing in and out through the modem.

To verify that Linux detects your system's serial port(s) correctly, check the boot messages with the dmesg command:

```
dmesg | grep ttyS*
```

If you see a message such as the following, Linux detects a serial port in your PC:

```
ttyS00 at 0x03f8 (irq = 4) is a 16550A
```

In this case, the message indicates that Linux detects the first serial port (COM1). It shows the serial port's I/O address (in hexadecimal), 0x3f8, and IRQ, 4. The last part of the message — 16550A — refers to the identifying number of the *universal asynchronous receiver/transmitter (UART)* chip, which is at the heart of all serial communications hardware. A UART converts each byte to a stream of 1's and 0's and then back to bytes when needed.

The boot messages are also stored in the /var/log/messages file. Therefore, you can search for the serial port's name in the /var/log/messages file with the grep command, as follows:

```
grep ttyS /var/log/messages
```

You can also check for the serial ports with the setserial command. Type the following command to see detailed information about the serial ports:

```
setserial -g /dev/ttyS?
```

Dialing Out with Minicom

**20 Min.
To Go**

After you complete the physical installation of the modem and verify that the necessary Linux device files exist, you can try to dial out through the modem. The best approach is to use the Minicom serial communications program included in the Red Hat Linux distribution on this book's CD-ROMs and installed in the /usr/bin directory. The Minicom program is a serial communications program with a text-based interface that emulates a VT102 terminal. Minicom is similar to other communications software, such as Procomm or Crosstalk, which you may have used under MS-DOS or Windows.

Running Minicom as the root user

To run Minicom, type minicom at the shell prompt in the terminal window or in a virtual console. If you run Minicom as a normal user (not root), Minicom displays the following error message and exits (unless the system manager has already set up Minicom for use by normal users):

```
minicom
minicom: there is no global configuration file /etc/minirc.dfl
Ask your sysadm to create one (with minicom -s).
```

Log in as root and then type

```
minicom -s
```

Minicom starts and displays a dialog box (see Figure 11-1) with a setup menu that enables you to configure various aspects of Minicom, including the serial port plus the modem and dialing commands. To enter the modem initialization commands, use the arrow key to highlight the Modem and Dialing item, as shown in Figure 11-1.

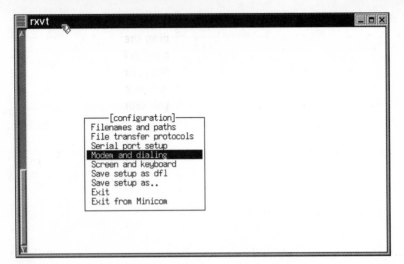

Figure 11-1   *Minicom's setup menu*

With the Modem and Dialing entry highlighted, press Enter. Minicom displays another menu (see Figure 11-2) with a list of settings that you can change. Minicom places the cursor on the first line, as shown in Figure 11-2. Press A to change the modem initialization string.

```
┌────rxvt───────────────────────────────────────────────────────┐
│≡ rxvt                                               _□x│
│                                                                 │
│    ┌───────[Modem and dialing parameter setup]───────────────┐  │
│    │ A - Init string ........ ~^M^AT S7=45 S0=0 L1 V1 X4 &c1 E1 Q0^M█│
│    │ B - Reset string ........ ^M^ATZ^M^                      │  │
│    │ C - Dialing prefix #1.... ATDT                           │  │
│    │ D - Dialing suffix #1.... ^M                             │  │
│    │ E - Dialing prefix #2.... ATDP                           │  │
│    │ F - Dialing suffix #2.... ^M                             │  │
│    │ G - Dialing prefix #3.... ATX1DT                         │  │
│    │ H - Dialing suffix #3.... ;X4D^M                         │  │
│    │ I - Connect string ...... CONNECT                        │  │
│    │ J - No connect strings .. NO CARRIER        BUSY         │  │
│    │                           NO DIALTONE       VOICE        │  │
│    │ K - Hang-up string ...... ~~+++~~ATH^M                   │  │
│    │ L - Dial cancel string .. ^M                             │  │
│    │                                                          │  │
│    │ M - Dial time .......... 45   Q - Auto bps detect ..... No│ │
│    │ N - Delay before redial . 2   R - Modem has DCD line .. Yes│ │
│    │ O - Number of tries ..... 10  S - Status line shows ... DTE speed│
│    │ P - DTR drop time (0=no). 1   T - Multi-line untag .... No│ │
│    │                                                          │  │
│    │ Change which setting?     (Return or Esc to exit)        │  │
│    └──────────────────────────────────────────────────────────┘  │
└─────────────────────────────────────────────────────────────────┘
```

Figure 11-2   *Setting modem and dialing parameters in Minicom.*

You can then use the Backspace key to edit that line and type the AT command you need to initialize the modem. For example, consider a 56K modem that the user initializes with the following AT command (check your modem manual for the appropriate initialization string):

```
AT &F1 E1 V1
```

After you enter the modem initialization string, press Enter to return to the top-level menu.

The AT *commands* are commands that you can use to control a modem and perform tasks such as dialing a number, turning the modem's speaker on or off, and setting the modem to answer an incoming call. These commands start with the two characters: AT (for attention). You can use AT commands for situations in which the communications software is primitive and all the software does is send the modem whatever you type.

After making your changes, if any, use the up and down arrow keys to highlight the item labeled Save as dfl (meaning save as default) and then press Enter. Minicom saves the settings in the /etc/minirc.dfl file — its default configuration file. You can exit Minicom by selecting Exit from Minicom and pressing Enter.

Running Minicom as an ordinary user

**10 Min.
To Go**

You also need to do the following before any user can run Minicom:

- Open the text file /etc/minicom.users in a text editor and verify that it has a line with the word, ALL. (This enables all users to access Minicom's default configuration file.) If not, add a line with the word, ALL.

- Assuming that you want all users to be able to dial out using the modem, enable any user to read from and write to the serial port where the modem is connected. For example, if the modem is on COM1 (/dev/ttyS0), type chmod o+rw /dev/ttyS0 to give everyone write permission for that device.

- Establish a link between the /dev/modem and the serial port device where the modem is connected. If the modem is on COM1 (/dev/ttyS0), you should type the following command:

```
ln -s /dev/ttyS0 /dev/modem
```

After that, you can run Minicom as an ordinary user. When Minicom first runs, it resets the modem. Figure 11-3 shows the result of running Minicom in a terminal window.

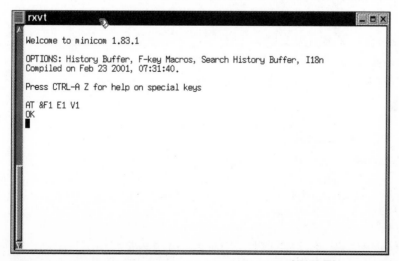

Figure 11-3   *The initial Minicom screen in a terminal window*

Press Ctrl+A to get the attention of the Minicom program. Then if you press Z, a help screen appears in the form of a text window (as shown in Figure 11-4).

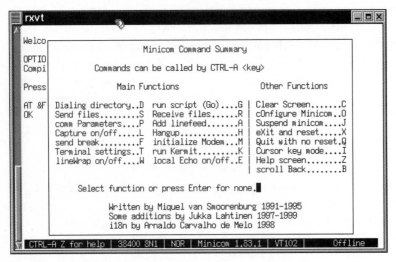

Figure 11-4   *The Minicom help screen*

In the help screen, you can get information about other Minicom commands. From the help screen, press Enter or Esc to return to online mode. In online mode, you can use the modem's AT commands to dial out. In particular, you can use the ATDT command to dial the phone number of another modem, such as your Internet Service Provider's (ISP's) computer or a system where you work (see Figure 11-5). Once you get the login prompt, you can log in as usual and use the remote system.

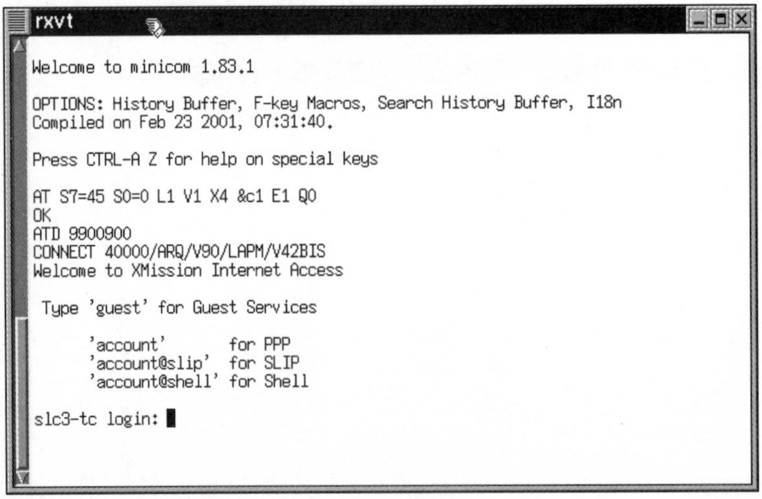

Figure 11-5   *Connecting to a remote system using Minicom*

When you log out of the other system and want to exit Minicom, press Ctrl+A and then type X to exit the program. Press Enter again in response to the Minicom prompt.

Troubleshooting

If setserial shows the UART as unknown, as you see in the following example, the kernel has not detected your serial port or the modem attached to it:

```
/dev/ttyS2, UART: unknown, Port: 0x03f8, IRQ: 10
```

This usually occurs because your PC's BIOS is set up to expect a Plug and Play (PnP) operating system. To solve the problem, reboot the PC and, as it powers up, press the key that permits you to access the system's BIOS. Typically, this is a function key, such as F2, but the exact key depends on your PC's BIOS. In the setup screen, locate the option for the PnP operating system (often labeled "Plug & Play O/S") and turn off that option. Then save the BIOS settings and exit. This causes the PC to reboot. This time, when Red Hat Linux boots, the kernel should be able to detect the PC's serial port correctly.

If your serial ports are correctly detected but the modem does not respond, make sure that /dev/modem is linked to the proper device file in /dev. This is especially common with PCI modem cards, which typically do not use COM1 (/dev/ttyS0) or COM2 (/dev/ttyS1) by default. For example, suppose dmesg | grep ttyS shows the following:

```
ttyS02 at port 0x6800 (irq = 10) is a 16550A
```

In this case, execute the following command to make sure that /dev/modem is linked to the proper device file:

```
ln -sf /dev/ttyS2 /dev/modem
```

If your modem does not appear to be detected, use the Windows Device Manager to obtain its IRQ and I/O address, and compare those values to the values the setserial command reports for that port.

Presently, some modems simply do not work with Linux. These are so-called "WinModems," which rely on the Windows operating system and a special, Windows-specific device driver to function. WinModems, also called *software modems*, rely on a device driver, rather than hardware, to function. In this case, your only recourse is to replace the modem with a hardware modem.

Done!

REVIEW

You started the session by learning the device names for serial ports in Red Hat Linux. You used the Minicom serial communications program to dial out with a modem. In the course of dialing out, you learned several AT commands used to control the modem.

QUIZ YOURSELF

1. What is the device name for the second serial port (COM2)? (See "Learning the serial port device names.")

2. How can you check to see if Linux detects any serial ports in your PC? (See "Checking if Red Hat Linux detects the serial devices.")

3. What program can you use to dial out through the modem? (See "Dialing Out with Minicom.")

4. What AT command do you use to make the modem dial a phone number? (See "Running Minicom as an ordinary user.")

5. What do you have to do to establish a link between the /dev/modem and the serial port device where the modem is connected? (See "Running Minicom as an ordinary user.")

Networking Your Red Hat Linux PC

30 Min.
To Go

Session Checklist

✔ Setting up an Ethernet LAN

✔ Configuring TCP/IP networking in Linux

✔ Using TCP/IP diagnostic commands in Linux

✔ Examining TCP/IP network configuration files

R
ed Hat Linux includes extensive built-in networking capabilities. In particular, Red Hat Linux supports TCP/IP (Transmission Control Protocol/Internet Protocol) networking over several physical interfaces, including Ethernet cards, serial ports, and parallel ports. You typically use an Ethernet network for your local area network (LAN). TCP/IP networking over the serial port enables you to connect to other networks by dialing out over a modem.

This session focuses on Ethernet LANs. You learn how to set up, configure, and monitor an Ethernet TCP/IP network. Much of what you learn also applies to TCP/IP networking over a dial-up connection, discussed in the next session.

Setting Up an Ethernet LAN

Ethernet is a standard way to move packets of data among two or more computers connected to a single cable. To set up an Ethernet LAN, you need an Ethernet card for each PC. Linux supports a wide variety of Ethernet cards for the PC.

Ethernet is a good choice for the physical data-transport mechanism because it's a proven, low-cost technology that provides good data transfer rates — typically 10 million bits per second (10 Mbps) although there is now 100 Mbps and even Gigabit (1000 Mbps) Ethernet.

In an Ethernet LAN, computers are connected to the network with cables. Nowadays, there are two popular forms of Ethernet cables. The first option is *10Base2*, sometimes called *ThinNet,* which uses a thin, flexible coaxial cable. 10Base2 cables appear identical to the cable through which cable television service is delivered. The other, more recent and more popular alternative is Ethernet over *unshielded twisted pair (UTP)* cable, known as *10BaseT.* A 10BaseT cable resembles a standard telephone cable with slightly fatter cables and wider connectors.

To set up a 10BaseT Ethernet, you need an Ethernet *hub*—a hardware box with RJ-45 jacks. You build the network by running twisted-pair wires from each PC's Ethernet card to this hub. (The twisted-pair wires are usually *Category 5,* or *Cat5,* cables.) Currently, you can buy an 8-port 10BaseT hub for about $50 (U.S.). Figure 12-1 shows a typical small 10BaseT Ethernet LAN that you might set up at a small office or your home.

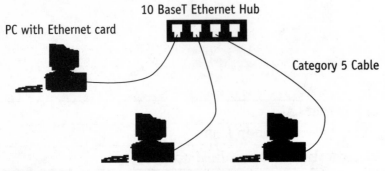

Figure 12-1   *A 10BaseT Ethernet LAN with a hub*

ThinNet Ethernet does not need a hub, which makes it attractive for small offices or home offices that have more than one PC. You can simply daisy chain the ThinWire cable from one PC to another and construct a small Ethernet LAN, as shown in Figure 12-2.

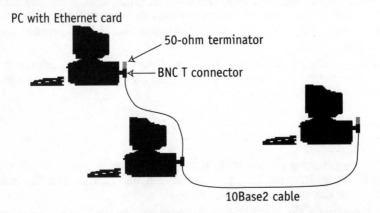

Figure 12-2   *A small ThinNet Ethernet LAN*

As Figure 12-2 shows, you need Ethernet cards in the PCs. The cards should have ThinNet connectors, known as *BNC connectors*. You also need segments of ThinNet cable (technically known as RG-58 thin coaxial cables with 50-ohm impedance). For each Ethernet card's BNC connector, you need a BNC *T-connector* (so called because the connector looks like a *T*). You also need two 50-ohm terminators for the two end points of the Ethernet network. Then all you have to do to complete your own Ethernet LAN is connect the parts in the manner shown in Figure 12-2. You could use this approach to connect several PCs and a workstation in your home office.

 You cannot simply connect two 10Base2 Ethernet cards with a cable to net-work two PCs. You have to use the BNC T-connectors and 50-ohm terminators even if you are connecting only two PCs on a 10Base2 LAN.

ThinNet is easy to set up, but it is inconvenient to connect many PCs this way. One problem is that any break in the cable causes the entire network to crash. Similarly, if one of the PCs on the cable experiences a problem with its network configuration, the entire network may be affected.

You can also connect a 10Base2 LAN with a 10BaseT LAN by using a hub that has a 10Base2 port and multiple 10BaseT ports.

When you install Red Hat Linux from this book's companion CD-ROMs on a PC connected to an Ethernet LAN, the installation program should install the appropriate drivers for the card, provided that the installation program successfully detects the Ethernet card. Otherwise, you can install Linux in expert mode, as described in Session 2.

Once properly installed, Linux should load the driver for the Ethernet card every time it boots. To verify that the Ethernet driver is loaded, use the dmesg command as follows:

```
dmesg | grep eth0
```

This command searches the boot messages for any line that contains the string eth0. (As discussed in the next session, "Configuring TCP/IP Networking," eth0 is the device name for the first Ethernet card in your Linux system.) A sample PC has a 3Com 3C503 Ethernet card installed. That system gets the following output when the user types dmesg | grep eth0 on his or her system:

```
eth0: 3c503 at i/o base 0x300, node  02 60 8c 8e c6 a9, using internal xcvr.
eth0: 3c503-PIO, 16kB RAM, using programmed I/O (REJUMPER for SHARED MEMORY).
```

You should see something similar showing the name of the Ethernet card and other relevant parameters. If the dmesg command does not show any Ethernet device, type grep eth0 /var/log/messages to look for the eth0 device name in the boot messages stored in the /var/log/messages file.

Configuring TCP/IP Networking

Like almost everything else in Red Hat Linux, TCP/IP setup is a matter of preparing a bunch of configuration files, which are text files that you can edit with any text editor. Most of these configuration files reside in the /etc directory. Red Hat Linux includes a network configuration utility that you can use to configure the network. First, you need to learn how to refer to the network devices.

Learning network device names

For most devices, Linux uses files in the /dev directory. The networking devices, however, have names that are defined internally in the kernel; no files for these devices exist in the /dev directory (or, for that matter, in any directory). Following are the common network-device names in Linux:

- *lo—the loopback device.* This device efficiently handles network packets that are sent from your system to itself (when, for example, an X client communicates with the X server on the same system).
- *eth0—the first Ethernet card.* If you have more Ethernet cards, they get device names eth1, eth2, and so on.
- *ppp0—the first serial port configured for a point-to-point link to another computer, using Point-to-Point Protocol (PPP).* If you have more serial ports configured for PPP networking, they are assigned the device names ppp1, ppp2, and so on.
- *sl0—the first serial port configured for Serial Line Internet Protocol (SLIP) networking.* SLIP establishes a point-to-point link to a TCP/IP network. If you use a second serial port for SLIP, it gets the device name sl1.

The loopback device (lo) is always present whether or not you have another network device, such as an Ethernet card or a modem, installed and configured. The loopback device passes data from one program to another without needing to access an external network. (This process is known as interprocess communication, or IPC.) In fact, the loopback device allows any application that requires a functioning network to work as long as the application uses only the local system.

Running Red Hat's network configuration tool

When you set up TCP/IP networking during Red Hat Linux installation, the installation program prepares all appropriate configuration files using the information you provide. However, Red Hat Linux comes with a graphical network configuration tool that you can use to add a new network interface or alter information such as name servers and host names.

To start the network configuration tool, log in as root and select Menu ⇨ System ⇨ Network Configuration. The Network Configurator displays the dialog box shown in Figure 12-3.

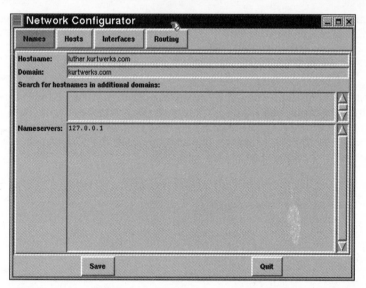

Figure 12-3   *Configuring a TCP/IP network with Network Configurator*

You can configure various aspects of your network through the four buttons at the top of the dialog box. Click each button to explore what entries you can add or edit. Specifically, these buttons enable you to do the following:

- *Names.* Enables you to enter the host name for your system and enter the IP addresses of name servers. The name server addresses are stored in the `/etc/resolv.conf` file. The host name is stored in a variable in the `/etc/sysconfig/network` file.

- *Hosts.* Shows you the current contents of the `/etc/hosts` file and enables you to add, remove, or edit entries. That file contains host names and corresponding IP addresses for each host.

- *Interfaces.* Enables you to add a new network interface, specify the IP address of the interface, and activate the interface. This information gets stored in various files in the `/etc/sysconfig` directory.

- *Routing.* Enables you to add static routes. Each route lists the gateway to use to reach a specified network.

To configure the network interfaces, you need to assign IP addresses to each interface. If you are running a private network, you may use IP addresses in the range, 192.168.0.0 to 192.168.255.255. There are other ranges of addresses reserved for private networks, but this range should suffice for most needs. For example, you could use the 192.168.1.0 address for a small private network.

Using TCP/IP Diagnostic Commands

20 Min.
To Go
After configuring, or reconfiguring, a TCP/IP network, you should verify the configuration. You can, of course, use network applications such as TELNET or FTP to verify that the

network is up and running, but Red Hat Linux includes a number of utility programs that help you monitor and diagnose problems.

Checking the interfaces

Type the /sbin/ifconfig command to view the currently configured network interfaces. The ifconfig command also configures a network interface (associates an IP address with a network device) during system startup. However, if you run ifconfig without any command-line arguments, the command displays information about the current network interfaces. Here is the result of a typical ifconfig invocation:

```
/sbin/ifconfig
eth0      Link encap:Ethernet  HWaddr 02:60:8C:8E:C6:A9
          inet addr:192.168.1.200  Bcast:192.168.1.255  Mask:255.255.255.0
          UP BROADCAST RUNNING MULTICAST  MTU:1500  Metric:1
          RX packets:3007 errors:0 dropped:0 overruns:0 frame:0
          TX packets:1140 errors:0 dropped:0 overruns:0 carrier:0
          collisions:0 txqueuelen:100
          Interrupt:5 Base address:0x300

lo        Link encap:Local Loopback
          inet addr:127.0.0.1  Mask:255.0.0.0
          UP LOOPBACK RUNNING  MTU:3924  Metric:1
          RX packets:54 errors:0 dropped:0 overruns:0 frame:0
          TX packets:54 errors:0 dropped:0 overruns:0 carrier:0
          collisions:0 txqueuelen:0
```

This output shows that two interfaces — the loopback interface (lo) and an Ethernet card (eth0) — are currently active on this system. For each interface, ifconfig displays the IP address and summary statistics about the interface's network activity. For an Ethernet device, ifconfig also reports the IRQ (shown as Interrupt: 5) and the base I/O port address (0x300). If the Red Hat Linux system had a dial-up PPP link up and running, you would also see an item for the ppp0 interface in the output.

Checking the IP routing table

Another network configuration command, /sbin/route, provides status information when you run it without any command-line argument. If you are having trouble connecting to another host, even if you use its IP address, check the IP routing table to see if a default gateway is specified. The *IP routing table* is a list of IP addresses that identifies the path a packet from one network should take in order to reach another network. Then, check the gateway's routing table to ensure that paths to an outside network appear in that routing table.

Output from the /sbin/route typically resembles the following:

```
/sbin/route
Kernel IP routing table
Destination     Gateway         Genmask         Flags Metric Ref    Use Iface
192.168.1.200   *               255.255.255.255 UH    0      0        0 eth0
192.168.1.0     *               255.255.255.0   U     0      0        0 eth0
127.0.0.0       *               255.0.0.0       U     0      0        0 lo
default         192.168.1.1     0.0.0.0         UG    0      0        0 eth0
```

This routing table shows that the local network uses the eth0 Ethernet interface and the default gateway is also that Ethernet interface. The *default gateway* handles packets addressed to any network other than the one in which the Linux system resides. In this example, packets addressed to any network address other than ones that begin with 192.168.1 are sent to the gateway, which has the IP address 192.168.1.1. The gateway forwards those packets to other networks, assuming, of course, the gateway is connected to another network.

Checking connectivity to a host

To see if you can connect to a specific host, use the ping command. The ping command is a widely used TCP/IP tool that employs a series of *Internet Control Message Protocol* (*ICMP*, often pronounced as *eye-comp*) messages. ICMP provides an Echo message to which every host responds. Using the ICMP messages and replies, ping can determine whether the other system is alive and then compute the *round-trip delay* — how long it takes a packet to travel from the source system to the destination system, and back to that system.

The following example shows how one user runs ping to see whether one of the systems on his network is alive:

```
ping -c 4 192.168.1.50
PING 192.168.1.50 (192.168.1.50): 56 data bytes
64 bytes from 192.168.1.50: icmp_seq=0 ttl=32 time=2.2 ms
64 bytes from 192.168.1.50: icmp_seq=1 ttl=32 time=1.2 ms
64 bytes from 192.168.1.50: icmp_seq=2 ttl=32 time=1.2 ms
64 bytes from 192.168.1.50: icmp_seq=3 ttl=32 time=0.8 ms

--- 192.168.1.50 ping statistics ---
4 packets transmitted, 4 packets received, 0% packet loss
round-trip min/avg/max = 0.8/1.3/2.2 ms
```

The ping command displays statistics showing the time it takes to send a packet between the two systems followed by a short summary report. By default, Red Hat Linux's ping runs continually until you press Ctrl+C to stop it, so the example used the -c 4 option to limit the number (count) of packets it sent to 4. On some systems, ping simply reports that a remote host is alive. However, you can still get the timing information with appropriate command-line arguments.

10 Min.
To Go

Examining TCP/IP Configuration Files

Configuring the network during installation or running the Red Hat network configuration tool may be enough to get TCP/IP configured on your system. However, you should also be familiar with the configuration files so that you can edit them if necessary. For example, you can specify the name servers through the network configuration tool, but suppose you want to add an alternative name server. To do so, you can simply add these names directly to the /etc/resolv.conf file — the configuration file that stores the IP addresses of name servers.

In the remainder of this session, you'll familiarize yourself with the basic TCP/IP configuration files. Each of these configuration files is a text file that you can examine with the cat or more command and edit using any text editor.

/etc/hosts

The /etc/hosts configuration file contains a list of the IP addresses and host names of all the systems on your local network. In the absence of a name server, programs on your system that need to access another system consult this file to determine its IP address. Type the cat /etc/hosts command to view the contents of this file.

Following is the /etc/hosts file from a sample system, showing the IP addresses and names of other hosts on the user's LAN:

```
127.0.0.1          localhost          localhost.localdomain
# Other hosts on the LAN
192.168.1.100      lnb486
192.168.1.50       lnbp133
192.168.1.200      lnbp200
192.168.1.233      lnbp233
192.168.1.40       lnbp400
192.168.1.60       lnbp600
192.168.1.25       mac        lnbmac
192.168.1.1        lnbp75
```

Each line in the file starts with an IP address, followed by the host name for that IP address. You can have more than one host name for a given IP address.

/etc/host.conf

The /etc/host.conf configuration text file specifies how Linux obtains the IP addresses corresponding to host names. Type cat /etc/host.conf to view the contents of this file. Typically, this file contains the following lines:

```
order hosts, bind
multi on
```

The entries in the /etc/host.conf file tell the resolver library what services to use, and in which order, to convert host names to IP addresses. The order option indicates the order of services. The sample entry specifies that the resolver library should first consult the /etc/hosts file and then check the name servers to resolve a name. The name servers are listed in the /etc/resolv.conf file, which you'll examine next.

The multi on **option specifies that hosts listed in the** /etc/hosts **file can have multiple IP addresses. Hosts that have more than one IP address are called** *multihomed* **because the presence of multiple IP addresses implies that the host has several network interfaces. In other words, the host "lives" in several networks simultaneously.**

/etc/resolv.conf

The /etc/resolv.conf configuration file is another text file that the resolver uses. This file is a library that determines the IP address corresponding to a host name. Type cat /etc/resolv.conf to view the contents of this file.

Following is a sample /etc/resolv.conf file:

```
search xyz.com
nameserver 164.109.1.3
nameserver 164.109.10.23
```

The search line specifies the names of systems the resolver uses to search for host names. The nameserver line provides the IP addresses of name servers for your domain. If you have multiple name servers, you should list them on separate lines. They are queried in the order in which they appear in the file. Typically, you list in the /etc/resolv.conf file the name servers provided by your Internet Service Provider (ISP).

/etc/hosts.allow

The /etc/hosts.allow configuration file identifies the systems allowed to use the Internet services (such as Telnet and FTP) that may be running on your system. The program that starts some, but not all, Internet services consults the /etc/hosts.allow file before starting, and begins a service only if the entries in the hosts.allow file permit the requesting host to use that specific service.

The entries in /etc/hosts.allow are in the format of *server*: *IP address* in which *server* refers to the name of the program providing a specific Internet service. *IP address* identifies the host allowed to use that service. For example, if you want all hosts in your local network (which has the address 192.168.1.0) to access the FTP service (which is provided by the in.ftpd program), add the following line in the /etc/hosts.allow file:

```
in.ftpd:192.168.1.
```

If you want to let all local hosts have access to all Internet services, use the ALL keyword and rewrite the line as follows:

```
ALL:192.168.1.
```

Finally, to open up all Internet services to all hosts, you can replace the IP address with ALL as follows:

```
ALL:ALL
```

You can also use host names in place of IP addresses.

 Security experts vigorously and emphatically discourage allowing all hosts access to all services on your system. For a more secure system, you should deny all hosts access and then allow selected hosts access to your system. This means that you should first deny all hosts access to your system using the ALL:ALL directive in /etc/hosts.deny (covered in the next section). You should then list each system or group of systems permitted to access your system in /etc/hosts.allow.

/etc/hosts.deny

The /etc/hosts.deny configuration file is just the opposite of /etc/hosts.allow. Whereas hosts.allow specifies which hosts may access Internet services (such as Telnet and FTP) on your system, the hosts.deny file identifies the hosts that must be denied services. The program that starts Internet services consults the /etc/hosts.deny file if it does not find any rules in the /etc/hosts.allow file that apply to the requesting host. The program denies service if it finds a rule in the hosts.deny file that applies to the host.

The entries in the /etc/hosts.deny file follow the same format as those in the /etc/hosts.allow file. They are in the form of a *server*: *IP address* format in which *server* refers to the name of the program providing a specific Internet service and *IP address* identifies the host allowed to use that service.

Assuming that you already set up entries in the /etc/hosts.allow **file to allow access to specific hosts, you can place the following line in** /etc/hosts.deny **to deny all other hosts access to any service on your system:**

```
ALL:ALL
```

Troubleshooting

If you are unable to access hosts on a networ⬛⬛⬛ sure you have at least one name server listed in /etc/resolv.conf.

If an external system cannot connect to y⬛⬛⬛ tem, remember the order in which the hosts.allow and hosts.deny files are read⬛⬛⬛ plied. The program that starts Internet services consults /etc/hosts.allow first. I⬛⬛⬛ rappers does not find a matching rule, it applies the first matching rule, if any, in /e⬛⬛⬛ ts.deny. If neither file contains a match, access will be granted.

REVIEW

Done!

This session showed you how to set up an Ethernet LAN using 10Base2 or 10BaseT cables. You explored Red Hat's network configuration tool that you can use to configure the network interfaces. You used a number of utility programs such as ping and route, to monitor the status of your TCP/IP network. Finally, you examined several TCP/IP configuration files that specify items such as host name, name servers, as well as which hosts can access services running on your system.

QUIZ YOURSELF

1. What is "ThinNet"? (See "Setting Up an Ethernet LAN.")
2. What is the name of the first Ethernet device in a Linux system? (See "Learning network device names.")
3. How do you start the Red Hat network configuration tool? (See "Running Red Hat's network configuration tool.")
4. What network utility do you use to check the connectivity to another system in the network? (See "Checking connectivity to a host.")
5. Which configuration file enables you to deny access to local Internet services? (See "/etc/hosts.deny.")

Connecting Your Red Hat Linux PC to the Internet

Session Checklist

✔ Learning the basics of dial-up networking

✔ Connecting to the Internet using PPP

✔ Using IP masquerading to share an Internet connection

**30 Min.
To Go**

After installing Red Hat Linux, you will probably want to connect your Red Hat Linux PC (and perhaps your LAN) to the Internet. You have the following popular options for connecting a small office or home office to the Internet: Digital Subscriber Line (DSL), cable modem, and dial-up networking. The DSL and cable modem options essentially involve connecting a special modem to an Ethernet card on your Linux system. In these cases, the setup procedures are the same as the ones discussed in Session 12.

This session focuses on the third option, dial-up access, which involves setting up a PPP connection from your Red Hat Linux PC to your ISP's system. You also learn how to use IP masquerading to share a Red Hat Linux system's Internet connection with other systems on a LAN.

Learning the Basics of Dial-up Networking

Dial-up networking refers to connecting a PC to a remote network (such as the Internet) by using a modem and a communication protocol such as PPP (*Point to Point Protocol*). A significant difference exists between dial-up networking and standard serial connections. Although both methods use a modem to connect two computers and establish a communication path, a serial connection makes your computer act like a terminal connected to the remote computer. A PPP connection makes your computer appear to be an independent, stand-alone system on the Internet. Together, PPP and the dial-up connection allow your Red Hat Linux system to become part of the network to which the remote computer belongs. You can have any number of network applications, such as Web browsers, Usenet news clients, e-mail clients, Telnet or FTP clients, and so forth, running at the same time. All of these applications can share the physical data transport capabilities of the dial-up PPP connection.

Dial-up networking involves TCP/IP data transfers over a dial-up connection. Like TCP/IP networking over a standard network connection, TCP/IP networking over a dial-up link is a matter of specifying the *protocol* — the convention — for packaging and sending a unit of data, known as a *packet*, over the communication link. These are the two most popular protocols for TCP/IP networking over dial-up connections

- *SLIP* is the Serial Line Internet Protocol, a simple protocol that specifies how to frame an IP packet on a serial line.
- *PPP* is the Point-to-Point Protocol, a more advanced protocol for establishing a TCP/IP connection over any point-to-point link, including dial-up serial links.

PPP is the most popular method of TCP/IP networking over a dial-up connection. The next section shows you how to use PPP to set up a network connection to a remote system.

Connecting to the Internet Using PPP

Most Internet Service Providers (ISPs) provide PPP access to the Internet. When you sign up for such a service, the ISP should provide you with the information that you need to make a PPP connection to the remote system. Typically, this information includes the following:

- The phone number to connect to the remote system.
- The user name and password that you must use to log into the remote system.
- The names, and perhaps the IP addresses, of the ISP's mail and news server.
- The IP addresses of the ISP's Domain Name Servers (DNS). Typically, the ISP gives you two IP addresses, one for the primary DNS server and one for the secondary DNS server.

Some ISPs may also give you an IP address for your side of the connection. Usually, though, your IP address is assigned dynamically and changes each time you connect to the ISP. Most ISPs also provide the IP addresses of the mail and news servers. However, these addresses are not important for the mechanics of setting up a PPP connection.

Before you set up a PPP connection, you must have an internal or external modem installed on your system. The modem should be connected to a phone line. You can use Minicom, as described in Session 11, to dial your ISP's phone number and make sure that the modem successfully establishes a connection. After you see a login prompt, you can hang up the modem and proceed to set up PPP.

Follow these steps to set up a PPP connection using Red Hat's graphical Dialup Configuration tool:

1. Log in as root and select Main Menu ⇨ Programs ⇨ Settings ⇨ Internet Configuration Wizard from the GNOME desktop. The Dialup Configuration tool displays the Select Device Type dialog box, shown in Figure 13-1. Click the device you are configuring (a modem) and then click the Next button to continue.

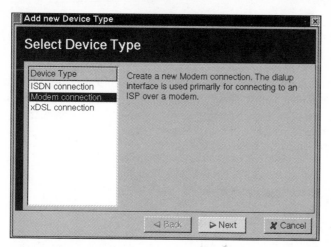

Figure 13-1 *Creating a new Internet connection with Red Hat's Internet Configuration Wizard*

2. In the Select Provider dialog box (see Figure 13-2), enter the connection information (phone number, the name of your ISP, your login name, and your password in the corresponding text boxes. Do not enter an area code unless you must dial it to access your ISP. Click Next to continue.

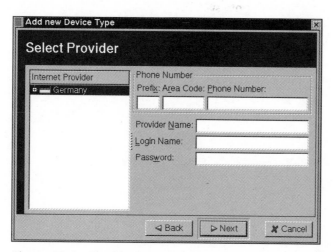

Figure 13-2 *Provide the connection information to connect to your ISP*

3. Click Finish to save the dial-up configuration information and close the Internet Configuration Wizard.

4. Click Main Menu ⇨ Applets ⇨ Network ⇨ Modem Lights to open the PPP dialer application. When you do so, the GNOME desktop will place the application on the panel, as shown in Figure 13-3.

Figure 13-3   *The Modem Lights PPP dialer starts as a panel applet*

5. Right-click on the Modem Lights applet, then select Properties to open the Modem
    Lights Settings dialog box (see Figure 13-4).

6. On the General tab, edit the Connect command and Disconnect command text
    boxes as shown in Figure 13-4. `ifup ppp0` and `ifdown ppp0` are the commands
    that start and stop the connection to your ISP.

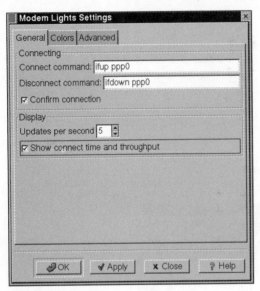

Figure 13-4   *Edit the connection and disconnection commands the Modem Lights
applet uses.*

7. On the Advanced tab, shown in Figure 13-5, change the name in the Modem lock
    file text box so that it reflects the device name of your modem. For example, on a
    sample system, the modem device name is /dev/ttyS4, as the following command
    shows:

    ```
    ls -l /dev/modem
    lrwxrwxrwx   1 root      root            10 Sep  6 08:18 /dev/modem ->
    /dev/ttyS4
    ```

    So, the last piece of the lock file name was changed to ttyS4.

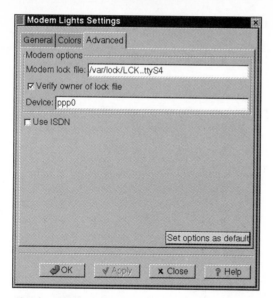

Figure 13-5   *Edit the lock file so that the Modem Lights applet can track your connection status.*

8. Click Apply and then OK to save your changes.
9. To establish a PPP connection, click the large button on the left-hand side of the Modem Lights applet, then click Yes in the dialog box shown in Figure 13-6.

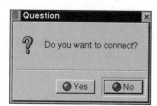

Figure 13-6   *Using Red Hat's PPP dialer to connect to the Internet*

Figure 13-7 shows the PPP dialer's connection monitor. The small window on the left shows your total connection time (in hours and minutes) and the window on the right shows current activity as a graphical display.

Figure 13-7   *The connection monitor displays current traffic graphically.*

Verifying that the PPP connection is up

After you connect using Linuxconf, you can verify that the PPP connection is up by typing
the /sbin/ifconfig command, which shows a listing such as this:

```
/sbin/ifconfig
eth0      Link encap:Ethernet  HWaddr 02:60:8C:8E:C6:A9
          inet addr:192.168.1.200  Bcast:192.168.1.255  Mask:255.255.255.0
          UP BROADCAST RUNNING MULTICAST  MTU:1500  Metric:1
          RX packets:4363 errors:0 dropped:0 overruns:0 frame:0
          TX packets:2111 errors:0 dropped:0 overruns:0 carrier:0
          collisions:0 txqueuelen:100
          Interrupt:5 Base address:0x300

lo        Link encap:Local Loopback
          inet addr:127.0.0.1  Mask:255.0.0.0
          UP LOOPBACK RUNNING  MTU:3924  Metric:1
          RX packets:50 errors:0 dropped:0 overruns:0 frame:0
          TX packets:50 errors:0 dropped:0 overruns:0 carrier:0
          collisions:0 txqueuelen:0

ppp0      Link encap:Point-to-Point Protocol
          inet addr:209.100.18.220  P-t-P:209.100.18.4  Mask:255.255.255.255
          UP POINTOPOINT RUNNING NOARP MULTICAST  MTU:1500  Metric:1
          RX packets:132 errors:2 dropped:0 overruns:0 frame:2
          TX packets:146 errors:0 dropped:0 overruns:0 carrier:0
          collisions:0 txqueuelen:10
```

Find the ppp0 device listed in the output. The ifconfig output also shows the IP
addresses of the local and remote ends of the PPP connection. This output confirms that the
PPP device is up and running.

Verifying that the routing table is set up correctly

To verify that the routing table is set up correctly, use the /sbin/route command without
any arguments, as follows:

```
/sbin/route
Kernel IP routing table
Destination    Gateway        Genmask          Flags Metric Ref Use Iface
209.100.18.4   *              255.255.255.255  UH    0      0   0   ppp0
192.168.1.200  *              255.255.255.255  UH    0      0   0   eth0
192.168.1.0    *              255.255.255.0    U     0      0   0   eth0
127.0.0.0      *              255.0.0.0        U     0      0   0   lo
default        209.100.18.4   0.0.0.0          UG    0      0   0   ppp0
```

In the routing table, the first line shows a route to the remote end of the PPP connection; this one should be set to the ppp0 device. Also, the default route should be set up so
that the remote end of the PPP connection serves as the gateway for your system (as the
last line of the routing table shows).

Verifying that Internet hosts can be reached

After checking the interface configuration (with the ifconfig command) and the routing
table (with the route command), verify that you can reach some well-known host. If your

ISP gives you the IP address of a name server or a mail server, you can try to ping those addresses. Otherwise, try to ping the IP address of a system at your workplace or your university.

The following example shows what you see if you try the ping command:

```
ping 140.90.23.100
PING 140.90.23.100 (140.90.23.100): 56 data bytes
64 bytes from 140.90.23.100: icmp_seq=0 ttl=243 time=143.2 ms
64 bytes from 140.90.23.100: icmp_seq=1 ttl=243 time=220.2 ms
64 bytes from 140.90.23.100: icmp_seq=2 ttl=243 time=140.2 ms
64 bytes from 140.90.23.100: icmp_seq=3 ttl=243 time=130.3 ms

--- 140.90.23.100 ping statistics ---
4 packets transmitted, 4 packets received, 0% packet loss
round-trip min/avg/max = 130.3/158.4/220.2 ms
```

The end of each line shows the round-trip time for a packet originating at your system to reach the designated IP address (140.90.23.100, in this case) and back to your system. For a PPP connection over dial-up lines, you can see times in hundreds of milliseconds.

You do not need an account on a system to ping its IP address. Although a system may disable the automatic response to ping messages, most systems respond to ping.

To see your connection speed, type tail -100 /var/log/messages | grep V42BIS. **This shows lines such as the following, with connection speed as reported by the modem:**

```
Mar 19 17:31:27 lnbp200 chat[1533]:  42666/ARQ/V90/LAPM/V42BIS^M
Mar 19 17:32:24 lnbp200 chat[1579]:  33333/ARQ/V90/LAPM/V42BIS^M
```

Closing the PPP connection

To use the PPP dialer to close your dial-up connection, click the button on the Modem Lights applet that has the green light in its center (see Figure 13-7). Then click the Yes button (see Figure 13-8) to confirm this decision.

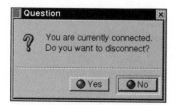

Figure 13-8   *Using the PPP dialer to close the PPP connection*

After a few moments, the connection closes and the PPP dialer's main screen goes blank. This is visual evidence that the PPP connection has closed and the modem has hung up.

10 Min.
To Go

Using IP Masquerading to Share an Internet Connection

Linux supports a feature called *IP masquerading* that enables you to connect an Ethernet LAN with a private IP address to the Internet. This occurs through a Linux PC (with an officially assigned IP address) that has a connection to the Internet. The Linux PC may be connected to the Internet by dial-up PPP or some other connection, such as DSL or cable modem.

With IP masquerading enabled, your Red Hat Linux PC acts as a stand-in for any of the other systems on the Ethernet LAN. As with the router setup, the Red Hat Linux PC is designated as the gateway for the Ethernet LAN. However, masquerading involves more than simply forwarding IP packets back and forth between the LAN and the Internet.

When the Red Hat Linux PC masquerades as another system on the LAN, it modifies outgoing packets so that they always appear to originate from the Red Hat Linux PC. When a response to one of the outgoing packets is received, the Red Hat Linux PC performs the reverse task — it modifies the packets so that they appear to come from the Internet directly to the system that sends the outgoing packet. The end result is that each system on the Ethernet LAN appears to have full access to the Internet, even though the Ethernet LAN uses a non-unique private IP address.

To enable and use IP masquerading, perform the following steps:

1. Make sure that the Linux kernel — the core operating system — supports IP firewall chains. This should be true for the version of Red Hat Linux you install from the companion CD-ROMs. If the file /proc/net/ip_fwchains exists, then the kernel supports IP firewall chains. (Type ls /proc/net/ip_fwchains to verify that the file exists.)

2. Make sure the Red Hat Linux PC has an Internet connection and a network connection to your LAN. The Red Hat Linux PC used for IP masquerading requires two network interfaces — an Ethernet card used to connect to and to communicate with the LAN and a dial-up PPP connection to the Internet (through an ISP).

3. Make sure that all other systems on your LAN use the Linux PC as the default gateway for TCP/IP networking. Use the same ISP-provided DNS addresses on all systems.

4. Enable IP forwarding in the kernel by typing the following command:

   ```
   echo "1" > /proc/sys/net/ipv4/ip_forward
   ```

   This is necessary because IP forwarding is disabled by default. To ensure that IP forwarding is enabled when you reboot your system, place this command in the /etc/rc.d/rc.local file. In Red Hat Linux, you can achieve the same result by changing the line FORWARD_IPV4=false to FORWARD_IPV4=true in the /etc/sysconfig/network file.

5. Run /sbin/ipchains — the IPCHAINS firewall administration program — to set up the rules that enable the Linux PC to masquerade for your LAN. For example, to enable masquerading for a LAN via the Linux PC's ppp0 network interface, you can use the following commands:

   ```
   /sbin/ipchains -P forward DENY
   /sbin/ipchains -A forward -i ppp0 -j MASQ
   ```

   If you want the IP masquerading set up at system startup, you should place these commands in the /etc/rc.d/rc.local file.

You may find IP masquerading a convenient way to provide Internet access to a small LAN at home or in your office. At home, you might use IP masquerading to connect an Ethernet LAN to the Internet through a Linux system. The Linux PC has an Ethernet card for the LAN connection and a modem to connect to the Internet via an ISP. (You need a valid IP address from the ISP.) With IP masquerading on the Linux PC, everyone in your family or small business will be able to access the Internet from any of the other PCs on the LAN.

Troubleshooting

If you can use ping to connect to an Internet host by IP address but not by name, make sure you have added the proper name servers to /etc/resolv.conf. However, if you first used the Red Hat netcfg tool to modify your network configuration, changes made with it override direct edits to /etc/resolv.conf.

If you have trouble using the PPP dialer to connect to your ISP, make sure that the permissions on the device file for your modem permit access. Suppose, for example, that your modem is on /dev/ttyS1. If ls -l /dev/ttyS1 does not show user and group permissions for everyone, as follows, you will not be able to use the modem unless you are the root user:

```
crw-rw----    1 root      uucp      4,  65 Mar 23 21:38 /dev/ttyS1
```

Use the following chmod command (as the root user) to make sure that normal users have read/write access to the modem:

```
chmod o+rw /dev/ttyS2
Ls -l /dev/ttyS1
crw-rw-rw-    1 root      uucp      4,  65 Mar 23 21:38 /dev/ttyS1
```

Done!

REVIEW

This session introduced you to dial-up networking, which is a method of establishing a network connection between your Linux PC and the Internet through a dial-up modem. You learned to use the Red Hat Dialup Configuration Tool to set up a PPP connection. Finally, this session showed you how to share a single Internet connection using the IP masquerading feature of the IPCHAINS firewall administration program.

QUIZ YOURSELF

1. What are dial-up networking and PPP? (See "Learning the Basics of Dial-up Networking.")
2. What information does an ISP typically provide for you to set up dial-up PPP connections? (See "Connecting to the Internet Using PPP.")

3. What tool do you use to set up a PPP connection? (See "Connecting to the Internet Using PPP.")

4. What program would you use to turn the PPP connection on and off? (See "Connecting to the Internet Using PPP".)

5. What is IP masquerading? (See "Using IP Masquerading to Share an Internet Connection.")

SESSION

14

Setting Up Internet Services

Session Checklist

✔ Understanding Internet services

✔ Using the e-mail server

✔ Setting up the Apache Web server

✔ Setting up the FTP server

30 Min.
To Go

You can use the Red Hat Linux PC as a server if it's connected to the Internet or an *intranet* (a private TCP/IP network). Both the Internet and intranets rely on Internet services. Each Internet service involves configuring and running one or more servers on the Red Hat Linux system. This session introduces you to the commonly used Internet services. It then focuses on the servers that implement the mail, Web, and file-transfer Internet services: the e-mail server, the Apache Web server, and the FTP server, respectively.

Understanding Internet Services

The term *Internet service* refers to a number of applications typically run on a network server that employ a client/server architecture to perform specific tasks. A *client/server architecture* uses two separate programs — a server that provides information, and one or more clients that request information to implement a service.

Many Internet services are specifically designed to deliver information from one system to another. This information may be in the form of mail messages, news items, or data files. As a user, you expect to access the following common Internet services from a typical Internet host:

- *Electronic mail (e-mail).* From an Internet host, you can send e-mail to any other user on the Internet using addresses such as president@whitehouse.gov.

- *World Wide Web.* You can use a Web browser to download and view Web pages using a Uniform Resource Locator (URL) address such as `http://www.whitehouse.gov/`. The Web pages are usually documents formatted in HyperText Markup Language (HTML).

- *Newsgroups.* You can read newsgroups and post news items to newsgroups with names such as `news://comp.os.linux.networking` or `news://comp.os.linux.setup`.

- *Information retrieval.* You can search for information with tools such as the World Wide Web browser. You also can download files with File Transfer Protocol (FTP). Reciprocally, users on other systems also can download files from your system, typically, through a feature known as anonymous FTP.

All Internet services rely on client and server software. For example, an e-mail server takes care of transferring mail from one system to another while you read e-mail using e-mail client software. Similarly, you use a Web browser client to download and view Web pages from a Web server.

The clients and servers that implement Internet services employ TCP/IP protocols to communicate with one another. You are already familiar with the IP address that identifies a host in a TCP/IP network. The IP address alone, however, cannot sufficiently distinguish among many services running on the same system. The concept of a port number (or, simply, *port*) is used to enable various Internet servers to communicate with clients. The port is not a physical entity; it's simply a number between 1 and 65,535 that uniquely identifies each end point of a TCP/IP communications link between two processes (typically, a server and a client). Thus, the combination of an IP address and a port number uniquely identifies each service running on each host on the Internet.

All well known Internet services have pre-assigned port numbers. For example, here are some commonly used Internet protocols and their assigned port numbers:

- *FTP (File Transfer Protocol)* allows transfer of files among computers on the Internet. FTP uses two ports; data is transferred on port 20, while control information is exchanged on port 21. FTP is the underlying protocol for file transfers.

- *HTTP (Hypertext Transfer Protocol)* is a recent protocol for sending HTML documents from one system to another. HTTP is the underlying protocol of the Web. By default, the Web server and client communicate on port 80.

- *SMTP (Simple Mail Transfer Protocol)* exchanges e-mail messages among systems. SMTP uses port 25 for information exchange. SMTP is the underlying protocol for the e-mail service.

- *NNTP (Network News Transfer Protocol)* distributes news articles in a store-and-forward fashion across the Internet. NNTP uses port 119. NNTP is the underlying protocol for the newsgroups service.

- *Telnet* enables a user on one system to log into another system on the Internet. The user must provide a valid user ID and password to log into the remote system successfully. Telnet uses port 23 by default. However, the Telnet client can connect to any specified port. Telnet is the underlying protocol for remote access.

- *SSH (Secure Shell)* is a newer, secure protocol designed to replace the Telnet protocol. It uses port 22.

- *NFS (Network File System)* shares files among computers. NFS uses Sun's *Remote Procedure Call (RPC)* facility, which exchanges information through port 111.

The /etc/services text configuration file stores the association between an Internet service and a port number, as well as the underlying data communications protocol. To see the contents of this file, use the more command as follows:

```
more /etc/services
```

The following is a small subset of entries in the /etc/services file of a Linux system:

```
ftp-data        20/tcp
ftp             21/tcp
fsp             21/udp         fspd
ssh             22/tcp                          # SSH Remote Login Protocol
ssh             22/udp                          # SSH Remote Login Protocol
telnet          23/tcp
# 24 - private
smtp            25/tcp         mail
# 26 - unassigned
time            37/tcp         timserver
time            37/udp         timserver
rlp             39/udp         resource         # resource location
nameserver      42/tcp         name             # IEN 116
whois           43/tcp         nicname
```

Each line starts with the name of a service followed by a port number and a data communications protocol (tcp or udp). The rest of the line shows another name, also known as an *alias*, for the service, if any. Anything following the pound sign (#) is interpreted as a comment.

Browsing through the entries in the /etc/services **file is instructive because they show the breadth of networking services available under TCP/IP.**

During Red Hat Linux installation from this book's companion CD-ROMs, you can opt to install the necessary packages for mail, Web, and news. All you need to do is select the Mail/WWW/News Tools package group from the installation screen that shows the package groups. *Mail* refers to the e-mail Internet service; *WWW* refers to the World Wide Web Internet service; and *News* refers to the newsgroups Internet service.

If you install the mail and news software during Red Hat Linux installation, you do not have to do much more to begin using the mail, Web, and news services. Otherwise, you can use the Red Hat Package Manager (RPM) to install individual packages.

Session 23 describes how to use the rpm **program for installing new software.**

Using the E-mail Server

E-mail is one of the most popular services on the Internet. E-mail started as a simple mechanism in which messages were copied to a user's mailbox file. In Red Hat Linux, your mail messages are stored in the /var/spool/mail directory in a text file with the same name as your user name.

Messages still are addressed to a user name. That means that if John Doe logs in with the user name jdoe, e-mail to him is addressed to jdoe. The only other piece of information needed to identify the recipient uniquely is the fully qualified domain name (FQDN) of the recipient's system. Thus, if John Doe's system is named someplace.net, his complete e-mail address is jdoe@someplace.net. Given that address, anyone on the Internet can send e-mail to John Doe.

Mail user agents and mail transport agents

To set up and use e-mail on your Red Hat Linux PC, you need two types of mail software:

- *Mail user agent* software (sometimes referred to using the acronym MUA) enables you to read your mail messages, write replies, and compose new messages. Typically, the mail user agent retrieves messages from the mail server using the POP3 or IMAP4 protocols. POP3 is Post Office Protocol version 3 and IMAP4 is the Internet Message Access Protocol version 4. The Red Hat Linux CD-ROMs include several popular mail user agents such as pine and elm.
- *Mail transport agent* (MTA) software actually sends and receives mail-message text. The exact method used for mail transport depends on the underlying network. In TCP/IP networks, the mail transport agent delivers mail using the Simple Mail Transfer Protocol (SMTP). This book's Red Hat Linux CD-ROMs include sendmail, a powerful and popular mail transport agent for TCP/IP networks.

Most mail transport agents run as *daemons*, background processes that run as long as your system is up. Because you or another user on the system can send mail at any time, the transport agent has to be there to deliver the mail to its destination. The mail user agent runs only when the user wants to read incoming mail, to write and send outgoing mail, or to check for new mail.

 Typically, a mail transport agent starts after the system boots. The system startup files for Red Hat Linux are set up so that the sendmail **mail transport agent starts when the Linux system is in multiuser mode. The shell script file** /etc/rc.d/init.d/sendmail **starts** sendmail.

sendmail

Because the system is already set up to start sendmail at boot time, all you have to do is use an appropriate sendmail configuration file to get e-mail going on your Linux system. You cannot send or receive e-mail until the sendmail mail transport agent is configured properly. The sendmail transport agent has the reputation of being a complex, but complete, mail-delivery system. If you take a quick look at sendmail's configuration file, /etc/sendmail.cf, you can see that sendmail is indeed complex. Luckily, you do not have to be an expert on the sendmail configuration file. All you need are the predefined configuration files from this book's companion CD-ROMs.

If you install the Mail/WWW/News Tools component during the Red Hat Linux installation, your system should have the working sendmail configuration file, /etc/sendmail.cf. The default file assumes an Internet connection and a name server. Provided you have an

Internet connection, you should be able to send and receive e-mail from your Linux PC once you connect it to the Internet. Then you can use a mail user agent such as elm to compose and send mail messages.

Setting Up the Apache Web Server

20 Min.
To Go

You probably already know how it feels to use the Web. However, you may not know how to set up a Web server so that you can provide information to the world through Web pages. To become an information provider on the Web, you have to run a Web server on your Red Hat Linux PC on the Internet.

Web servers provide information by using the HyperText Transfer Protocol (HTTP). Web servers are also known as *HTTP daemons* because they are continuously running server processes that use HTTP. In fact, most Web server programs, including the Apache Web server you learn about in this session, are usually named httpd.

Among the freely available Web servers, Apache Web server is the most popular. Apache is freely available over the Internet and it accompanies Red Hat Linux on this book's companion CD-ROMs.

When you install Red Hat Linux from this book's companion CD-ROMs, you also have the option of installing the Apache Web server. If you install the Mail/WWW/News Tools package during Red Hat Linux installation, then Red Hat Linux automatically starts the Apache Web server during system boot.

Perform the following steps to verify that the Apache Web server software is installed and running on your system:

1. Type the following command to check whether the Apache Web server is installed:

   ```
   rpm -q apache
   apache-1.3.19-5
   ```

   If the output shows an apache package name, you have the Apache software installed on your system.

2. Type the following command to check whether the httpd process is running; the name of the Apache Web server program is httpd:

   ```
   ps ax | grep httpd
   ```

   The output should show a number of httpd processes. It is common to run one parent and several child Web server processes so that HTTP requests can be handled efficiently by assigning each request to an httpd process.

3. Use the telnet program on your Linux system and execute the HTTP HEAD command to query the Web server as follows:

   ```
   telnet localhost 80
   Trying 127.0.0.1...
   Connected to localhost.
   Escape character is '^]'.
   HEAD / HTTP/1.0
   ... Press Enter once more to type a blank line
   HTTP/1.1 200 OK
   ```

```
Date: Sat, 19 Aug 2000 23:57:14 GMT
Server: Apache/1.3.12 (Unix)  (Red Hat/Linux)
Last-Modified: Mon, 07 Aug 2000 10:21:07 GMT
ETag: "328fe-b4a-398e8d93"
Accept-Ranges: bytes
Content-Length: 2890
Connection: close
Content-Type: text/html

Connection closed by foreign host.
```

If you get a response such as the preceding, your system already has the Apache Web server installed and set up correctly. All you have to do is understand the configuration so that you can place the HTML documents in the proper directory.

4. Use a Web server to load the home page from your system. Start Netscape Navigator by clicking the big "N" icon on the GNOME Panel, use the URL `http://localhost/`, and then see what happens. You should see a Web page with the title, Test Page for the Apache Web Server on Red Hat Linux.

The Apache Web server is set up to serve the HTML documents from the `/var/www/html` directory. Therefore, you should place your Web pages in that directory. In particular, edit or replace the `/var/www/html/index.html` file with your own home page.

In addition to the HTML files, the Apache Web server also supports *Common Gateway Interface (CGI)* programs, which the Web server can invoke to access other files and databases. You should place any CGI programs in the `/var/www/cgi-bin` directory.

Also note the following useful information about the Apache Web server:

● The Apache Web server configuration files are located in the `/etc/httpd/conf` directory. The configuration file, `httpd.conf`, controls how the server runs, what documents it serves, and who can access these documents.

● The `/var/log/httpd` directory is where the Apache Web server's access-log and error-log files are located.

● The `/etc/rc.d/init.d/httpd` script starts the `httpd` process as your Red Hat Linux system boots.

10 Min.
To Go

Setting Up the FTP Server

Besides e-mail and Web services, *anonymous FTP* is a common service on an Internet host. You may be familiar with FTP, which you can use to transfer files from one system to another on the Internet. When you use FTP to transfer files to or from a remote system, you have to log into the remote system before you can use FTP.

If you install Red Hat Linux from this book's companion CD-ROMs, you should have anonymous FTP set up on your system and the FTP server configured to run when needed. The default setup also employs the necessary security precautions.

Type the following command to check whether the FTP server is installed:

```
rpm -q wu-ftpd
wu-ftpd-2.6.1-16
```

If the output shows a `wu-ftpd` package name, you have the FTP server software installed on your system.

Anonymous FTP refers to the user name anonymous, which anyone can employ with FTP to transfer files from a system. Anonymous FTP is a common way to share files on the Internet. Many businesses use anonymous FTP to support their customers.

Type the following command to check whether anonymous FTP support is installed on your system:

```
rpm -q anonftp
anonftp-4.0-7
```

If the output shows an `anonftp` package name, your system supports incoming anonymous FTP.

If you have used anonymous FTP to download files from various Internet sites, you already know the convenience of that service. Anonymous FTP enables you to make information available to anyone on Internet. Even if you haven't used anonymous FTP explicitly, your Web browser often employs anonymous FTP to download files. (You simply might click a link; the Web browser does the rest.)

To see anonymous FTP in action, you can try accessing your system using an FTP client. For example, here's a sample session from when one user accesses his system from another PC on the LAN (his input appears in bold text):

```
ftp lnbp200
Connected to lnbp200
220 lnbp200.lnbsoft.com FTP server (Version wu-2.6.0(1) Fri Feb 4 23:37:48 EST 2
000) ready.
220 lnbp200 FTP server (Version wu-2.6.1(1) Wed Aug 9 05:54:50 EDT 2000) ready.
Name (lnbp200:): anonymous
331 Guest login ok, send your complete e-mail address as password.
Password:
230 Guest login ok, access restrictions apply.
Remote system type is UNIX.
Using binary mode to transfer files.
ftp> bye
221-You have transferred 0 bytes in 0 files.
221-Total traffic for this session was 299 bytes in 0 transfers.
221-Thank you for using the FTP service on lnbp200.
221 Goodbye.
```

When you log in with anonymous FTP successfully, you access the home directory of a user named `ftp` (the default directory is `/var/ftp`). You should place the publicly accessible files in the `/var/ftp/pub` directory.

Troubleshooting

If the Apache Web server is not installed on your system, use the following instructions to install it:

1. Log in as the root user.
2. Mount the Red Hat Linux installation CD-ROM (disk 1).
3. Type the following command to install Apache and its supporting packages (replace /mnt/cdrom with the mount point of your CD-ROM drive if it is different):

    ```
    # rpm -ivh /mnt/cdrom/RedHat/RPMS/apache*rpm
    ```

To start the Apache Web server if it is not running, type the following command as root:

```
/etc/rcd./init.d/httpd start
```

If the FTP server is not installed on your system, use the following instructions to install it:

1. Log in as the root user.
2. Mount the Red Hat Linux installation CD-ROM (disk 1).
3. Type the following command to install Apache and its supporting packages (replace /mnt/cdrom with the mount point of your CD-ROM drive if it is different):

    ```
    # rpm -ivh /mnt/cdrom/RedHat/RPMS/wu-ftpd*rpm*
    ```

If anonymous FTP support is not installed on your system, use the following instructions to install it:

1. Log in as the root user.
2. Mount the Red Hat Linux installation CD-ROM (disk 1).
3. Type the following command to install Apache and its supporting packages (replace /mnt/cdrom with the mount point of your CD-ROM drive if it is different):

    ```
    # rpm -ivh /mnt/cdrom/RedHat/RPMS/anonftp*rpm
    ```

Done!

REVIEW

This session introduced you to Internet services. You learned how to use the mail server (sendmail) to exchange e-mail with other systems on the Internet. You also examined the setup of the Apache Web server, as well as where to place the HTML documents and where to look for the log files. Finally, you explored how anonymous FTP is set up on your Red Hat Linux system.

QUIZ YOURSELF

1. Which configuration file stores the association between Internet services and port numbers? (See "Understanding Internet Services.")

2. What is a mail transfer agent? (See "Using the E-mail Server.")

3. From which directory does the Apache Web server serve the Web pages (HTML files)? (See "Setting Up the Apache Web Server.")

4. Where are the Web server's configuration files stored? (See "Setting Up the Apache Web Server.")

5. In which directory should you place the files that you want others to download using anonymous FTP? (See "Setting Up the FTP Server.")

Using Red Hat Linux as a Workgroup Server

Session Checklist

✔ Sharing files with NFS

✔ Setting up your Red Hat Linux PC as a Windows server with Samba

**30 Min.
To Go**

A low-end Pentium PC (or even a 486) configured with Red Hat Linux (from this book's companion CD-ROMs) makes a very capable workgroup or office server. A *workgroup* is a small local area network (LAN) of perhaps a dozen or so PCs. You can configure the Red Hat Linux PC to be the file and print server and the other PCs as the clients. The client PCs can run Windows instead of Linux.

This session introduces you to the Samba package, which comes with Red Hat Linux and provides everything you need to set up your Red Hat Linux PC as a server in a Windows network. However, first you learn about file sharing through Network File Sharing (NFS), which provides another way of sharing files besides Samba.

Sharing Files with NFS

Sharing files with NFS is simple, involving two basic steps:

1. On the Red Hat Linux server, export one or more directories by listing them in the /etc/exports file, thereby making them available to the client system.
2. On each client system, mount the directories exported by the Red Hat Linux server using the mount command.

The only problem in using NFS for file sharing is that each client system must support NFS. Most PCs do not come with NFS. That means you have to buy NFS software separately if you want to share files using NFS. It makes sense to use NFS if all systems on your LAN run Linux or other variants of UNIX with built-in NFS support. This session walks you through NFS setup using an example of two Red Hat Linux PCs on a LAN.

Exporting a file system with NFS

On the server, you must run the NFS service and also designate one or more file systems to *export*, or make available to the client systems. You can perform both tasks using the Linuxconf graphical system administration tool.

Perform these steps to start Linuxconf:

1. Log in as root and select Main Menu ➪ Programs ➪ System ➪ Linuxconf from the GNOME menu. Or, again as root, open a terminal window, and type linuxconf at the command prompt.

2. Click the Config tab and then select Networking ➪ Server Tasks ➪ Exported File Systems (NFS). Linuxconf then displays the Exported File Systems tab, which shows the current contents of the /etc/exports file. If /etc/exports is empty, the display should resemble Figure 15-1.

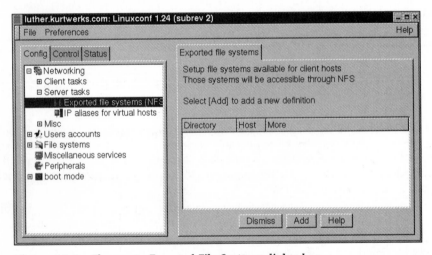

Figure 15-1   *The empty Exported File Systems dialog box*

3. Click the Add button. This adds the One Exported File System tab to the display, which allows you to define the details of the exported file system. You specify the file system with a full pathname, as shown in Figure 15-2.

   In this dialog box, you should also enter the names of client systems that may mount this exported file system. In the example shown in Figure 15-2, the /home/public directory is being exported and the host named katie can mount this file system for read and write operations.

4. Enter the information and click the Accept button. Linuxconf returns to the dialog box shown in Figure 15-1, but now it displays summary information about the exported file system.

5. Click the Dismiss button to finish defining exported file systems.

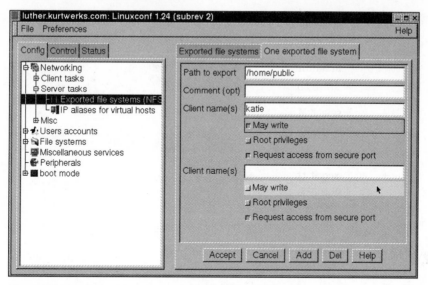

Figure 15-2   *Entering information about exported file systems in Linuxconf*

As a result of this session, Linuxconf adds the following entry to the /etc/exports file:

```
/home/public katie(rw)
```

To verify that the exported directories are listed in the /etc/exports file, type cat /etc/exports in a terminal window.

Now you should turn on the NFS server. To do this, click the Control tab, then select Control Panel ⇨ Control Service Activity. Linuxconf displays the Service Control screen with a list of all the services and their statuses, as shown in Figure 15-3.

Each line has three fields: one provides the name of a service, another indicates whether the service is enabled to run automatically or manually, and the last reveals whether the service is already running. Scroll down the list and locate the entry named nfs for the NFS service. In this case, the NFS service is not running yet. Click that entry. This causes Linuxconf to display the Service nfs tab, shown in Figure 15-4.

The buttons in this tab enable you to start, stop, or restart the service. In this case, click the Start button to start the NFS service. Then click Accept to return to the previous dialog box (Figure 15-3). Now the Service Control screen should show the status of the nfs entry as Running. Click Dismiss to exit this dialog box.

 If you ever make any changes to the exported file systems listed in the /etc/exports file, remember to restart the NFS service. Click the Restart button in the dialog box shown in Figure 15-4.

If you prefer to start the NFS service using a command, log in as root and type the following command in a terminal window:

```
/etc/rc.d/init.d/nfs start
```

That sets up the server side of NFS. Now you can try to mount the exported file system from the client system.

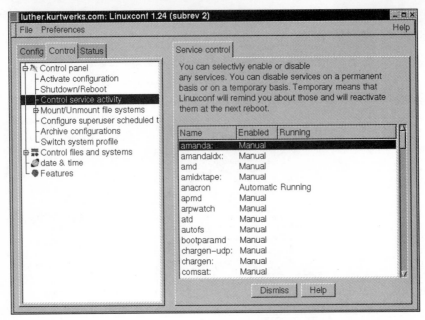

Figure 15-3 *Viewing the services and their statuses in the Service Control screen in Linuxconf*

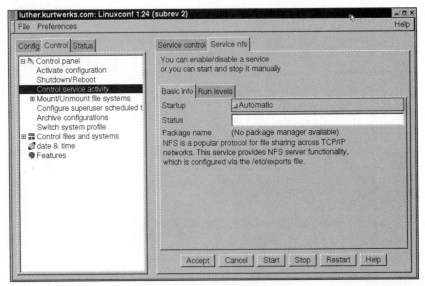

Figure 15-4 *Starting the NFS service through Linuxconf Service nfs tab*

Mounting an NFS file system

You can use Linuxconf on the client system to mount an exported NFS file system. However, the easiest way to perform the mount operation is to log in as root and use the mount command. For example to mount the /home/public file system from the luther system on the /mnt/luther directory of the client system named katie, type

```
mount luther:/home/public /mnt/luther
```

To confirm that the NFS file system is indeed mounted, log in as root on the client system and type mount in a terminal window. You should see a line similar to the following one about the NFS file system:

```
luther:/home/public on /mnt/luther type nfs (rw,addr=192.168.1.200)
```

Setting Up Your Linux PC as a Windows Server with Samba

**20 Min.
To Go**

If your business relies on Windows for file and print sharing, you probably use Windows in your servers and clients. You can move to a Red Hat Linux PC as your server without losing the Windows file and printer sharing because you can set up a Linux PC as a Windows server. When you install Red Hat Linux from this book's companion CD-ROMs, you also get a chance to install the Samba software package, which performs that task. All you have to do is select the DOS/Windows Connectivity package group during installation.

After you install and configure Samba on your Red Hat Linux PC, client PCs running Windows 95/98/NT/2000 can access disks and printers on the Red Hat Linux PC by using the *Server Message Block (SMB)* protocol, which is the underlying protocol in Windows file and print sharing.

With the Samba package installed, you also can make your Red Hat Linux PC a Windows client. This means that the Red Hat Linux PC can access the disks and printers managed by a Windows server. The Samba software package consists of these major components:

- smbd is the SMB server that accepts connections from Windows clients and provides file and print sharing services.
- nmbd is the NetBIOS name server that clients use to look up servers. *NetBIOS* stands for *Network Basic Input/Output System*. NetBIOS is an interface that applications use to communicate with network transports such as TCP/IP.
- /etc/samba/smb.conf is the Samba configuration file that the SMB server uses.
- testparm is a program that ensures that the Samba configuration file is correct.
- smbclient is the Windows client, which runs on Red Hat Linux and allows Red Hat Linux to access the files and printers on any Windows server.
- smbprint is a script that enables printing on a printer on an SMB server.
- smbadduser is a program that adds users to the SMB password file.
- smbpasswd is a program that changes the password for an SMB user.
- smbstatus is a command that lists the current SMB connections for the local host.

The following sections describe how to install Samba from the companion CD-ROMs. They also discuss the process of setting up a printer on the Red Hat Linux PC to print through Windows.

Checking if Samba is installed, and installing Samba

Before installing Samba, first check whether Samba is already installed by typing the following command in a terminal window:

```
rpm -qa | egrep samba
samba-common-2.0.7-36
samba-client-2.0.7-36
samba-2.0.7-36
samba-swat-2.0.7-36
```

If the rpm command displays a package name that begins with samba, then Samba is already installed on your system and you should skip the rest of this section. Otherwise, follow these steps to install Samba from this book's companion CD-ROMs:

1. Log in as root and make sure that the companion CD-ROM is in the drive and mounted. If not, use the umount /mnt/cdrom command to dismount the current CD-ROM, replace it with the companion CD-ROM, and then mount it with the mount /mnt/cdrom command.

2. Use the following command to change the directory to the CD-ROM where the Red Hat Package Manager (RPM) packages are located:

   cd /mnt/cdrom/RedHat/RPMS

3. Use the following rpm command to install Samba:

   ```
   rpm -ivh samba*
   ```
   If Samba is already installed, this command gives an error message. Otherwise, the rpm command installs Samba on your system by copying various files to their appropriate locations.

These steps complete the unpacking and installation of the Samba software. Now, to use Samba, you simply configure it.

Configuring Samba

To set up the Windows file- and print-sharing services, you have to provide a configuration file named /etc/samba/smb.conf. The configuration file is a text file that looks like a Microsoft Windows 3.1 INI file.

Like the Windows INI files, the /etc/samba/smb.conf file consists of sections with a list of parameters in each section. Each section of the smb.conf file begins with the name of the section in brackets ([]). The section continues until the next one begins or the file ends.

Each line in a section specifies the value of a parameter using this syntax:

name = value

As in Windows INI files, comment lines begin with a semicolon (;). In the /etc/samba/smb.conf file, comments may also begin with a hash mark (also known as the number sign), #.

 Text editors are covered in Session 9.

The Samba software comes with a configuration file that you can edit to get started. To prepare the configuration file, log in as root and use your favorite text editor to edit the file /etc/samba/smb.conf. Here's a sample configuration file without any comments:

```
[global]
workgroup = KurtWerks
server string = Samba Server
hosts allow = 192.168. 127.
guest account = kwall
log file = /var/log/samba/%m.log
max log size = 0
security = user
smb passwd file = /etc/samba/smbpasswd
encrypt passwords = yes
unix password sync = no
socket options = TCP_NODELAY SO_RCVBUF=8192 SO_SNDBUF=8192
remote browse sync = 192.168.0.255
remote announce = 192.168.0.255
local master = yes
os level = 33
name resolve order = lmhosts bcast
dns proxy = no
ssl CA certFile = /usr/share/ssl/certs/ca-bundle.crt

[printers]
comment = All Printers
path = /var/spool/samba
browseable = yes
guest ok = yes
writable = no

[homes]
comment = Home Directories
browseable = yes
writable = yes
printable = yes

[tmp]
comment = Temporary file space
path = /tmp
read only = no
public = yes
```

```
[public]
comment = Public Stuff
path = /home/samba
browseable = yes
public = yes
guest ok = yes
writable = yes
printable = no
available = yes
guest only = no
user = kwall
only user = yes
```

Change the workgroup name to one of your choosing. Change the user and guest account entries from kwall to your user name. Also make sure that all directories mentioned in the configuration file actually exist. For example, create the /home/samba directory with the command mkdir /home/samba.

After editing the Samba configuration file, add two users to the Samba password file. First add your user name. Here's how one user adds himself:

```
smbadduser kwall:kwall
----------------------------------------------------------
ENTER password for kwall
New SMB password:           type the password
Retype new SMB password:    type password again
Added user kwall.
```

Next add the root user with the command smbadduser root:root and then provide a password. (This does not change the password of your Red Hat Linux system's root user.)

After making the changes to the /etc/samba/smb.conf file, type testparm to verify that the file is OK. The testparm command checks the /etc/samba/smb.conf file and reports if the file is OK or not. After that, restart the SMB services with the following command:

```
/etc/rc.d/init.d/smb restart
Shutting down SMB services: [  OK  ]
Shutting down NMB services: [  OK  ]
Starting SMB services: [  OK  ]
Starting NMB services: [  OK  ]
```

The first two lines may show [FAIL] **if SMB services were not already running. You can ignore this error message.**

Accessing the Samba server

**10 Min.
To Go**

You can now try to access the Samba server on the Red Hat Linux system from one of the Windows systems on the LAN. Perform these steps to do so:

1. Double-click the Network Neighborhood icon on the Windows desktop. This should open up the Network Neighborhood window (see Figure 15-5) with all the other Windows systems on the LAN.

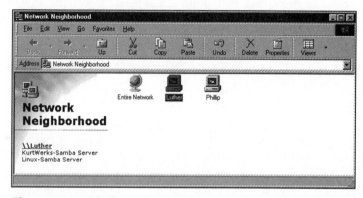

Figure 15-5 *Viewing a Red Hat Linux Samba server in the Windows Network Neighborhood*

2. Click the Red Hat Linux Samba server's icon to see its server string. Notice from the comment in the lower-left corner of Figure 15-5 that luther is actually a Linux system, as specified in the Samba configuration file.

3. If you do not see the Red Hat Linux Samba server in the Network Neighborhood screen in Windows, select Start ⇨ Find ⇨ Computer. Then type in the Linux system's host name (see Figure 15-6) and click the Find Now button. The Red Hat Linux Samba server should then show up on the screen.

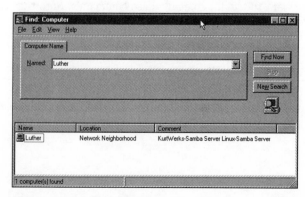

Figure 15-6 *Searching for a Linux Samba server from Windows*

Once you see the Linux Samba server, you can open it by double-clicking the icon. This should show folders for each shared directory in the Linux Samba server. You can then open these folders to further explore the contents of the directories. When you finish browsing the Samba server, you can close the Network Neighborhood.

Accessing Windows resources with smbclient

You can use the smbclient program to access shared directories and printers on Windows systems on the LAN as well as to check that your Linux Samba server is working. One quick way to check is to use the smbclient -L command to view the list of services on the Linux Samba server itself.

If you have other Windows servers on the LAN, you can look at their services with the smbclient program. Here is the smbclient command that one user types to view the services on a Pentium II PC running Windows 98:

```
smbclient -L phillip
```

You can also use smbclient to access a disk on a Windows server, as well as send a file to a Windows printer. The smbclient program is similar to ftpin that you connect to a Windows server and then use commands to exchange files and send files to the printer.

The following example shows how one user implements smbclient to access a disk on his Windows 98 PC and view its directory (he types the command in a terminal window):

```
smbclient //phillip/c kwall
added interface ip=192.168.0.1 bcast=192.168.0.255 nmask=255.255.255.0
Got a positive name query response from 192.168.0.2 ( 192.168.0.2 )smb: \> dir *.txt
    BOOTLOG.TXT                    AH    131754  Wed Jul 18 01:14:06 2001
    FRUNLOG.TXT                    A       1012  Wed Jul 18 00:59:32 2001
    SETUPLOG.TXT                   AH    146146  Wed Jul 18 01:07:06 2001
    NETLOG.TXT                     A      16076  Wed Jul 18 01:07:06 2001
    DETLOG.TXT                     AHS    69573  Wed Jul 18 01:01:58 2001

        34728 blocks of size 131072. 26814 blocks available
smb: \> quit
```

To see a list of smbclient commands, type help at the smb: \> prompt. To familiarize yourself with smbclient, you may want to try out some of these commands. Note that the smbclient commands are similar to MS-DOS commands.

Done!

REVIEW

This session showed you how to use NFS to share files among a Red Hat Linux system and other Linux or UNIX systems. Then you learned how to configure your Red Hat Linux system as a Windows server using the Samba software package.

QUIZ YOURSELF

1. What are the basic steps in sharing files through NFS? (See "Sharing Files with NFS.")

2. How do you export a file system using NFS? (See "Exporting a file system with NFS.")

3. How do you check if Samba is installed on your system? (See "Checking if Samba is installed, and installing Samba.")

4. How do you configure your Linux system to provide Windows file-sharing services? (See "Configuring Samba.")

5. How do you access Windows resources from your Linux system? (See "Accessing Windows resources with smbclient.")

Accessing Windows and DOS Files from Red Hat Linux

Session Checklist

✔ Mounting and accessing a DOS/Windows partition from Red Hat Linux

✔ Mounting and accessing a DOS/Windows floppy disk from Red Hat Linux

✔ Accessing and using DOS floppy disks with the `mtools` utility program

**30 Min.
To Go**

Typically, you install Linux on a PC that previously had Microsoft Windows installed on it. If you happen to work in Windows as well as in Red Hat Linux, you probably want to access the DOS/Windows files from Red Hat Linux. This session shows you how to do this, as well as how to mount and access MS-DOS/Windows floppy disks. You also learn about a package called `mtools`, which enables you to access and use MS-DOS/Windows files on a floppy disk in Red Hat Linux.

Mounting and Accessing a DOS/Windows File System

Red Hat Linux has built-in support for MS-DOS files. As Session 5 explained, the Red Hat Linux file system starts at the root directory and is denoted by a single slash (/). Even if you have multiple partitions on a single disk or a separate hard disk, their contents appear logically somewhere in the Red Hat Linux file system. *Mounting*, as discussed in Session 7, causes a physical storage device such as a hard disk partition or a CD-ROM, to appear as part of the Red Hat Linux file system.

Mounting DOS/Windows file systems during installation

During installation, the Red Hat installation program runs the Disk Druid program. This program finds any DOS/Windows partitions by checking the hard disk's partition table. You can use Disk Druid to specify where you want to mount each DOS partition. For example, you might mount the first DOS partition as /dosc, the second one as /dosd, and so on. You can name these mount points anything you want. If you specify them, Disk Druid performs the necessary steps to ensure that the DOS partitions are mounted automatically whenever you boot Linux.

To see whether your DOS/Windows hard disk partition is mounted automatically, follow these steps:

1. Use the grep command to look for the string vfat in the file /etc/fstab. Note the result you get with grep on a particular Linux PC:

```
grep vfat /etc/fstab
/dev/hda1  /dosc  vfat    defaults   0 0
```

2. If the output shows one or more lines that contain vfat, your Linux system mounts DOS/Windows hard disk partitions automatically. In this example, the output shows a matching line whose first field is the partition name /dev/hda1 (the first partition on the first IDE disk); the second field, /dosc, shows where that partition is mounted.

3. If the grep command does not show any lines that contain the string vfat in /etc/fstab, your system does not mount any DOS/Windows hard disk partitions automatically. An explanation, of course, may be that your hard disk does not have any DOS partitions.

 You do not have to be the root user to perform the preceding steps.

Another quick way to find out about the mounted devices is to type mount (without any arguments) at the shell prompt. Following is the output of the mount command on a sample system:

```
/dev/hda3 on / type ext2 (rw)
none on /proc type proc (rw)
/dev/hda1 on /dosc type vfat (rw)(Windows partition mounted on /dosc)
none on /dev/pts type devpts (rw,mode=0622)
```

If you see vfat anywhere in the output, those lines indicate MS-DOS file systems mounted on Red Hat Linux. In this case, a MS-DOS partition is mounted on the Linux directory /dosc.

 Even if you don't have any DOS/Windows partitions on your hard disk, you should learn how to access a DOS/Windows file system from Red Hat Linux because you may have to access a DOS/Windows floppy disk under Red Hat Linux. Understanding the concept of mounting is key to using a DOS file system in Red Hat Linux.

Mounting a DOS/Windows file system with the mount command

As discussed in Session 7, you can use the mount command to mount a device on the Linux file system manually at a specified directory. That directory is referred to as the *mount point.* You can use any directory as the mount point. However, if you mount a device on a non-empty directory, you lose the ability to access the files originally in that directory until you unmount the device with the umount command. Therefore, you should always use an empty directory (such as /mnt/cdrom) as the mount point.

If your DOS/Windows partition is the first partition on your IDE drive and you want to mount it on /dosc, use the following mount command:

```
mount -t vfat /dev/hda1 /dosc
```

The -t vfat part of the mount command specifies that the device you mount, /dev/hda1, has an MS-DOS file system. Linux has built-in support for MS-DOS files. Figure 16-1 illustrates the effect of this mount command.

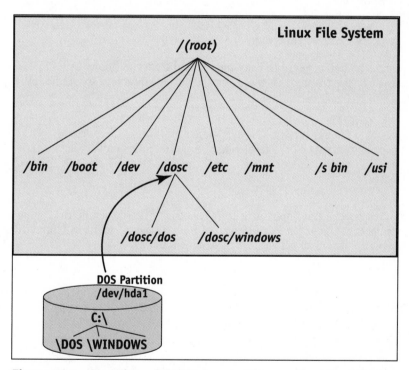

Figure 16-1 *Mounting a DOS/Windows partition on the /dosc directory*

Figure 16-1 also shows how directories in your DOS partition are mapped to the Linux file system. What once was the C:\DOS directory under DOS now becomes /dosc/dos under Linux. Similarly, C:\WINDOWS is now /dosc/windows. You probably can see the pattern. To convert a DOS filename to Linux (for this specific case, when you mount the DOS partition on /dosc), perform the following steps:

1. Change the DOS names to lowercase.
2. Change C:\ to /dosc/.
3. Change all backslashes (\) to slashes (/).

Mounting and Accessing DOS/Windows Floppy Disks

**20 Min.
To Go**

Just as you can mount a DOS/Windows hard disk partition under Linux, you can mount a DOS/Windows floppy disk. Usually, you have to log in as root to mount a floppy, but you can follow the steps shown later in this session to set up your system so that any user can mount a DOS/Windows floppy disk. You also need to know the device name for the floppy drive. By default, Linux defines two generic floppy device names:

- /dev/fd0, which is the A: drive (the first floppy drive)
- /dev/fd1, which is the B: drive (the second floppy drive, if you have one)

As for the mount point, an existing directory named /mnt/floppy is meant specifically for this type of temporary mount operation. Thus, you can mount the DOS floppy disk on the /mnt/floppy directory with the following command:

```
mount -t vfat /dev/fd0 /mnt/floppy
```

After the floppy is mounted, you can copy files to and from the floppy using Linux's copy command (cp). To copy the file gnome1.pcx from the current directory to the floppy, type the following:

```
cp gnome1.pcx /mnt/floppy
```

Similarly, to see the contents of the floppy disk, type the following:

```
ls /mnt/floppy
gnome1.pcx
```

When you want to remove the floppy disk from the drive, first dismount the floppy drive. This action disconnects the floppy disk's file system from its mount point in Linux's file system. Use the umount command to dismount a device, as follows:

```
umount /dev/fd0
```

 You can also type umount /mnt/floppy **to dismount the floppy disk.**

You can set up your Linux system so that any user can mount a DOS floppy. You simply log in as root and add a line in the /etc/fstab file. For example, to enable users to mount a DOS floppy in the A: drive on the /a directory, perform these steps:

1. Log in as root.
2. Create the /a directory with the following command:
   ```
   mkdir /a
   ```
3. Edit the /etc/fstab file in a text editor (such as vi or Emacs) and insert the following code:
   ```
   /dev/fd0   /a   vfat   noauto,user   0 0
   ```

Then save the file and quit the editor. The `user` option enables all users to mount DOS floppy disks. The first field identifies the device (`/dev/fd0`), the second one is the mount point (`/a`), and the third field shows the type of file system (`vfat`).

4. Log out and then log back in as a normal (not `root`) user.

5. To test that you can mount a DOS floppy without being `root`, insert a DOS floppy in the A: drive and type the following command:

   ` mount /a`

   Notice that you use the mount directory as an argument for the `mount` command. The mount operation should succeed, and you should see a listing of the DOS floppy when you type the command `ls /a`.

6. To unmount the DOS floppy, type `umount /a`.

Before you remove a mounted floppy disk, regardless of its file system type, you must first unmount it. Otherwise, you will not be able to use that floppy device for another floppy disk. Moreover, because Linux caches disk reads and writes, simply removing the floppy disk may cause you to lose data; a `umount` command causes Linux to write any outstanding data to disk.

Accessing and Using DOS/Windows Floppy Disks with mtools

So far, you've learned one way to access the MS-DOS file system: mount the DOS hard or floppy disk using the `mount` command and then use regular Linux commands, such as `ls` and `cp`. This approach to mounting a DOS file system is fine for hard disks. Linux can mount the DOS partition automatically at startup, and you can access the DOS directories on the hard disk anytime.

If you want to get a quick directory listing of a DOS floppy disk, however, you might find the mount process tedious. This is where the `mtools` package comes to the rescue. The `mtools` package is a collection of utilities that implements most of the common DOS commands for a Linux system. The commands have the same names as in DOS, except that you add an m prefix to each command. So, for example, `mdir` retrieves a directory listing and `mcopy` copies files. The best part of `mtools` is the fact that you do not have to mount the floppy disk to use the `mtools` commands.

Because the `mtools` commands write to and read from the physical device (floppy disk), you have to log in as `root` to perform these commands. If you want any user to access the `mtools` commands, you have to alter the permission settings for the floppy-drive devices. Execute the following command (as `root`) to permit anyone to read from and write to the first floppy drive:

```
chmod o+rw /dev/fd0
```

Verifying if mtools is installed

The `mtools` package comes with the Red Hat Linux distribution on this book's companion CD-ROMs. When you install Red Hat Linux, `mtools` is installed automatically as part of the base Linux. The `mtools` executable files are in the `/usr/bin` directory. To see whether you have mtools installed, type ls /usr/bin/mdir at the shell prompt. If the ls command shows that this file exists, you should have mtools available on your system.

You also can type the following rpm command to verify that mtools is installed on your system:

```
rpm -q mtools
mtools-3.9.7-4
```

If mtools is installed, the output shows you the full name of the mtools package. The sample output shows that mtools version 3.9.7-4 is installed on the system.

To try mtools, follow these steps:

1. Log in as root, or type su and then enter the root password.
2. Place an MS-DOS floppy disk in your system's A: drive.
3. Type mdir. You should see the directory of the floppy disk in the standard DOS directory listing format.

Checking the /etc/mtools.conf file

The mtools package should work with the default setup; but if you get any errors, you should check the /etc/mtools.conf file. This file contains the definitions of the drives (such as A:, B:, and C:) that the mtools utilities see. Following are a few lines from a typical /etc/mtools.conf file:

```
drive a: file="/dev/fd0" exclusive 1.44m mformat_only
drive b: file="/dev/fd1" exclusive 1.44m mformat_only

# First SCSI hard disk partition
#drive c: file="/dev/sda1"

# First IDE hard disk partition
drive c: file="/dev/hda1"

# IDE Zip drive
drive X: file="/dev/hdd4" exclusive
```

The pound sign (#) indicates the start of a comment. Each line defines a drive letter, the associated Linux device name, and some keywords that indicate how the device is accessed. In this example, the first two lines define drives A: and B:. The third non-comment line defines drive C: as the first partition on the first IDE (Integrated Drive Electronics) drive (/dev/hda1). If you have other DOS drives (D:, for example), you can add another line that defines drive D: as the appropriate disk partition.

**10 Min.
To Go**

If your system's A: drive is a high-density, 3.5-inch drive, you do not have to change anything in the default /etc/mtools.conf file.

Understanding the mtools commands

Recall from earlier in this chapter, the mtools package is a collection of utilities. So far, you have seen the command mdir, which is the mtools counterpart of the DIR command in DOS.

If you know the MS-DOS commands, using the mtools **commands is very easy. Type the DOS command in lowercase letters, and add** m **in front of each command. Because the Linux commands and filenames are case-sensitive, use all lowercase letters when you type the** mtools **commands.**

Table 16-1 summarizes the various mtools utilities and some of their corresponding commands available in mtools version 3.9.6.

Table 16-1 *Common* mtools *Commands*

mtools **Utility**	**MS-DOS Command**	**Action**
mattrib	ATTRIB	Changes MS-DOS file-attribute flags
mcd	CD	Changes an MS-DOS directory
mcopy	COPY	Copies files between MS-DOS and Linux
mdel	DEL or ERASE	Deletes an MS-DOS file
mdeltree	DELTREE	Recursively deletes an MS-DOS directory
mdir	DIR	Displays an MS-DOS directory listing
mformat	FORMAT	Places an MS-DOS file system on a low-level formatted floppy disk; uses fdformat to perform a low-level format on a floppy in Linux
mlabel	LABEL	Initializes an MS-DOS volume label
mmd	MD or MKDIR	Creates an MS-DOS directory
mmove	MOVE	Moves or renames an MS-DOS file or subdirectory
mrd	RD or RMDIR	Deletes an MS-DOS directory
mren	REN or RENAME	Renames an existing MS-DOS file
mtype	TYPE	Displays the contents of an MS-DOS file
xcopy	XCOPY	Recursively copies a DOS directory into another

You can use the mtools commands just as you use the corresponding DOS command. For example, the mdir command works like the DIR command in DOS. The same goes for all the other mtools commands shown in Table 16-1.

Formatting a DOS/Windows floppy disk

Suppose you have to copy some files to an MS-DOS/Windows floppy disk. If you already have a formatted MS-DOS/Windows floppy, you can simply mount that floppy and copy the files to the floppy using the Linux cp command. What if you do not have a formatted DOS floppy? The mtools package again comes to the rescue.

The `mtools` package provides the `mformat` utility, which can format a floppy disk for use under MS-DOS. Unlike the DOS `format` command that formats a floppy in a single step, the `mformat` command requires you to follow a three-step process:

1. Use the `fdformat` Linux command to perform a low-level format on a floppy disk. The `fdformat` command expects the floppy device name to be the argument; the device name includes all the parameters necessary for formatting the floppy disk. To format a 3.5-inch high-density floppy disk in your system's A: drive, type `fdformat /dev/fd0H1440`.

2. Use the `mformat` command to put an MS-DOS file system on the low-level formatted floppy disk. If the floppy is in drive A:, type the following command:

   ```
   mformat a:
   ```

3. Use the `mcopy` command to copy the files to the floppy disk. For example:

   ```
   mcopy *.pcx a:
   ```

Troubleshooting

If you get an error message that the VFAT (Virtual File Allocation Table) file system, the Windows file system, is not supported when using the `mount` command to mount a DOS/Windows floppy disk, log in as the `root` user and execute the following command:

```
/sbin/modprobe vfat
```

This command will load the necessary modules that Red Hat Linux needs in order to provide support for DOS/Windows file systems.

If you get a "device busy" error message when trying to unmount a floppy disk with the `umount` command, make sure your current directory is not located on the floppy disk (use the `pwd` command). Red Hat Linux cannot unmount a file system or disk of any sort if a process is using it, which includes having a current working directory located anywhere on the file system.

If you accidentally remove a floppy disk from a mounted drive without first unmounting it, in many cases, you can simply reinsert the floppy disk and execute the appropriate `umount` command to unmount the drive properly.

Done!

REVIEW

This session showed you how to access and mount the DOS/Windows file systems from Red Hat Linux and how to mount a DOS/Windows file system with the `mount` command. You also learned how to use the `mtools` utility programs to format and access a DOS/Windows floppy disk directly from Red Hat Linux without first having to mount the floppy disk.

QUIZ YOURSELF

1. How do you check if your Red Hat Linux system is set up to mount any DOS disk partitions automatically? (See "Mounting and Accessing a DOS/Windows File System.")

2. What mount command do you use to mount a DOS partition with the device name /dev/hda1 on the mount point /dosc? (See "Mounting a DOS/Windows file system with the mount command.")

3. What is mtools? (See "Accessing and Using DOS/Windows Floppy Disks with mtools.")

4. What are some of the mtools commands? (See "Understanding the mtools commands.")

5. How do you format a DOS/Windows floppy disk in Red Hat Linux? (See "Formatting a DOS/Windows floppy disk.")

PART

III

Saturday
Afternoon

1. What are the Linux device names for serial ports COM1 and COM2? What are the IRQ and I/O port address of COM1?

2. Describe how you would dial a remote system using the Minicom program.

3. Before using Minicom as an ordinary (non-root) user, what steps must you take?

4. What commands can you use to determine if the Linux kernel has detected your serial port(s)?

5. What peripheral(s) do you need to connect your Red Hat Linux system to an Ethernet local area network? What is the difference between 10Base2 and 10BaseT?

6. What diagnostic command can you use to see if your network interfaces are functioning? How do you determine if your Linux system can send network packets to another host?

7. What is the difference between a PPP connection to an Internet host and a regular serial connection with another system?

8. What information do you need from your ISP in order to establish a PPP connection from your system?

9. What are the programs you can use to set up and establish a PPP connection?

10. Suppose you have a Linux system that can connect to the Internet either using PPP or a DSL connection. How would you allow other computers on your LAN to use that connection? How do the other computers have to be configured in order to use a shared connection?

11. Name some common Internet services and the primary configuration file that connects those services to a port. What is a port?

12. What are the two software components necessary to provide or use e-mail service?

13. What are the default locations of the Apache Web server's configuration and log files?

14. Which script must you execute to enable and disable the Apache Web server?

15. How do you download a file using anonymous FTP?

16. Provide an overview of how to configure a server to provide file system access using the Network File System (NFS).

17. What must you do on a client system to enable it to use a file system made available from an NFS server?

18. What is Samba? Briefly describe how to set up a Red Hat Linux system as a Samba server.

19. What is the command to mount a Windows VFAT hard disk partition named /dev/hda4 on the Linux file system at the mount point /mnt/dosc?

20. How would you copy a file from your home directory to a DOS-formatted floppy disk without mounting the floppy disk?

PART

IV

Saturday Evening

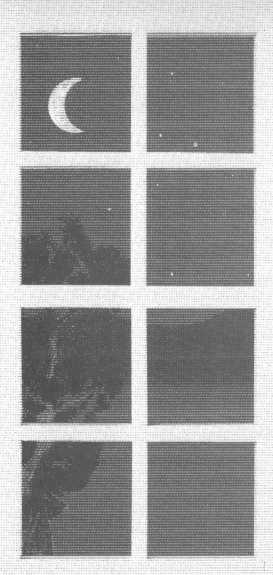

SESSION

Working with Screen Savers and Playing Games

Session Checklist

✔ Activating screen savers

✔ Playing games in GNOME

✔ Playing games in KDE

**30 Min.
To Go**

N ow that you know how to customize the GNOME and KDE graphical desktops and switch from one to the other, you can have some fun. You should have the games installed on your system, assuming that you selected the Games package group when you installed Red Hat Linux from this book's companion CD-ROMs in Session 1.

Both GNOME and KDE desktops in Red Hat Linux come with quite a few games and screen savers. In this session, you'll learn how to set up and activate the screen savers and explore some games.

Activating Screen Savers

By default, your Red Hat Linux system uses a randomly selected screen saver. Whenever you do nothing for some time (usually 20 minutes), the screen saver comes on. The screen saver can also act as a *screen-locking program*, which means you must type your password to get back to the graphical desktop.

Setting up a screen saver in GNOME

To select and try out a screen saver from the GNOME desktop, start the GNOME Control Center by clicking the toolbox icon on the GNOME Panel. Then select Desktop ⇨ Screen Saver from the tree menu in the Control Center. A dialog box appears in the Control Center's workspace from which you can select a screen saver. The small screen in the upper-right corner of the dialog box shows how the selected screen saver looks, as you can see in Figure 17-1.

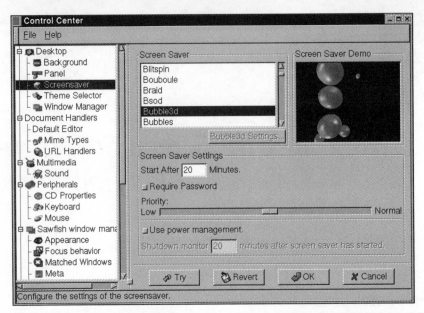

Figure 17-1 *Selecting and previewing a screen saver in the GNOME Control Center*

From the dialog box in Figure 17-1, you can also select several other screen saver settings. For example, you can set the number of minutes of inactivity after which the screen saver comes on. If you click the Require Password button, then the screen saver locks the screen and forces you to enter your password before you can return to the desktop.

The scrollbar labeled Priority enables you to specify the priority of the screen saver program. You should leave it at the default setting (which is midway between Low and Normal) or make it low; this ensures that other processes have higher priority. After all, just because there is no mouse or keyboard activity it does not mean that your Linux system is idle. You may be compiling a huge program when the screen saver activates. In that case, you don't want the screen saver to use up too much of the processor's time.

The button labeled Use Power Management applies if your PC supports power management features. If you click this button, the screen saver puts the system and monitor in a "sleep" mode that draws less power than normal operation.

Setting up a screen saver in KDE

If you use the KDE desktop, you can select and test screen savers from the KDE Control Center. Start it by clicking the monitor and circuit board icon on the KDE Panel or select K ⇨ Control Center. Then select Look & Feel ⇨ Screensaver from the tree menu in the KDE Control Center. The Screensaver tab appears in the Control Center's workspace from which you can select and preview screen savers (see Figure 17-2).

Many screen savers have their own setups. To set up the selected screen saver, click the Setup button in the KDE Control Center's Screensaver tab. (If the Setup button is not enabled, the screen saver is not configurable.) This brings up that screen saver's Setup dialog box, from which you can set up that screen saver's configurable parameters.

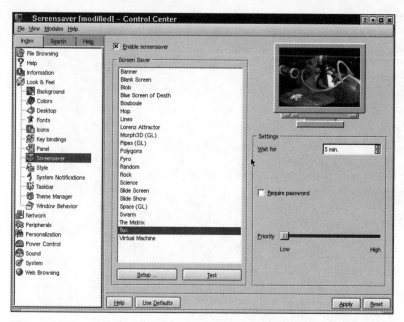

Figure 17-2 *Selecting and previewing a screen saver in the KDE Control Center*

You can also easily test a screen saver from the KDE Control Panel's Screensaver tab. Simply click the Test button that appears under the list of screen savers. This causes the screen saver to activate as a full screen. You can return to the desktop by pressing a key or moving (or clicking) the mouse. The Test button makes it very easy to test the KDE screen savers.

The KDE Control Center's Screensaver tab also enables you to set other parameters that control the screen saver. Specifically, you can set the number of minutes of inactivity after which the screen saver should start in the Wait For box. You can also click the checkbox labeled Require Password to make the screen saver require a password before returning to the desktop. Additionally, you can set the priority of the screen saver process.

Playing Games in GNOME

**20 Min.
To Go**

Now, try some games that come with Red Hat Linux. You can access them from the GNOME or KDE desktops. Look at some of the GNOME games first. To do so, select Main Menu (Foot) ➪ Programs ➪ Games to view the menu of available games. Figure 17-3 shows a typical Games menu in GNOME. As you can see, the GNOME desktop's Games menu offers almost 30 games on the Main menu, plus many more under the xpuzzles selection near the bottom of the Games menu. Select Main Menu ➪ Games ➪ xpuzzles to view the available puzzles.

In addition to these games, you can also play all the KDE games from the GNOME desktop. Simply select Main Menu (Foot) ➪ KDE Menus ➪ Games to view the KDE Games menu. The rest of this section describes some of the popular GNOME games.

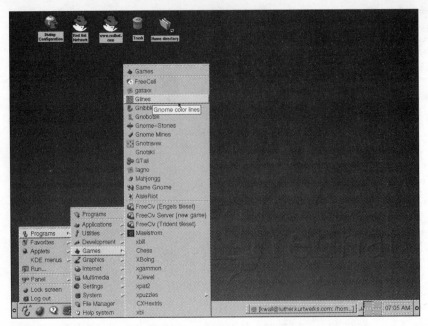

Figure 17-3   *The Games menu in GNOME*

Card games

If you like card games such as Solitaire, you'll like the AisleRiot game. AisleRiot is a card program that can play 30 different card games including such well-known ones as FreeCell and Klondike.

To start AisleRiot, select Main Menu (Foot) ⇨ Programs ⇨ Games ⇨ AisleRiot. AisleRiot's default game is Klondike.

If you want to play a different card game in AisleRiot, select Game ⇨ New Game from the menu. This causes AisleRiot to display a long list of card games.

Now you can choose another card game from this list. If you need help, select Help ⇨ AisleRiot. This brings up the AisleRiot help in the GNOME Help browser.

GNOME also comes with a stand-alone FreeCell card game. You can play that game by selecting Main Menu ⇨ Programs ⇨ Games ⇨ FreeCell. After the main window appears, click the New button on the toolbar to start a new game. Now you can play the game.

Gnome-Stones

Gnome-Stones is a game in which you run around a cave collecting diamonds and avoid being crushed by rocks. Select Main Menu ⇨ Programs ⇨ Games ⇨ Gnome-Stones to start the game. You can select Settings ⇨ Preferences to choose the type of cave you want to explore. Then select Game ⇨ New game to start a game. Use the arrow keys to move the little person around and collect the diamonds.

GNOME Mahjongg

Select Main Menu ⇨ Programs ⇨ Games ⇨ Mahjongg to start the GNOME Mahjongg game. In this version of Mahjongg, your goal is to find and click matching pairs of tiles, which are then removed from the game board.

If you have trouble locating matching tiles, click the Hint button on the toolbar. The game program then flashes two matching tiles for a short time. You can then click those tiles one after another. Of course, the point of the game is for you to figure out which tiles to remove, so you should use the Hint button sparingly.

Chess game

Select Main Menu ⇨ Programs ⇨ Games ⇨ Chess to start a game of chess. By default, the computer plays black and you play white. You get the first move. To make your move, click and drag a white piece to its new position. The chess program checks and stops you from making any illegal moves.

Once you move, the computer responds with its move. Initially, the computer responds promptly, but the moves take longer as the game progresses. A timer counts down the time for whoever has the current turn.

**10 Min.
To Go**

Playing Games in KDE

To try out the games available on the KDE desktop, log in after selecting KDE as the current desktop. (Remember to select Session ⇨ KDE from the login window.) From the KDE desktop, select K ⇨ Games to view the menu of available games. Figure 17-4 shows a typical menu of games in KDE.

As the menu shows, KDE includes over 30 games on the Games menu. You can try any of these games by selecting one from this menu.

> **KDE includes its own version of Mahjongg, which is similar to the GNOME version of Mahjongg introduced earlier in this session.**

Now that you know where to find and how to start the games, you can try them out at your leisure. In the remainder of this session, you can play a few KDE games.

Minesweeper

Minesweeper is a popular game that you may have played on your PC (because it comes with Microsoft Windows). In Minesweeper, your goal is to locate all the mines in a minefield represented by squares arranged in a grid. You are supposed to uncover all the squares that do not contain mines and mark the squares that contain mines.

To run the KDE version of Minesweeper, select K ⇨ Games ⇨ Minesweeper. To play, click squares to clear them. When you uncover a square that does not have any adjacent mines, Minesweeper clears out all other neighboring squares that also do not touch any squares with mines. The number on an uncovered square tells you how many mines are located in the adjacent squares. To mark a square that you suspect has a mine, click the right mouse button on that square. When you mark a square by right-clicking, a red flag appears on that square.

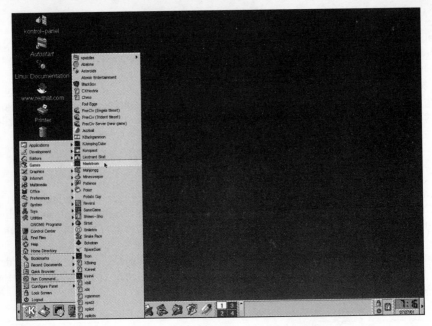

Figure 17-4   *The Games menu in KDE*

 The Games menu in GNOME also includes a Minesweeper game called Gnome Mines.

Patience

Patience is another Solitaire card game, similar to GNOME's AisleRiot. In Patience, you can play several card games including Klondike and FreeCell. To run Patience, select K ⇨ Games ⇨ Patience. By default, Patience starts a Klondike card game. To play another card game, select Game ⇨ Choose New Game and pick a game from the resulting menu.

Shisen-Sho

Shisen-Sho is a Mahjongg-like game. To start a game, select K ⇨ Games ⇨ Shisen-Sho. To play the game, select matching tiles that can be connected by horizontal or vertical lines without crossing over any other tile.

Troubleshooting

If you have selected a screen saver but cannot test it; or, it either runs as slow molasses in winter or refuses to start at all, you may not have the proper video hardware. Try selecting a less demanding screen saver. In both GNOME and KDE, 3D and OpenGL screen savers perform poorly, if at all, unless you have a hardware-accelerated graphics card that XFree86 supports.

If you really ruin the configuration of your screen savers and want to restore their default settings, you can delete or, better still, rename the following files in your home directory:

- .xscreensaver (may not exist)
- .gnome/Screensaver
- .kde/share/config/kdesktoprc

The second entry is GNOME-specific. The third file is for KDE. Note that kdesktoprc also controls other elements of your KDE desktop, so you might simply want to edit it (it is a text file) and remove all of the entries in the section that begin with the heading [ScreenSaver].

Done!

REVIEW

In this session, you learned how to select, configure, and preview screen savers in both GNOME and KDE desktops. Then you explored some games in the GNOME desktop. Finally, you spent some time trying out a few games in KDE.

QUIZ YOURSELF

1. How do you select and try out a screen saver in GNOME? (See "Setting up a screen saver in GNOME.")
2. How do you configure a screen saver in KDE? (See "Setting up a screen saver in KDE.")
3. How can you make sure that a GNOME screen saver "locks the screen?" (See "Setting up a screen saver in GNOME.")
4. How do you access and start the games available in GNOME? (See "Playing Games in GNOME.")
5. What games are available in KDE and how do you start them? (See "Playing Games in KDE.")

Working with Multimedia Applications

Session Checklist

✔ Configuring the sound card

✔ Playing audio CDs

✔ Working with graphics and images

**30 Min.
To Go**

R ed Hat Linux comes with quite a few multimedia applications that enable you to play audio CDs and manipulate graphics and images. In this session, you'll try out several multimedia applications and learn how to work with graphics and images. You start the session by configuring your PC's sound card in Red Hat Linux because you'll need a working sound card for listening to audio CDs.

Configuring the Sound Card

Your PC must have a sound card and speakers to play audio CDs according to the instructions from the PC's manufacturer. Red Hat Linux needs a sound driver to access and control the sound card. The sound drivers are provided as modules that you can load after booting Red Hat Linux. You can configure the sound card by running the /usr/sbin/sndconfig utility. This is a text-mode configuration program, so you should run it from a text console using the following procedure:

1. Log in as root.

2. In a terminal window or one of the virtual consoles, type /usr/sbin/sndconfig. A message informs you that the utility will probe for sound cards. Press Enter to continue with the probing.

3. The utility displays the result of probing for sound cards. Press Enter to continue with the configuration.

4. The utility then displays one or more dialog boxes that indicate existing configuration files will be replaced. Press Enter to continue with each step.

5. A dialog box informs you that sndconfig will play a sound sample. Press Enter.

6. If all goes well, you should hear Linus Torvalds pronounce Linux the way it should be pronounced (*his* way, of course!). A dialog box asks you if you hear the sound. If you hear the sound, press Enter to select Yes. Otherwise, press Tab to select No and then press Enter.

7. If you selected No in Step 6, sndconfig shows a dialog box from which you can manually select the interrupt request number (IRQ), I/O port addresses, and direct memory access (DMA) channels.

8. The utility then plays a *MIDI, Musical Instrument Digital Interface*, sound sample. You should now hear the MIDI sound sample. You can go through and confirm this part as well.

You can play audio CDs and other sound files even if you cannot hear the MIDI sample play.

9. After you exit sndconfig, type **exit** to log out.

Once you configure your sound card for use with Red Hat Linux, you can play audio CDs and other sound files on your Red Hat Linux system.

Playing Audio CDs

You need a special application to play audio CDs in Red Hat Linux. Red Hat Linux comes with several CD-player applications, including xplaycd, an X application providing a graphical Control Panel for playing audio CDs. Additionally, both GNOME and KDE come with CD players.

Before using any CD-player program, make sure that you dismount any CD-ROM currently in the drive (use the umount /mnt/cdrom **command introduced in Session 7) and place an audio CD in the drive.**

To try out the xplaycd program, type xplaycd in a terminal window from the GNOME or KDE desktop. The graphical user interface (GUI) of xplaycd is easy to understand because it resembles the interface of a hardware CD player. Try out the buttons to see how they work. Click the Exit button to quit the program.

If you are using the GNOME desktop, you can play audio CDs using the GNOME CD Player application. To launch the GNOME CD Player, select the Main Menu ⇨ Programs ⇨ Multimedia ⇨ CD Player. Figure 18-1 shows this CD player playing a track from an audio CD.

As you can see, the GNOME CD Player displays the title of the CD and the name of the current track. The GNOME CD Player gets the song titles from FreeDB, an Internet-based CD database. This means that you need an active Internet connection for the CD Player to download song information from the CD database. The GNOME CD Player will still work even without an Internet connection; it just will not display the CD's title and track information.

Figure 18-1 The GNOME CD Player playing a track from an audio CD

Once the CD Player downloads information about a particular CD, it caches that information in a local database for future use. The CD player's user interface is easy to learn; if you do not know what a button does, you can hold the mouse over it for a moment to view pop-up balloon help briefly describing the purpose of the button. One nice feature of the GNOME CD Player is that it allows you to select a track by title.

 To learn more about CDDB, read the Frequently Asked Questions about CDDB at http://www.cddb.com/FAQs.html.

If you want to log in as a normal user and play audio CDs on the CD-ROM drive, you should first log in as root and set the CD-ROM device's permissions to allow anyone to read it. Follow these steps to do so:

1. Log in as root. If you are already logged in, you can type the su command and enter the super user's password to assume the identity of root.
2. Make the CD-ROM device readable by all users using the chmod command as follows (the example assumes that /dev/hdc is your CD-ROM device):

        chmod o+r /dev/hdc

 Anyone who has access to your Red Hat Linux PC can now play audio CDs and access the CD-ROM drive.

If you use KDE as your desktop, you can find a similar audio CD player in KDE. Start the KDE CD Player by selecting K ⇨ Multimedia ⇨ CD Player. You can then use the KDE CD player to play a track from an audio CD.

Working with Graphics and Images

20 Min. To Go

The applications in this category enable you to prepare, view, modify, and print graphics and images. In the remainder of this session, you'll try out a few graphics and image manipulation applications.

The GIMP

The *GIMP (GNU Image Manipulation Program)* is an image-manipulation program written by Peter Mattis and Spencer Kimball and released under the GNU General Public License (GPL).

It is installed if you select the Graphics Manipulation package when you install Red Hat Linux from this book's companion CD-ROMs.

Follow this procedure to try out the GIMP:

1. Select Main Menu ⇨ Programs ⇨ Graphics ⇨ The GIMP from the GNOME desktop. (From the KDE desktop, select K ⇨ Red Hat ⇨ Graphics ⇨ The GIMP.) The GIMP starts and displays a window with licensing information. Click the Continue button to proceed.

2. The next screen previews what the GIMP will do in order to complete a personal installation. A personal installation involves creating a directory called .gimp-1.2 in your home directory and placing a number of files and subdirectories in that directory. This directory essentially holds information about any changes to user preferences that you might make to the GIMP. Click the Continue button to proceed.

3. The next dialog box shows a log explaining what the installation process did. Click the Continue button to proceed.

4. Click the Continue button in the next dialog box, GIMP Performance Tuning, to accept the default settings.

5. Select the checkbox next to Get Resolution from Windowing System and click the Continue button. This step completes the installation and opens the initial GIMP window, which is the toolbox shown in Figure 18-2.

Figure 18-2   *The GIMP toolbox*

From now on, the GIMP will start straightaway. You only have to perform the workstation or personal installation the first time you run the GIMP.

The GIMP then loads any existing *plug-ins*, which are external modules that enhance its functionality. After finishing the startup, the GIMP displays a Tip of the Day in a window. You can browse the tips and then click the Close button to exit the tip window. At the same time that it displays the Tip of the Day window, the GIMP displays the toolbox shown in Figure 18-2 and may also display a few other windows. For the purposes of this session, click the Close button on each of the other windows so that the only open GIMP window is the one shown in Figure 18-2.

The toolbox has three menu items on the menu bar: File, Xtns (extensions), and Help. The File menu includes options to create a new image, open an existing image, and quit the GIMP. The Xtns menu gives you access to a whole lot of extensions to the GIMP. The exact content of the Xtns menu depends on which extensions are installed on your system. The Help menu items enable you to get help.

The Toolbox

The toolbox in Figure 18-2 also has a large number of buttons, each with an icon, that represent the tools you use to edit images and apply special effects. You can get pop-up help on each tool button by placing the mouse pointer on the button. You can select a tool by clicking the tool button and then you can apply that tool's effects on an image.

To open an image file in the GIMP, select File ⇨ Open. This brings up the Load Image dialog box, which enables you to select an image file. You can change directories and select the image file you want to open. The GIMP can read most common image-file formats such as GIF, JPEG, TIFF, PCX, BMP, PNG, and PostScript. After you select the file and click the OK button, the GIMP loads the image into a new window. Figure 18-3 shows an image that the GIMP has opened.

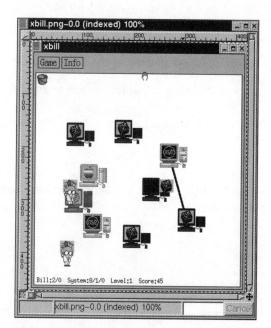

Figure 18-3 *Displaying an image with the GIMP*

For your convenience, the GIMP displays a pop-up menu when you right-click your mouse on the image window. The pop-up menu has most of the options from the File and Xtns menus in the toolbox. You also can pick some additional options such as printing or mailing the image. You can then select specific actions from these pop-up menus.

You can do much more than just load and view images with the GIMP, but you have to spend quite a bit of time learning all of its features. To learn more about GIMP, select Xtns ⇨ Web Browser ⇨ GIMP.ORG ⇨ Documentation. This brings up the Web browser with the online documentation for the GIMP. Of course, you will need an active Internet connection for this to work.

**10 Min.
To Go**

Ghostscript

Ghostscript is a utility for previewing and printing PostScript documents. Ghostscript enables you to print PostScript documents on many non-PostScript devices. At its heart, Ghostscript is an implementation of the PostScript language. Ghostscript includes the interpreter that processes PostScript input and generates output on an output device. A Ghostscript device can be a printer or display screen as well as an image-file format such as BMP or PCX.

Ghostscript is distributed under the GNU GPL, but is copyrighted and maintained by Aladdin Enterprises. Some Ghostscript documentation is installed in the /usr/doc directory. To change to the appropriate directory, type cd /usr/doc/ghostscript*. The exact directory name depends on the version of Ghostscript installed on your system. You can find the latest contact information in the README file in that directory. That directory also contains some other Ghostscript documentation. All of these documentation files are text files that you can view using the more command.

You typically use Ghostscript to load and view a PostScript file. To see how Ghostscript renders a PostScript document, you can use any available PostScript document you have. One good solution is to use one of the sample PostScript files in the /usr/share/ghostscript/5.50/examples directory with the gs command. (Replace 5.50 with whatever version of Ghostscript is installed on your system.) For example, type the following command in a terminal window:

```
gs /usr/share/ghostscript/5.50/examples/golfer.ps
```

Ghostscript opens that file, processes its contents, and displays the output in another window (as shown in Figure 18-4).

In this case, the output is a picture of a golfer. After displaying the output, Ghostscript produces the following message:

```
>>showpage, press <return> to continue<<
```

Press Enter to continue. For a multiple-page PostScript document, Ghostscript then shows the next page. After all the pages are displayed, you return to the Ghostscript prompt. Type quit to exit Ghostscript.

Ghostview

Ghostview is an X-based graphical front end to the Ghostscript interpreter. Ghostview is ideal for viewing and printing PostScript documents. For a long document, you can even print selected pages. You also can view the document at various levels of magnification by zooming in or out.

To run Ghostview, select Main Menu ⇨ Graphics ⇨ Ghostview (if you are running GNOME), or type ghostview & in a terminal window. Both methods open a Ghostview window. The window is divided into three parts:

- Along the window's top edge, you see eight buttons. The first six buttons are menu buttons.

- Down the window's left side, you see several more buttons, text boxes for information display, and scrollbars for scrolling the image.

Figure 18-4 *Ghostscript displaying a PostScript file*

- The large area occupying most of the Ghostview window is the work area where Ghostview displays the PostScript document.

To load and view a PostScript document in Ghostview, select File ⇨ Open or click the Open button on the left side of the Ghostview window. This action causes Ghostview to display a file-selection dialog box. You can choose one of the PostScript files that come with Ghostscript. For example, select the file tiger.ps in the /usr/share/ghostscript/5.50/examples directory. If your system has a version of Ghostscript later than 5.50, you have to use the new version number in place of 5.50.

To open the selected file, click the Open File button in the file-selection dialog box. Ghostview opens the selected file, processes its contents, and displays the output in its window as shown in Figure 18-5.

In the last two buttons on the upper-right corner of the window, Ghostview displays the current filename and the date the file was created. As you move the mouse over the image, Ghostview displays the coordinates of the mouse pointer in a button along the upper-left corner of the window, which is helpful if you want to select a specific area of the image to edit, copy, or delete.

Figure 18-5   *Ghostview displaying a PostScript file*

Ghostview is useful for viewing documentation that comes in PostScript format, which typically uses the `.ps` filename extension. This format is also used for viewing files saved with Adobe's PDF (Portable Document Format) format, which is an increasingly popular file format on the Internet and the World Wide Web. It is very handy to have a single program that can read both file formats. For example, you can use Ghostview to view the documentation for the CVS program, which comes in several PostScript files that you can find in the `/usr/share/doc/cvs*` directory. When viewing such documents in Ghostview, use the magnification button, which is labeled 1.000 in Figure 18-5. If you click that button and hold down the mouse, a menu appears with a number of magnification factors from 0.1 to 10.0. You may have to select a magnification of 2.000 or more to make the document legible onscreen.

Troubleshooting

If you have trouble persuading xplaycd to play CDs for you, you may need to give yourself permission to use the CD-ROM device. To do so, log in as root and execute the following command:

```
chmod 666 /dev/cdrom
```

This command gives all users read and write permission to the CD-ROM drive.

If the previous tip brings you no aural joy, try using the actual CD-ROM device, rather than /dev/cdrom, which is only a symbolic link. For example, on a sample system /dev/cdrom is a symbolic link to /dev/hdc, so it would be necessary to execute the following command:

```
chmod 666 /dev/hdc
```

If your system has less than 64MB of RAM *and* you want to use GIMP, setting its *tile cache* — the amount of RAM it uses for image storage — to a low value, such as 16MB, will improve your system's speed. However, this gain comes at the expense of GIMP's performance, especially if you intend to work with large images. To change the tile cache size, following these steps:

1. Select File ⇨ Preferences from the GIMP toolbar.
2. Click the Environment item on the Categories tree menu.
3. Enter a new value for Tile Cache Size.
4. Enable the Conservative Memory Usage checkbox.
5. Click OK to save your changes and close the dialog box.

Done!

REVIEW

This session showed you how to configure the sound card and use a few CD-player applications to hear CDs on your Red Hat Linux system. You also familiarized yourself with the GIMP, Xpaint, Ghostscript, and Ghostview applications for working with image files of various formats.

QUIZ YOURSELF

1. How do you employ the /usr/sbin/sndconfig utility to configure the sound card for use in Red Hat Linux? (See "Configuring the Sound Card.")
2. What steps do you have to perform so that any user can play audio CDs on the CD-ROM drive? (See "Playing Audio CDs.")
3. What is "The GIMP" and what can you do with it? (See "The GIMP.")
4. How do you view PostScript files with Ghostscript? (See "Ghostscript.")
5. How is Ghostview related to Ghostscript (See "Ghostview.")

Working with the Office Tools in Red Hat Linux

Session Checklist

✔ Using the Gnumeric spreadsheet

✔ Exploring KOffice applications

✔ Maintaining calendars

✔ Working with calculators

✔ Utilizing the spelling checker

**30 Min.
To Go**

This session focuses on the applications that you need for day-to-day office work. This book's companion CD-ROMs include all of the Red Hat Linux office tools discussed in this session: calendars, calculators, and spelling checkers. I also introduce you to several prominent commercially available office applications for Linux that are not included on the companion CD-ROMs.

Using the Gnumeric Spreadsheet

The GNOME desktop comes with *Gnumeric*, which is an X-based graphical spreadsheet program. To try out Gnumeric, select Main Menu ⇨ Programs ⇨ Applications ⇨ Gnumeric Spreadsheet from the GNOME Panel. The Gnumeric program displays its main window, which looks similar to Windows-based spreadsheets such as Microsoft Excel. In fact, Gnumeric can read and write Excel 95 spreadsheet files.

You use Gnumeric the same way as Microsoft Excel. You can type entries in cells, use formulas, and format the cells, specifying the type of value and the number of digits after the decimal point.

You might want to type in a sample spreadsheet to get used to Gnumeric. Try some formulas that you normally use in Microsoft Excel. For example, use the formula SUM(D2:D6) to add up the entries from cell D2 to D6. To set cell D2 as the product of the entries A2 and C2, type =A2*C2 in cell D2.

To learn more about the functions available in Gnumeric, select Help ⇨ Gnumeric function reference from the menu. This brings up the GNOME Help Browser with information about the Gnumeric functions. You can browse the list of functions and click one to read more about that function. Figure 19-1 shows a small spreadsheet created using Gnumeric.

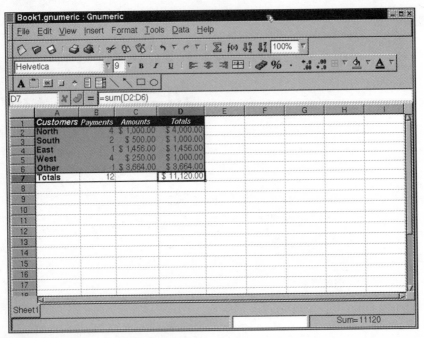

Figure 19-1 *A Gnumeric spreadsheet*

When you're finished preparing the spreadsheet, select File ⇨ Save As to save it. A dialog box appears from which you can specify the file format, the directory location, and the name of the file. Gnumeric can save the file in a number of formats including XML (eXtensible Markup Language), Excel 95, a simple text file, and Adobe's Portable Document Format (PDF) file. You cannot read the file back into Gnumeric unless you save it as an XML or Excel 95 file. Gnumeric's default file format is XML, which is a text-based format. However, Gnumeric compresses the resulting XML file using the GNU Zip (gzip) compression program. Gnumeric assigns a .gnumeric extension to files stored in the compressed XML format.

Save the spreadsheet in Excel 95 format. Then transfer that file to a Windows system and try to open it using Microsoft Excel. Notice that the file loses some of the text styles (such as bold and justification) in the translation. However, the basic elements, such as the numbers and the formulas, stay intact when you save the spreadsheet in Excel 95 format.

Exploring KOffice Applications

Red Hat Linux includes KOffice, a complete suite of office productivity applications, including the following:

- *KWord* for word processing
- *KSpread* for spreadsheets
- *KChart* for creating charts and graphs
- *KPresenter* for presentations
- *KIllustrator* for drawing vector graphics

We do not have enough time to discuss all of the KOffice applications, so we'll only introduce you to KSpread and KWord. Figure 19-2 shows KSpread with the same spreadsheet shown in Figure 19-1. To start KSpread from KDE, select K ➪ Office ➪ KSpread.

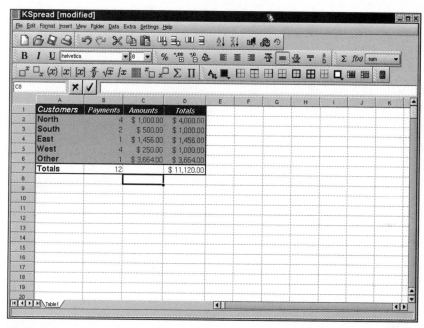

Figure 19-2 *The KSpread spreadsheet*

As you can see in Figure 19-2, KSpread's interface is similar to Microsoft Excel's and, in its default configuration, most of the functions you will need are already available. KSpread can open about a dozen spreadsheet formats, including Excel 97, but will only save new sheets in its own format, .ksp, or as *CSV (comma separated value)* data.

Even though KOffice was written with KDE in mind, it runs just fine under GNOME. To start KOffice applications while using the GNOME desktop, select Main Menu ➪ KDE Menus ➪ Office, and then select the application you want to run.

Figure 19-3 shows a KWord document with part of the worksheet from Figure 19-2 embedded in it. In fact, to edit the worksheet in KSpread, you can simply click on the sheet to make KSpread active.

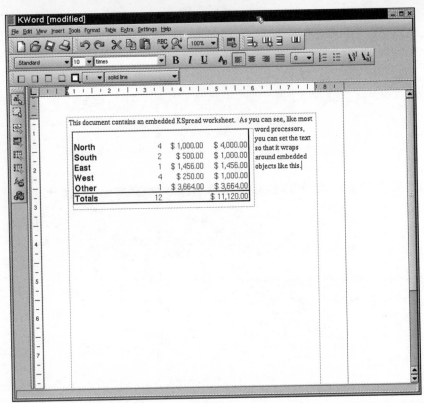

Figure 19-3 *KWord allows you to embed objects from other KOffice applications.*

To start KWord from KDE, select K ⇨ Office ⇨ KWord. You can experiment with the components of the KOffice suite and discover everything that it is capable of doing.

Maintaining Calendars

20 Min. To Go

The companion CD-ROMs contain several calendar programs. The GNOME desktop comes with its own calendar program. Additionally, when you install the X Window System following the steps outlined in Session 1, you also install ical, which is an X Window System-based calendar program. You can start both calendars from the GNOME Panel's Main Menu button or the KDE main menu.

ical calendar

To start ical, select Main Menu ⇨ Programs ⇨ Applications ⇨ ical from the GNOME desktop. (You can also simply type ical in a terminal window.) The program displays a full-screen window where you can click a date to view that day's schedule. To add appointments for a specific time, click the time and type a brief description of the appointment.

You can go to a different month or year by clicking the arrows next to the month and the year. After you finish adding events and appointments, select File ⇨ Save to save the calendar.

GNOME calendar

To start the GNOME calendar program, select Main Menu ⇨ Programs ⇨ Applications ⇨ Calendar from the GNOME Panel. The GNOME calendar's main window appears. The GNOME calendar has a different, more intuitive, user interface than the ical program. Figure 19-4 shows the GNOME calendar in its default Day view.

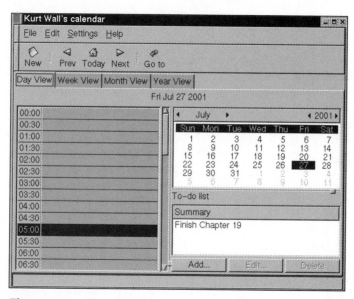

Figure 19-4   *The GNOME calendar shows daily, weekly, monthly, and yearly calendar views.*

The To-do list contains a task item to finish writing this chapter today. To create a new task, click the Add button. Use the Edit button to change an existing task. You can click the Delete button to remove the highlighted task.

The GNOME Calendar's toolbar buttons give you quick access to the most commonly needed functions, such as moving to a different date or adding a new appointment. Underneath the toolbar, a number of tabs display the appointments in four different views: Day View, Week View, Month View, and Year View. If you are unsure about what a button does, simply hover the mouse pointer over the button and a small pop-up help message gives you some information.

To add an appointment, you can double-click the date in the right side of the window and then click the New button on the toolbar. This brings up a dialog box where you can enter information about the appointment. Select File ⇨ Save to store the appointments on disk.

Working with Calculators

You have a choice of three calculators that you can use with Red Hat Linux:

- xcalc, the X calculator that comes with the X Window System
- GNOME calculator
- KDE calculator

All of these calculators are scientific calculators capable of performing typical functions such as square root and inverse, as well as trigonometric functions such as sine, cosine, and tangent.

xcalc calculator

The xcalc calculator is styled after the Texas Instruments TI-30 model. To use the xcalc calculator, type xcalc & in a terminal window. Figure 19-5 shows the resulting calculator. You can use it by clicking its buttons or by entering the numbers on the keyboard.

Figure 19-5   *The* xcalc *TI-30-style calculator*

If you prefer the Reverse Polish Notation (RPN) of the Hewlett-Packard calculators, you can get a calculator modeled after the HP-10C by typing the xcalc -rpn & command. In RPN, the operands precede the operation. For example, to add 2.25 to 9.95 on an HP-10C calculator, you press the keys in the following order: 2.25 ENTER 9.95 +.

GNOME calculator

The GNOME calculator is based on xcalc, but with a nicer user interface. To run the GNOME calculator, select Main Menu ⇨ Programs ⇨ Utilities ⇨ Simple Calculator in the GNOME Panel. Figure 19-6 shows the resulting display of the GNOME calculator.

If you compare Figure 19-5 with Figure 19-6, you see that both xcalc and the GNOME calculator have the same set of buttons, except that GNOME calculator's buttons are easier to read.

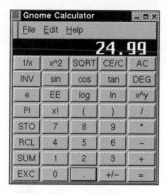

Figure 19-6   *The GNOME calculator*

KDE calculator

KDE also includes a scientific calculator with more features than xcalc and the GNOME calculator. For example, it can perform calculations in hexadecimal, decimal, octal, and binary format. From the KDE desktop, you can start the KDE calculator by selecting K ⇨ Utilities ⇨ Calculator (or Main Menu ⇨ KDE Menus ⇨ Utilities ⇨ Calculator from the GNOME Panel).

With the KDE calculator, you can convert a number from one base to another by simply entering the number with one of the buttons selected and then clicking the desired base. For example, to convert the hexadecimal value FF to decimal, click the Hex button and enter FF. Then click the Dec button to see the answer, which should be 255.

Utilizing the Spelling Checker

The aspell utility is an interactive spelling checker. When you install Red Hat Linux from the companion CD-ROMs, you have the opportunity to install aspell.

Using aspell to check the spelling of words in a text file is simple. To do so, simply type aspell check *filename*. To try out aspell, type some notes and save them in a text file named notes.txt. To run the spelling checker on that file, type the following command in a terminal window:

```
aspell check notes.txt
This note describes the *concensus* reached during the August 16 meeting.
1) consensus            6) consensus's
2) con census           7) consensuses
3) con-census           8) consciences
4) condenses            9) condensers
5) concerns             0) consensual
i) Ignore               I) Ignore all
r) Replace              R) Replace all
a) Add                  x) Exit
?
```

When aspell starts, it scans the file named notes.txt until it finds a misspelled word (any word that does not appear in aspell's dictionary). As the output shows, aspell displays the sentence with the misspelled word (*concensus*) and highlights that word by enclosing it in a pair of asterisks (*). Below that sentence, aspell lists possible corrections, numbering them sequentially from 1. In this case, the utility lists *consensus* — the right choice — as the first correction for *concensus*. The list also includes a few items labeled with a letter that mean specific actions such as ignore the misspelling or accept the misspelled word for the rest of the file.

At the end of the list of choices, aspell displays a question mark (?) prompt. You should press one of the numbers or letters from the list shown in aspell's output to indicate what you want aspell to do. If you press a number, aspell uses the corresponding word to replace the misspelled one. Select i or I to ignore the misspelling; r to replace just this occurrence; R to replace all instances of this misspelling; a to add the word to your private dictionary; or x to exit aspell.

> To read the aspell **manual, start the Web browser and select File ⇨ Open Page and click the Choose File button from the Open Page dialog box. Go to the** /usr/share/doc **directory and look for a directory name that begins with** aspell; **the complete name depends on the** aspell **version number. From the** man_html **subdirectory of that directory open the** 1_Introduction.html **file.**

Done!

REVIEW

This session introduced you to office applications for Linux. You tried out a few common office tools — spreadsheets, calendars, calculators, and spelling checkers — that come with Red Hat Linux. You also learned about several commercially available office application suites for Linux — WordPerfect Office 2000 for Linux, Applixware Office, and StarOffice. These commercial applications are not part of Red Hat Linux, but you learned how to find out more about each product in case you need a Linux office suite for your home or business.

QUIZ YOURSELF

1. What is the default file format and file extension of the Gnumeric spreadsheet? (See "Using the Gnumeric Spreadsheet.")
2. How do you add an appointment to the GNOME Calendar? (See "GNOME calendar.")
3. What choice of calculators do you have with Red Hat Linux? (See "Working with Calculators".)
4. What utility do you use to check the spellings in a text file? (See "Utilizing the Spelling Checker.")
5. What are some commercially available office applications for Linux? (See "Exploring Koffice Applications.")

Using the Red Hat Network

Session Checklist

✔ Registering with the Red Hat Network

✔ Running the Software Manager

✔ Using the Update Agent

**30 Min.
To Go**

O ne of the biggest challenges of maintaining your Red Hat Linux system is keeping up with software updates that add new features, fix bugs, and, most importantly, address real and potential security risks. In this session, you'll learn how to use the Red Hat Network to keep your Red Hat Linux system up-to-date and secure.

Registering with the Red Hat Network

The Red Hat Network is a system management tool developed and administered by Red Hat for Red Hat Linux systems. Its only service, at this time, is the Software Manager. Software Manager consists of several services, including a software update subscription service, automatic Red Hat Package Manager (RPM) updates, and e-mail notification of bugs and security alerts.

Of course, the Red Hat Network is a fee-based service, not a free one. Red Hat Linux users who purchase versions 6.2 and 7.x are permitted a free subscription to Software Manager for one system. Additional subscriptions for other systems cost $19.95 per month, per system.

For complete information about subscribing to the Red Hat Network, visit its Web site at http://www.redhat.com/network/.

In order to use the Red Hat Network, you have to create a system profile and then register it with the Red Hat Network. A *system profile* is a database of software and hardware information that Red Hat Network uses to customize the updates and notifications you receive. Then, after a quick trip to the Red Hat Network to activate your Software Manager subscription, you can use the Update Agent to obtain the latest updates for your system. To create the system profile and register with the Red Hat Network, follow this procedure:

1. Using the GNOME desktop, select Main Menu ⇨ Programs ⇨ System ⇨ Red Hat Network. This opens the Red Hat Registration screen, shown in Figure 20-1.

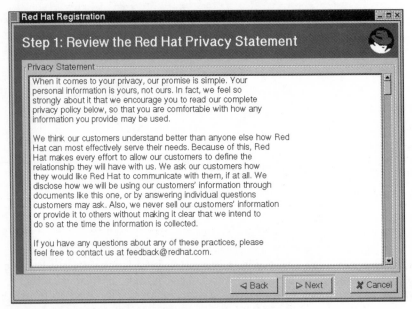

Figure 20-1   *The Red Hat Network privacy policy*

2. After you read the privacy policy, click the Next button.
3. Fill out the form shown in Figure 20-2 to register your system, and then click the Next button.

When selecting a password for the account you create, *do not use* the password of any account on your system. Should your Red Hat Network account information be compromised somehow, using a different password will maintain the security of your system – using the same passwords gives the person with your Red Hat Network password access to your Red Hat Linux system.

4. If you wish, provide the additional information requested in the next dialog box. Doing so is optional, though. Click the Next button to continue.
5. The following dialog box allows you to name the system profile. The default name is your system's host name. This dialog box also shows the hardware information that will be stored in the profile. Figure 20-3 shows the profile for a sample system. Click the Next button to continue.

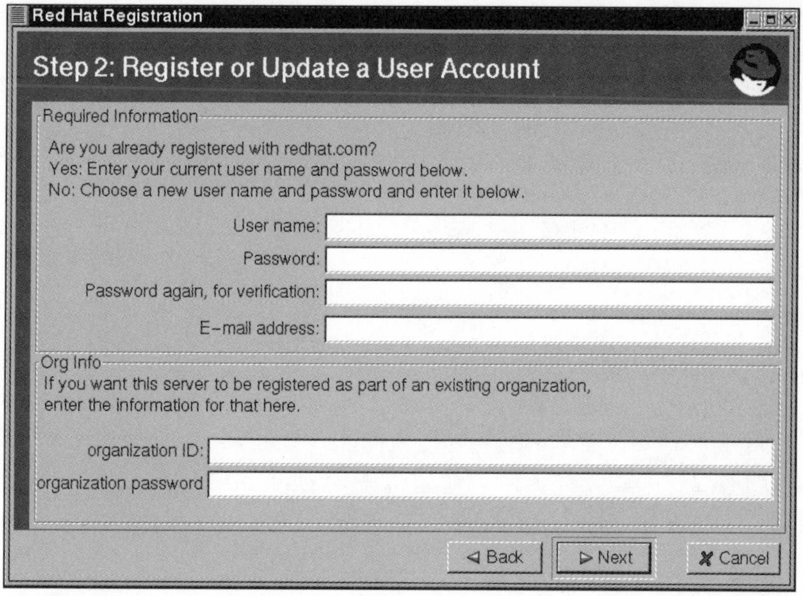

Figure 20-2 *Fill out the registration form to create an account for yourself.*

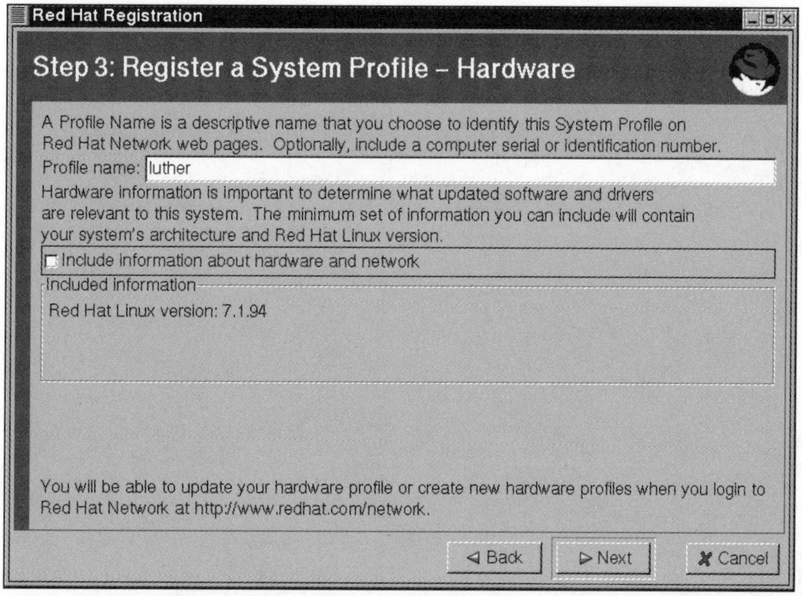

Figure 20-3 *The hardware profile and profile name are specific to your system.*

6. After a short pause, the next screen shows a list of the packages installed on your system (see Figure 20-4). You should check the checkbox at the top of the dialog so that the Software Manager can store this information in the profile and use it to update packages installed on your system. Click the Next button to continue.

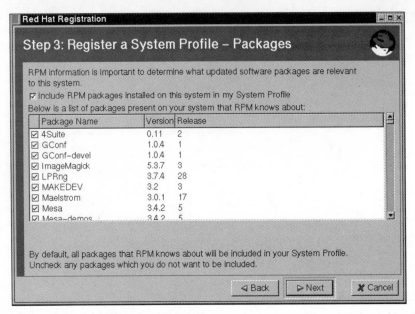

Figure 20-4   The software profile enables the Software Manager to update RPMs.

7. In the following dialog box, click Next to send the profile information to Red Hat and to register with the Red Hat Network (see Figure 20-5). You can click the Cancel button to cancel the registration.

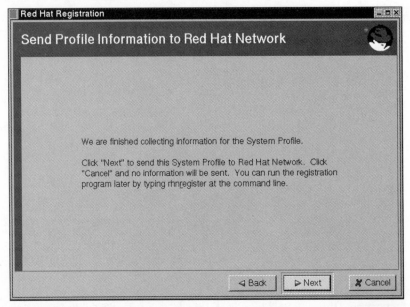

Figure 20-5   Send the system profile to the Red Hat Network to register.

8. Depending on the speed of your network connection, you may see a progress dialog, as shown in Figure 20-6. When the process completes, you will see the screen shown in Figure 20-7. Click the Finish button to complete the registration process.

Figure 20-6 *The progress dialog monitors the registration process.*

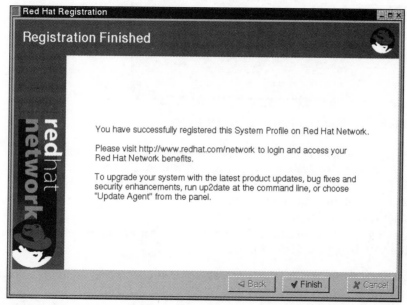

Figure 20-7 *Clicking the Finish button completes the registration process.*

Running the Software Manager

**20 Min.
To Go**

After registering with the Red Hat Network, follow this procedure to subscribe to the Software Manager:

1. Open the Red Hat Network home page at `http://rhn.redhat.com/`. Enter the user name and password you created when you registered with the Red Hat Network (see Step 3 in the previous section). Then click the Login button.

2. Click the Entitlements button under the Your RHN category on the left-hand side of the screen. The Entitlement Manager tells you how many entitlements you have left (see Figure 20-8).

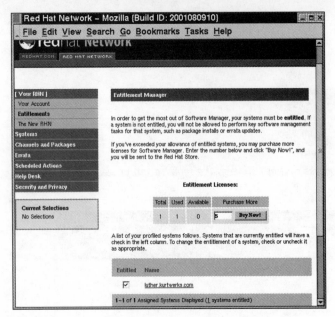

Figure 20-8   *The Red Hat Network Entitlement Manager*

3. If you have one or more Entitlements left, place a check mark in the checkbox next to the name of the system that you just registered.

4. Click the Update Entitlements button at the bottom of the page. The number of entitlements remaining will decrease, and your system is now ready to use the Red Hat Update Agent and Software Manager.

5. After updating your account, click the Log Out button in the upper left-hand corner of the page to log out of the Red Hat Network.

You are now ready to use the Update Agent, as described in the next section, to update your Red Hat Linux system's software packages.

Using the Red Hat Update Agent

Once you have activated your Software Manager subscription, you can use the Update Agent to download and install the latest updates and security fixes. Start the Update Agent by logging in as root and selecting Main Menu ⇨ Programs ⇨ System ⇨ Update Agent on the GNOME desktop. When prompted to do so, click Yes to import the Red Hat PGP key (see Figure 20-9).

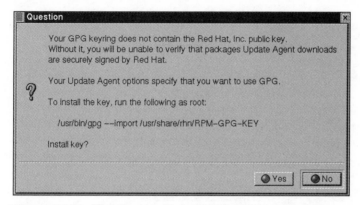

Figure 20-9   *Click Yes to add the Red Hat, Inc. public key.*

When you see the Welcome screen, click the Next button to continue. If you are connected to the Internet, the Update Agent compares the installed packages to the latest available patches. After a few moments, you will see a screen resembling Figure 20-10. It shows all of the available software updates based on what is currently installed on your system.

You can check the Select All Packages checkbox to install all of the new packages or scroll through the list and select packages individually. After making your selections, click the Next button to start the download. A dialog box will show the download's progress for each package selected and the overall progress of the update.

After the Update Agent downloads the selected packages, click the Next button to install them. Once the installation is complete, click the Next button to show a dialog box listing the packages that were just installed (see Figure 20-11). After reviewing the list, click the Finish button to close the dialog box and end the Update Agent session.

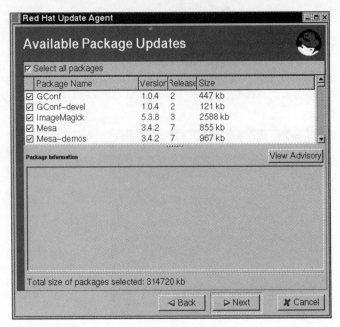

Figure 20-10 *The Update Agent lists the upgrades available for your system.*

Troubleshooting

When you click Yes to import the Red Hat public key, the Update Agent may not continue. Simply restart the Update Agent after importing the public key to restart the update process.

If the Update Agent starts but displays an error message that it is not configured properly, log into the Red Hat Network and activate your Software Manager subscription. The Update Agent requires a valid Software Manager subscription in order to function.

If the Update Agent does not show all of the RPMs installed on your system, log in as root, open a terminal window, and execute the command up2date -p to synchronize the system profile with the list of packages installed and maintained by the RPM database.

Figure 20-11 *The Update Agent lists the packages it installed.*

Done!

REVIEW

This session introduced you to the Red Hat Network. After you learned how to create a system profile and register with the Red Hat Network, you learned how to activate your Software Manager subscription. Then, you used the Red Hat Update Agent to download and install software package updates.

QUIZ YOURSELF

1. What is a system profile and what does it do? (See "Registering with the Red Hat Network.")
2. What is the URL for the Red Hat Network Web site? (See "Registering with the Red Hat Network.")
3. How do you activate your Software Manager subscription? (See "Running the Software Manager.")
4. What is the Update Agent? (See "Using the Red Hat Update Agent.")
5. How can you download all available updates? (See "Using the Red Hat Update Agent.")

PART

IV

Saturday Evening

1. Name some of the features of the GNOME desktop that you can configure. What application can you use to do so?

2. What is Sawfish? What is its relationship to GNOME?

3. How do you change your default desktop from GNOME to KDE and vice versa?

4. Name some of the features of the KDE desktop that you can configure. What application can you use to do so?

5. Explain how to choose and configure a screensaver using the GNOME desktop.

6. Describe how to select and customize a KDE screensaver.

7. How do you play games using the GNOME desktop? What are some of the games that you can play?

8. Name some of the games you can play if you use the KDE desktop and describe how to start them from KDE.

9. How would you access KDE games while running the GNOME desktop?

10. What is the name of the command you use to configure your sound card?

11. Name three applications you can use to play audio CD-ROMs.

12. What steps must you take to permit normal users to use the CD-ROM to play audio CDs?

13. What is CDDB? What multimedia applications, if any, use it?

14. List the names of at least two programs that you can use to view or manipulate graphics.

15. What is Ghostscript?

16. What is the name of the spreadsheet application that comes with the GNOME desktop? Does it produce files that are compatible with Microsoft Excel?

17. How would you check the spelling of a text file named `report.txt`?

18. What is the Red Hat Network?

19. Provide an overview of how to register with the Red Hat Network.

20. Briefly explain how to update your system with the latest software updates using the Red Hat Network.

☑ Friday

☑ Saturday

☑ Sunday

PART

V

Sunday Morning

Configuring the X Window System

Session Checklist

✔ Setting up the X Window System

✔ Controlling the X server

✔ Changing the default color depth

**30 Min.
To Go**

This morning's sessions focus on various system administration tasks such as configuring X, learning the Red Hat Linux boot sequence, installing new software packages from RPM and tar files, building a new kernel, scheduling jobs to run at specific times, and performing system backups. This session shows you the steps involved in configuring the X Window System, or X for short. It's important to learn how to configure X because graphical desktops such as GNOME and KDE require X in order to work.

Setting Up the X Window System

The *X Window System, X* for short, refers to the various components that facilitate the Red Hat Linux graphical interface. Although their two GUIs may bear superficial resemblance to each other, X and Microsoft Windows are different in two fundamental ways. Significant portions of the Microsoft Windows graphical system are tightly integrated into the operating system. X, on the other hand, is just another program that runs on top of the Linux kernel. This distinction is not important in the context of this session, but it helps explain why Linux is much more stable than Windows: the Linux kernel is unaffected by misbehaving X applications, but a poorly written Windows application can easily crash the Windows operating system.

The other key difference is that the X Window System conforms to a client/server model while Windows is *monolithic*, that is, the entire display subsystem is a single, complex, and large application. The functionality of the X Window System is partitioned into a server component and one or more client components. This session concerns itself exclusively with the X server piece. Other sessions focus on X clients, the games, word processors, screen savers, and additional applications that use the services that the X server provides.

The X Window System for Red Hat Linux comes from the XFree86 Project; see the XFree86 home page at http://www.xfree86.org/.\. **The XFree86 Project consists of a group of programmers who maintain the free version of the X Window System for Intel-based PCs. As a result, the Linux version of X is called XFree86.**

Understanding the X server

At the heart of X is the *X server*, which is a process or program just like any other, such as the vi editor or a calendar program. Rather than editing text or telling you the date, though, the X server application provides the fundamental services necessary to create and manage a graphical interface. These services include controlling the video adapter; interpreting input from keyboards, mice, and other input devices; drawing windows; moving them around, scribbling in them; and responding to requests from X clients.

X clients are the typical sort of applications, such as word processors, Web browsers, or e-mail programs that run in the graphical environment the X server maintains. When X clients need to display output or show a dialog box, they do so by communicating with the X server, which is solely responsible for drawing on the screen. X clients rely on the X server for screen output because they have no independent capability to do so.

Finally, the X server runs on your computer and controls the monitor, keyboard, and mouse. X clients, on the other hand, may run locally or on remote systems.

Configuring X requires you to create the server's configuration file, /etc/X11/XF86Config-4. This file contains information about your video card, monitor, keyboard, mouse, and other input devices. Red Hat Linux comes with XFree86 version 4.0.3, which itself includes a configuration utility named xf86cfg, which simplifies creating a working configuration file.

In Session 2, you learned how to use the Xconfigurator **utility to create the X configuration file.**

The next part of this session walks you through the X configuration process using the xf86cfg program so that you can see the configuration options in detail, and understand the format and purpose of the configuration file. If the Anaconda installer incorrectly configured X or if you would like to experiment with your X configuration, you can use xf86cfg and the information in the next part of this session to reconfigure X using the new XFree86 configuration tool, xf86cfg.

**20 Min.
To Go**

Using xf86cfg

To run xf86cfg, log in as root and type xf86cfg at the shell command prompt or in a terminal window, if X is already running. (The rest of this session assumes that you are using xf86cfg while running X.) The initial screen should resemble Figure 21-1.

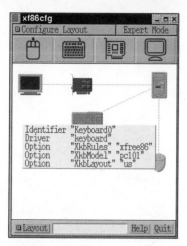

Figure 21-1 *Buttons and icons in* xf86cfg *allow you to configure the corresponding items.*

You can use the buttons across the top of the window to add a mouse, keyboard, video card, or monitor to the configuration. You can use the icons in the main window to reconfigure the components in the current configuration. The icons may be arranged differently on your system. Notice in Figure 21-1 that hovering the mouse cursor over one of the icons (the keyboard icon in this case) pops up balloon help, showing that item's current configuration values.

The following steps show you how to reconfigure X using xf86cfg.

1. Right-click the keyboard icon and select configure.

2. Select your keyboard language and layout from the scroll boxes.

3. If you wish, you can type a new name in the Identifier text box at the top of the dialog box, but this step is optional.

4. Click the Apply Change button if it is enabled, and then click Ok to return to xf86cfg's main screen.

5. Right-click the mouse icon and select Configure. The resulting dialog box should resemble Figure 21-2.

6. Select the mouse device and mouse protocol in the scroll boxes in the dialog box. For example, Figure 21-2 shows that /dev/ttyS0 is the mouse device (a serial mouse in this case) and that it uses the standard Microsoft mouse protocol.

7. If you do not have a three-button mouse, click the Emulate 3 Buttons box at the bottom of the dialog box. This will enable you to *chord*, or press simultaneously, the left and right buttons on a two-button mouse to emulate a third (middle) mouse button.

8. If you wish, you can type a new name in the Identifier text box at the top of the dialog box, but this step is optional.

9. Click the Apply Changes button if it is enabled and then the Ok button to return to the main screen of xf86cfg.

Figure 21-2   *xf86cfg's mouse configuration dialog box*

10. Right-click the video adapter icon and select Configure. The resulting dialog box should resemble Figure 21-3.

Figure 21-3   *The configuration dialog box for* xf86cfg *video adapters*

11. The scroll box in the center of the dialog box contains over 700 video card models. To reduce the number of entries displayed, you can filter the list by typing the first few letters of your card's name in the Card model filter list box and then pressing Enter. For example, you could type ati, press Enter, and then select the card highlighted in Figure 21-4, which is an ATI Xpert@Play 98. Selecting this video card causes the text ATI Mach64 text to appear in the Identifier text box — the Identifier text describes the chipset used in the selected card.

If your video card's vendor and model do not appear in the list, but you know the video chipset, try selecting an entry that corresponds to the chipset rather than the specific card model.

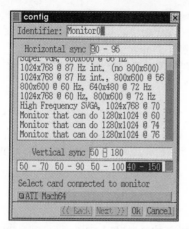

Figure 21-4 *The configuration dialog box for* xf86cfg *monitors*

12. If you wish, you can type a new name in the Identifier text box at the top of the dialog box, but this step is optional. The text ATI Mach64 that appears in Figure 21-3 is the default text that xf86cfg inserts when you select a card based on the Mach64 graphics chipset.

13. Click the Ok button to return to the main screen of xf86cfg.

14. Right-click the monitor icon and select Configure. The resulting dialog box should resemble Figure 21-4.

15. The scroll box in the center of the dialog lists about a dozen standard monitor frequencies. You can select one of these or enter values specific to your monitor in the Horizontal Sync and Vertical Sync text boxes. Your monitor's manual contains this information, or you can obtain it from the manufacturer's Web site.

Do not specify a horizontal synchronization range that is beyond the capabilities of your monitor. A wrong value can damage the monitor.

16. If you use multiple video adapters in your system, you can select the card for this monitor configuration from the drop-down list box at the bottom of the screen. Otherwise, xf86cfg uses the card you configured in Steps 10–13. Note that the name appearing in this box is the identifier value.

17. If you wish, you can type a new name in the Identifier text box at the top of the dialog box, but this step is optional.

18. Click the Ok button to return to the main screen of xf86cfg.

19. The configuration is now complete and your changes have been saved, so click the Quit button to exit xf86cfg.

To test the new configuration, you must restart the X server. If you use the graphical login, you can restart the X server in one of two ways. First, log out. Then, you can either reboot the system as you learned in Session 4, or press Ctrl+Alt+Backspace to restart the X server. The next section, "Controlling the X Server," explains what Ctrl+Alt+Backspace does.

If you do not use the graphical login, simply exit X as shown in Session 4 and type startx to restart X. In every case, the X server will restart using the new configuration.

Controlling the X Server

10 Min.
To Go

There are some special keystrokes that you can use to control the X server. You can force the server to terminate immediately or switch from one resolution to another without needing to restart the server.

Aborting X

Aborting an action means to terminate or kill it immediately without going through the orderly, normal shutdown process. Sometimes, it is necessary to abort a process because it does not respond to a normal shutdown request. For example, if your newly configured X server does not allow you to log out normally, you can abort it by pressing Ctrl+Alt+Backspace. If your system is not set up for a graphical login screen, you return to the text display.

However, if you selected the graphical login option, the X server immediately restarts. In this case, pressing Ctrl+Alt+R might disable the graphical login screen and return you to the text mode screen. If not, use the following procedure to abort X:

1. Press Ctrl+Alt+F1 to get a text mode login screen.
2. Log in as root and execute the command telinit 3 to terminate the X server.

If you cannot seem to type on the console after executing telinit 3, **press Alt+F1 to return to the text mode screen you used. Sometimes, changing run levels between graphical and text modes causes the console terminal to change from the default.**

3. Reconfigure the X server using xf86cfg as explained in the previous section. The xf86cfg program will start a generic X session in order to enable the configuration process.
4. After the configuration is complete, execute the command telinit 5 to restart the graphical login using the new (hopefully corrected) configuration options.

Switching screen modes

If your video adapter and monitor support it, you can switch between screen resolutions (not color depths) on the fly using Ctrl+Alt+Keypad+ and Ctrl+Alt+Keypad-. (Keypad + and Keypad - refer to the plus and minus keys on the numeric keypad.) You can try it now. If it does not work at all, only one resolution is defined for the current color depth. If it does work, but the resulting screen is off-center or sized strangely, rerun xf86cfg, and make sure you select the correct video adapter and provide the correct monitor frequencies for your monitor.

Color depth is discussed later in this session.

To understand how switching between screen modes works, use the more command as follows to view /etc/X11/XF86Config-4:

```
more /etc/X11/XF86Config-4
```

and scroll through the display until you find the part that begins with the line Section "Screen". For example, Listing 21-1 shows an excerpt from /etc/X11/XF86Config-4 on the system configured earlier in the session.

Listing 21-1   *The Screen Section in* /etc/X11/XF86Config-4

```
Section "Screen"
        Identifier    "Screen0"
        Device        "ATI Mach64"
        Monitor       "Monitor0"
        SubSection    "Display"
            Depth     24
            Modes     "800x600" "1024x768" "1280x1024"
        EndSubSection
        SubSection    "Display"
            Depth     16
            Modes     "800x600" "1024x768" "1280x1024"
        EndSubSection
EndSection
```

Notice the Display subsections, in particular the entries that begin with Modes. Each Display subsection describes the video *modes*, or resolutions, that your particular combination of video adapter and monitor support for a specific color depth. For example, in Listing 21-1, you can see that the monitor and card can display resolutions of 800 × 600, 1024 × 768, and 1280 × 1024 *dpi* (dots per inch) at color depths of 16 and 24 *bpp* (bits per pixel).

When the X server starts, it selects the highest possible color depth available in the Display subsections and the first resolution listed on the corresponding Modes line. In this case, that would be 800 × 600 dpi at 24 bpp. When you press Ctrl+Alt+Keypad+, the X server switches to the next mode in the list, in this case, 1024 × 768. Pressing Ctrl+Alt+Keypad+ again switches to 1280 × 1024 mode. Do it a third time and you return to the original mode. Pressing Ctrl+Alt+Keypad- causes the X server to cycle backward through the modes listed in the Modes entry.

You can make the X server start in any of the supported modes. If you want the X server to start at the highest-resolution mode, edit the Modes entry so that the desired resolution appears first. In this case, the Modes entry is changed as follows:

```
Modes    "1280x1024" "800x600" "1024x768"
```

This change makes X start in 1280 × 1024 dpi.

Changing the Default Color Depth

Some applications only work properly in a specific *color depth*, the number of colors displayed on the screen. Most systems will run faster if you reduce the color depth (or the resolution). By default, the X server starts in the highest possible color depth and resolution that your system supports, subject to the configuration defined in /etc/X11/ XF86Config-4. This section shows you how to change this default behavior. To make the X server start in a specific color depth, follow these steps:

1. Edit /etc/X11/XF86Config-4 file using your favorite text editor.

2. Locate the Screen section. Immediately above the first Display subsection, insert or change the following line:

    DefaultDepth N

    This line sets the default color depth that the X server uses to N bits per pixel. N can be 8, 16, or 24. For example, referring back to Listing 21-1, if you want the default color depth to be 24bpp, you would add DefaultDepth 24 above the first Display subsection. Listing 21-2 illustrates this modification (the change is shown in bold text).

 The keyword DefaultDepth **can also be** DefaultColorDepth **for purposes of backward compatibility with older versions of XFree86, but support for the older configuration keyword may disappear.**

3. Save the change and exit the editor.

4. Restart X using one of the methods described in "Controlling the X Server" earlier in this session, and the server will start using the specified color depth.

Listing 21-2   *Setting the Default Color Depth to 24bpp*

```
Section "Screen"
        Identifier   "Screen0"
        Device       "ATI Mach64"
        Monitor      "Monitor0"
        DefaultDepth 24
        SubSection   "Display"
            Depth    24
            Modes    "800x600" "1024x768" "1280x1024"
        EndSubSection
        SubSection   "Display"
            Depth    16
            Modes    "800x600" "1024x768" "1280x1024"
        EndSubSection
    EndSection
```

Troubleshooting

If xf86cfg does not start or is not installed, you can use the older, text-based program xf86config to configure the X server. Be sure to use the filename /etc/X11/XF86Config-4 when you save the configuration file.

If you still have trouble creating a working configuration file, try the command XFree86 -configure. This causes the X server to detect the video hardware, create a basic configuration file in your home directory, and then start the X server using that configuration file.

If you do not know the exact specifications of your video adapter, such as the chipset or the amount of video RAM it has, run the command SuperProbe or SuperProbe -v. The SuperProbe program probes the installed hardware and displays a report indicating what it finds. This information will help you create a basic configuration that enables X to start. You might want to save SuperProbe's output by piping it to a file like this:

```
SuperProbe > SuperProbe.report.
```

When troubleshooting problems with X, disable the graphical login and work from the command line. (Refer to Session 22 to find out how to disable the graphical login.) In addition, you will find it useful to save X's startup messages because they provide valuable information that can help you locate and fix the problem you want to solve. To save this information, use the following command:

```
startx > log 2> err
```

This command redirects normal output to the file named log and sends error messages to the file named err (both files will be in the current directory). Use the more command to browse these files.

Done!

REVIEW

This session showed you how to configure the X Window System. You learned how to reconfigure X using the xf86cfg program, how to abort the X server using Ctrl+Alt+Backspace, and how to cycle through the available screen resolutions using Ctrl+Alt+Keypad+ and Ctrl+Alt+Keypad-. Finally, you read about how to change the X server's default color depth.

QUIZ YOURSELF

1. What is the X server and what does it do? (See "Understanding the X server.")
2. What is xf86cfg and how do you start it? (See "Using xf86cfg.")
3. How do you kill the X server? (See "Aborting X.")
4. What keystroke causes the X server to use the next available screen resolution? (See "Switching screen modes.")
5. How do you make the X server start in a specific color depth? (See "Changing the Default Color Depth.")

Understanding How Red Hat Linux Boots

Session Checklist

✔ Understanding the init process

✔ Understanding the Red Hat Linux startup scripts

30 Min. To Go

I t is important to learn the sequence in which Red Hat Linux starts processes as it boots. You can use this knowledge to start and stop services such as the Web server and Network File System (NFS), and to troubleshoot startup-related problems. This session provides you with an overview of how Red Hat Linux boots and starts the initial set of processes. You also become familiar with the shell scripts that start various services and how to control the services that Red Hat Linux runs.

Understanding the init Process

When Red Hat Linux boots, it loads and runs the *kernel* from the hard disk. The kernel is the core of the operating system. However, the kernel is designed to run other programs. A process named init starts the initial set of processes on your Linux system.

To see the processes currently running on the system, type the command ps ax | more. The first column in the output has the heading PID, and that column shows a number for each process. *PID* stands for *process ID* (identification), which is a sequential number assigned by the Linux kernel to each process (program) when the process starts. Right at the beginning of the list of processes, you notice a process with a PID of 1:

```
PID TTY     STAT   TIME COMMAND
  1 ?        S     0:05 init [5]
```

As you can see, init is the first process and it has a PID of 1. Also, init starts all other processes in your Linux system. That's why init is referred to as the *mother of all processes*.

What the init process starts depends on the following:

- The *run level*, which designates a system configuration in which only a selected group of processes exists
- The contents of the /etc/inittab text file, which specifies the processes to start at different run levels
- A number of shell scripts (located in the /etc/rc.d directory and its subdirectories) that are executed at a specific run level

The current run level, together with the contents of the /etc/inittab file, controls which processes init starts. For example, Linux has seven run levels: 0, 1, 2, 3, 4, 5, and 6. By convention, some of these levels indicate specific processes that run at that level. Run level 1 denotes a single-user, stand-alone system. Run level 0 means the system is halted, and run level 6 means the system is being rebooted. Run levels 2 through 5 are multiuser modes with various levels of capabilities.

The initial default run level is 3 for text-mode login screens and 5 for the graphical login screen. As the following section explains, you can change the default run level by editing a line in the /etc/inittab file.

To check the current run level, type the following command /sbin/runlevel. The output will show the current and previous run levels:

```
/sbin/runlevel
N 5
```

The runlevel command prints two alphanumeric characters as output. The first character of the output shows the previous run level (N means there was no previous run level), and the second character shows the current level (5).

Examining the /etc/inittab *file*

The /etc/inittab file is the key to understanding the processes that init starts at various run levels. You can look at the contents of the file by using the more command as follows:

```
more /etc/inittab
```

**20 Min.
To Go**

When looking at the contents of the /etc/inittab **file with the** more **command, you do not have to log in as** root.

The following is a listing of the /etc/inittab file on a sample Red Hat Linux system that is set up for a graphical login screen:

```
#
# inittab       This file describes how the INIT process should set up
#               the system in a certain run-level.
#
# Author:       Miquel van Smoorenburg, <miquels@drinkel.nl.mugnet.org>
#               Modified for RHS Linux by Marc Ewing and Donnie Barnes
#
```

```
# Default runlevel. The runlevels used by RHS are:
#   0 - halt (Do NOT set initdefault to this)
#   1 - Single user mode
#   2 - Multiuser, without NFS (The same as 3, if you do not have networking)
#   3 - Full multiuser mode
#   4 - unused
#   5 - X11
#   6 - reboot (Do NOT set initdefault to this)
#
id:5:initdefault:

# System initialization.
si::sysinit:/etc/rc.d/rc.sysinit

l0:0:wait:/etc/rc.d/rc 0
l1:1:wait:/etc/rc.d/rc 1
l2:2:wait:/etc/rc.d/rc 2
l3:3:wait:/etc/rc.d/rc 3
l4:4:wait:/etc/rc.d/rc 4
l5:5:wait:/etc/rc.d/rc 5
l6:6:wait:/etc/rc.d/rc 6

# Things to run in every runlevel.
ud::once:/sbin/update

# Trap CTRL-ALT-DELETE
ca::ctrlaltdel:/sbin/shutdown -t3 -r now

# When our UPS tells us power has failed, assume we have a few minutes
# of power left.  Schedule a shutdown for 2 minutes from now.
# This does, of course, assume you have power installed and your
# UPS connected and working correctly.
pf::powerfail:/sbin/shutdown -f -h +2 "Power Failure; System Shutting Down"

# If power was restored before the shutdown kicked in, cancel it.
pr:12345:powerokwait:/sbin/shutdown -c "Power Restored; Shutdown Cancelled"

# Run gettys in standard runlevels
1:2345:respawn:/sbin/mingetty tty1
2:2345:respawn:/sbin/mingetty tty2
3:2345:respawn:/sbin/mingetty tty3
4:2345:respawn:/sbin/mingetty tty4
5:2345:respawn:/sbin/mingetty tty5
6:2345:respawn:/sbin/mingetty tty6

# Run xdm in runlevel 5
# xdm is now a separate service
x:5:respawn:/etc/X11/prefdm -nodaemon
```

Confused? Don't be. The /etc/inittab file is easy to understand once you are comfortable with its format. Each line in /etc/inittab specifies the action that init should take when switching to a given run level. Each entry in the inittab file has four fields, separated by colons (:), in the following format:

id:*runlevels*:*action*:*process*

The fields have the following meanings:

- *id* is a unique, one- or two-character identifier. The init process uses this field internally. You can use any identifier you want. However, you cannot use the same identifier on more than one line. For example, si, x, and 1 are all valid identifiers.

- *runlevels* is a sequence of zero or more characters, each denoting a run level. For example, the line with the identifier 1 applies to run levels 1 through 5. So, the *runlevels* field for this entry is 12345. This field is ignored if the action field is set to sysinit, boot, or bootwait.

- *action* tells the init process what to do with that specific entry. For instance, if this field is initdefault, init interprets the *runlevels* field as the default run level. If this field is set to wait, init starts the process specified in the *process* field and waits until that process exits. Table 22-1 summarizes the valid action values you can use in the *action* field.

- *process* specifies the process that init has to start. Of course, some settings of the *action* field require no process field. For example, when *action* is set to initdefault, a *process* field is unnecessary.

Table 22-1   *Valid Actions in /etc/inittab*

Action	Description
respawn	Restarts the process whenever it terminates.
boot	Executes the process as the system boots, regardless of the run level; the *runlevels* field is ignored.
bootwait	Executes the process as the system boots and init waits for the process to exit; the *runlevels* field is ignored.
initdefault	Starts the system at this run level after it boots. The *process* field is ignored for this action.
sysinit	Executes the process as the system boots, before any entries with the boot or bootwait actions; the *runlevels* field is ignored.
ctrlaltdel	Executes the process when init receives the SIGINT signal, which occurs when you press Ctrl+Alt+Del. Typically, the *process* field should specify the /sbin/shutdown command with the -r option to reboot the PC.
kbdrequest	Executes the process when init receives a signal from the keyboard driver that a special key combination has been pressed. The key combination should be mapped to KeyboardSignal in the keymap file.

Lines that start with a hash mark (#) are comments. The first non-comment line in the /etc/inittab is the following:

```
id:5:initdefault:
```

Thus, the default run level is 5, which corresponds to the graphical login you have used throughout this book. If you want your system to run at level 3 after startup (for a plain text-mode login screen), all you have to do is change 5 to 3.

 Type `man inittab` **to see the detailed syntax of the entries in the** `inittab` **file.**

You can specify a variety of values in the *action* field. Table 22-1 lists the valid *action*s and briefly describes what each *action* does.

The *process* field is typically specified in terms of a shell script, which, in turn, can start several processes. For example, the l5 entry is specified as follows:

```
l5:5:wait:/etc/rc.d/rc 5
```

This entry indicates that `init` should execute the file `/etc/rc.d/rc` with 5 as an argument. If you look at the file `/etc/.rc.d/rc`, you notice that it is a shell script file. You can study the file `/etc/rc.d/rc` to see how it starts various processes for run levels 1 through 5.

Getting back to the subject of the graphical login screen, the last line of the `/etc/inittab` file starts the graphical login process with the following entry:

```
x:5:respawn:/etc/X11/prefdm -nodaemon
```

This command runs `/etc/X11/prefdm`, which is a symbolic link to a specific display manager. For the GNOME graphical desktop (the default in Red Hat Linux), `/etc/X11/prefdm` is a symbolic link to `/usr/bin/gdm` — the GNOME display manager. If you use the KDE desktop as your default, `/etc/X11/prefdm` is a symbolic link to `/usr/bin/kdm` — the KDE display manager. This means that regardless of your choice of GUI, `init` starts a display manager at run level 5. The display manager, in turn, displays the graphical login dialog box and enables you to log into the system.

 If you do not enable the graphical login screen during Red Hat installation (covered in Session 1), you can do so now by editing the `/etc/inittab` **file. Locate the line containing** `initdefault` **and make sure that it reads as follows (the run level appearing between two colons should be 5):**

```
id:5:initdefault:
```

Before you edit the `/etc/inittab` file, you should know that any errors in this file may prevent Red Hat Linux from starting up to a point at which you can log in. If you cannot log in, you cannot use your system. As explained in the next section, you can always try out a specific run level with the `init` command before you actually change the default run level in the `/etc/inittab` file.

 Never set `initdefault` **to** 0 **or** 6**! If you set the default runlevel to** 0**, your Red Hat Linux system will boot, then shut down and halt. Similarly, setting** `initdefault` **to** 6 **will cause your system to reboot each time it boots.**

Trying out a new run level with the `init` command

To try a new run level, you do not necessarily have to change the default run level in the `/etc/inittab` file. If you log in as `root`, you can change the run level (and, consequently, the set of processes that run in Linux) with the `init` command. It has the following format:

```
init runlevel
```

Here, *runlevel* must be a single character denoting the run level that you want. To put the system in single-user mode, for example, type the following:

```
init 1
```

Assuming that your system is not set up for a graphical login screen yet, if you want to try run level 5 without changing the `/etc/inittab` file, enter the following command at the shell prompt:

```
init 5
```

The system should end all current processes and enter run level 5. By default, the `init` command waits 20 seconds before stopping all current processes and starting the new processes for run level 5.

 To switch to run level 5 immediately, type the command `init -t0 5`**. The number after the** `-t` **option indicates the number of seconds that** `init` **waits before changing the run level.**

You can also use the `telinit` command, which is simply a symbolic link to `init`. If you make changes to the `/etc/inittab` file and want `init` to reload its configuration file, use the command `telinit q`.

Understanding Red Hat Linux Startup Scripts

The `init` process runs a number of scripts at system startup. Notice the following lines that appear near the beginning of the `/etc/inittab` file:

```
# System initialization.
si::sysinit:/etc/rc.d/rc.sysinit
```

As the comment on the first line indicates, the second line causes `init` to run the `/etc/rc.d/rc.sysinit` script, which is the first Red Hat Linux startup script that `init` runs. The `rc.sysinit` script performs many initialization tasks such as mounting the file systems, setting the clock, configuring the keyboard layout, starting the network, and loading many other driver modules. The `rc.sysinit` script performs these initialization tasks by calling many other scripts and reading configuration files located in the `/etc/sysconfig` directory.

After executing the `/etc/rc.d/rc.sysinit` script, the `init` process runs the `/etc/rc.d/rc` script with the run level as an argument. For example, for run level 5, the following line in `/etc/inittab` specifies what `init` has to execute:

```
l5:5:wait:/etc/rc.d/rc 5
```

This says that `init` should execute the command `/etc/rc.d/rc 5` and wait until that command completes.

The `/etc/rc.d/rc` script is somewhat complicated. Here is how it works:

- It changes to the directory corresponding to the run level. For example, to change to run level 5, the script changes to the `/etc/rc.d/rc5.d` directory.
- In the directory that corresponds with the run level, it looks for all files that begin with a K and executes each of them with a `stop` argument. This kills currently running processes. Then it locates all files that begin with an S and executes each file with an argument of `start`. This starts the processes needed for the specified run level.

To see what gets executed at run level 5, type the command `ls -l /etc/rc.d/rc5.d`. The output, shown in the following listing, is truncated because it is repetitive:

```
ls -l /etc/rc.d/rc5.d
total 0
lrwxrwxrwx  1 root     root     15 Aug 14 16:24 K01pppoe -> ../init.d/pppoe
lrwxrwxrwx  1 root     root     14 Aug 14 16:08 K05innd -> ../init.d/innd
lrwxrwxrwx  1 root     root     13 Aug 19 22:18 K20nfs -> ../init.d/nfs
lrwxrwxrwx  1 root     root     16 Aug 14 16:24 K20rstatd -> ../init.d/rstatd
lrwxrwxrwx  1 root     root     17 Aug 14 16:24 K20rusersd ->
../init.d/rusersd
lrwxrwxrwx  1 root     root     16 Aug 14 16:24 K20rwalld -> ../init.d/rwalld
lrwxrwxrwx  1 root     root     15 Aug 14 16:24 K20rwhod -> ../init.d/rwhod
...part of listing deleted...
lrwxrwxrwx  1 root     root     18 Aug 14 16:26 S80sendmail ->
../init.d/sendmail
lrwxrwxrwx  1 root     root     13 Aug 14 16:07 S85gpm -> ../init.d/gpm
lrwxrwxrwx  1 root     root     15 Aug 14 15:56 S85httpd -> ../init.d/httpd
lrwxrwxrwx  1 root     root     13 Aug 14 15:58 S90xfs -> ../init.d/xfs
lrwxrwxrwx  1 root     root     17 Aug 14 15:55 S95anacron ->
../init.d/anacron
lrwxrwxrwx  1 root     root     19 Aug 14 16:16 S99linuxconf ->
../init.d/linuxconf
lrwxrwxrwx  1 root     root     11 Aug 14 15:56 S99local -> ../rc.local
```

As the output shows, all files with names starting with K and S are symbolic links to scripts that reside in the `/etc/rc.d` and `/etc/rc.d/init.d` directories. In fact, the `/etc/rec.d/rc` script executes these files exactly in the order that they appear in the directory listing.

Note that the last file in the directory listing is a symbolic link to the `../rc.local` script. This means that `/etc/rc.d/rc.local` is executed after all other scripts. So you can place in that script any command you want executed whenever your Linux system boots.

Most of the startup scripts reside in the `/etc/rc.d/init.d` directory. You can manually invoke scripts in this directory to start, stop, or restart specific processes — usually servers. For example, to stop the Web server, type the following command:

```
/etc/rc.d/init.d/httpd stop
Shutting down http: [  OK  ]
```

You can enhance your system administration skills by familiarizing yourself with the scripts in the `/etc/rc.d/init.d` directory. To see the listing, type the following command:

```
ls /etc/rc.d/init.d
anacron    halt       keytable   netfs      pppoe       sendmail  ypbind
apmd       httpd      killall    network    random      single
yppasswdd
arpwatch   identd     kudzu      nfs        rawdevices  smb       ypserv
atd        innd       linuxconf  nfslock    rstatd      snmpd
crond      ipchains   lpd        pcmcia     rusersd     syslog
functions  isdn       mars-nwe   portmap    rwalld      xfs
gpm        kdcrotate  named      postgresql rwhod       xinetd
```

The script names give you some clue about what server the script can start and stop. For example, the `nfs` script starts and stops the processes required for NFS services. At your leisure, you may want to study some of these scripts to see what each one does. You don't have to understand all the shell programming; the comments should help you learn the purpose of each script.

Enabling and Disabling Startup Scripts

10 Min. To Go

As your Linux administration skills develop, you may want to modify the default Red Hat Linux startup sequence to change the set of services that you run. You can disable startup scripts, preventing them from executing at all, or you can exercise finer-grained control, enabling and disabling scripts in specific levels.

Disabling and enabling startup scripts in all run levels

In the previous section, you saw that the run level-specific directories, such as `/etc/rc.d/rc5.d`, contain symbolic links to scripts in `/etc/rc.d/init.d`. For example, `/etc/rc.d/rc5.d/S80sendmail` is a link to `/etc/rc.d/init.d/sendmail`. To disable a startup script in all run levels, remove its execute permissions using the `chmod` command. So, to disable the `sendmail` startup script, log in as the root user and execute the command `chmod a-x /etc/rc.d/init.d/sendmail`. Similarly, if you decide later to enable a script, use the `chmod` command to restore the execute permissions. You can use the following command to restore the `sendmail` script's execute permissions:

```
chmod a+x /etc/rc.d/init.d/sendmail
```

You can use this approach to disable any of the startup scripts in the `/etc/rc.d/init.d` directory.

Disabling and enabling startup scripts in specific run levels

If you want a startup script to execute in certain run levels, but not in others, use the Red Hat Linux chkconfig command. chkconfig is an easy-to-use tool for maintaining the scripts in the /etc/rc.d/ directory.

For example, suppose you want to find out the run levels in which the sendmail startup script executes. You can use the command chkconfig --list sendmail to obtain this information, as shown in the following example:

```
chkconfig --list sendmail
sendmail        0:off   1:off   2:on    3:on    4:on    5:on    6:off
```

The output displays the name of the script, sendmail, followed by the run level, and off or on to indicate whether sendmail runs in that run level. As you can see, the sendmail startup script is executed when the system enters run levels 2, 3, 4, and 5.

To change the behavior of a startup script on a given run level, you can use the following chkconfig command:

```
chkconfig --level runlevels scriptname on|off|reset
```

The *scriptname* entry is the name of the startup script (such as nfs or sendmail) that you want to modify. The *runlevels* entry indicates the levels you want to change. The on and off entries turn the service on or off for the specified run levels. The reset entry restores the script's default configuration. You may only use one of the options, on, off, or reset entry. For example, the following commands disable the sendmail startup script in run level 2; use the --list option to confirm that the sendmail script was disabled as directed; restore the original configuration; and then use the --list option to confirm the change:

```
chkconfig --level 2 sendmail off
chkconfig --list sendmail
sendmail        0:off   1:off   2:off   3:on    4:on    5:on    6:off
chkconfig sendmail reset
sendmail        0:off   1:off   2:on    3:on    4:on    5:on    6:off
```

 You can use chkconfig **to disable a startup script for all run levels by executing the command** chkconfig --level 0123456 sendmail off.

The chkconfig utility works by manipulating the symbolic links behind the scenes, saving you the tedious, potentially error prone process of updating them yourself. To extend your knowledge of the chkconfig command, you can read its manual page (man chkconfig).

Troubleshooting

Certain startup scripts, especially those that assume a functioning network, may appear to hang during boot. (The /etc/rc.d/init.d/sendmail script is a common example of this.) If this happens to you, use the chkconfig utility to disable the script that seems to be causing the problem. This will enable you to troubleshoot the problem without having to wait for long periods of time. Don't forget to reenable the script after fixing the problem!

If your system is set to boot to run level 5 but X Window is having trouble initializing, change initdefault in /etc/inittab to 3 while troubleshooting the problem and test your fixes using the init 5 command. Once you have solved the problem, change initdefault back to 5 to restore the graphical login when the system boots.

If you forget the syntax of the chkconfig command, type chkconfig and press Enter to see a short usage message.

Done!

REVIEW

This session provided an overview of how to use the init process. You learned about the /etc/inittab file, which controls init. You also learned about the Red Hat Linux startup scripts in the /etc/rc.d directory and its subdirectories. Finally, you learned how to use the chkconfig utility to control the startup sequence.

QUIZ YOURSELF

1. Why is init referred to as the "mother of all processes?" (See "Understanding the init Process.")

2. How can you determine the current run level of your Linux system? (See "Understanding the init Process.")

3. What can you do to make your Linux system start at run level 3 when you reboot the system? (See "Examining the /etc/inittab file.")

4. How do you figure out which scripts init executes for run level 5? (See "Understanding Red Hat Linux Startup Scripts.")

5. In what script do you place commands that you want executed every time your Linux system boots? (See "Understanding Red Hat Linux Startup Scripts.")

Installing Software Packages

Session Checklist

✔ Using Gnome RPM to install and remove packages

✔ Using the rpm command to install and remove packages

**30 Min.
To Go**

As a system administrator of your Linux system, you should know how to install or remove software packages distributed in the form of Red Hat Package Manager (RPM) files. In this session, you'll learn to install or remove RPMs using the Gnome RPM graphical tool and the RPM commands.

Using Gnome RPM to Install and Remove Packages

One of Red Hat's most significant contributions to Linux system administration is the *Red Hat Package Manager (RPM)*. RPM is a system for installing, maintaining, removing, and upgrading a software product using a single file referred to as an RPM, which contains all the necessary files for installing that product.

Red Hat Linux is distributed in the form of a large number of RPMs. All of the RPM files, or packages, are located in the /mnt/cdrom/RedHat/RPMS directory of the first two CD-ROMs included with this book. (This is assuming that you have mounted the CD-ROM on the /mnt/cdrom directory.) Gnome RPM is a graphical front end to RPM that functions as an interface for working with RPMs. The operations that you can perform with Gnome RPM are similar to what you can do with the rpm command from the command line. You'll learn the rpm command later in this session.

To start Gnome RPM, log in as root and then select Main Menu ⇨ Programs ⇨ System ⇨ GnoRPM. Figure 23-1 shows the initial Gnome RPM window. Gnome RPM has a standard GNOME user interface with a menu bar and a toolbar. The toolbar has buttons for common RPM operations: Install a New Package, Query a Package, or Uninstall a Package. The tree menu on the left of the window shows the currently installed packages organized in a hierarchy of package groups. A *package group* contains a number of RPMs. You can click the plus signs to view the hierarchy. If you click a specific package group, Gnome RPM displays all of the packages in that group in the area to the right of the tree menu. For example, Figure 23-1 shows the packages in the package group named Desktops. As Figure 23-1 shows, the Desktops package group contains the packages that make up the GNOME and KDE desktops along with the FVWM and WindowMaker window managers.

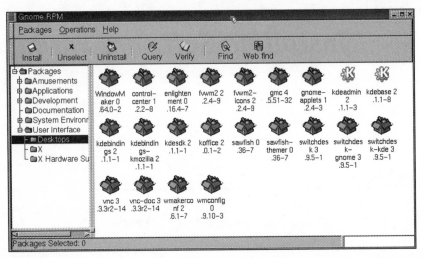

Figure 23-1 *Gnome RPM displaying the contents of the Desktops package group*

You typically select one or more packages and then perform tasks such as installing or uninstalling the package; querying the package to see when it was installed and finding out which files it contains; or verifying the package to confirm that none of the files have changed. To perform these operations, open the package group and select the package by clicking the package icon. Then click the Install, Uninstall, Query, or Verify button to initiate the operation. Each of these operations brings up a window in which Gnome RPM displays relevant information and provides buttons through which you can initiate further action. For example, when you query a package, Gnome RPM displays the information about that package in a window. From the information, you can see when the package was installed, when it was built, its size in bytes, a brief description, and what files make up the package (including the full pathname of each file). Figure 23-2 shows the query results Gnome RPM displays for the db3-utils RPM.

As you can see in Figure 23-2, the display includes an active URL where you can find more information about the db3-utils package. Gnome RPM displays the URL as a link that you can click to view that Web page in a Web browser. You can learn a lot about a package by browsing the information in the query results.

To uninstall or remove a package, select the package from the Gnome RPM window and click the Uninstall button on the toolbar (see Figure 23-1). Gnome RPM then displays a dialog box asking you to confirm if you want to remove the package. Click the Yes button to remove the package.

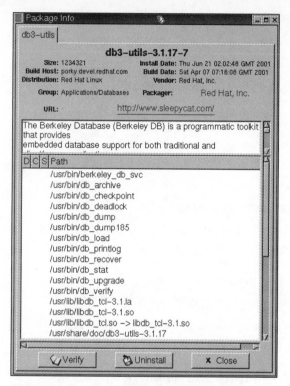

Figure 23-2 *Gnome RPM displaying the results of querying the db3-utils RPM*

To install a new package from any one of this book's companion CD-ROMs, mount the CD-ROM by typing mount /mnt/cdrom in a terminal window, and then click the Install button on the Gnome RPM toolbar. An empty Install dialog box appears. Click the Add button on the Install dialog box. Gnome RPM displays an Add Packages dialog box with the contents of the /mnt/cdrom/RedHat/RPMS directory in which all of the RPM files are located, as shown in Figure 23-3.

From this dialog box, you can select packages one by one and click the Add button to add them to the list of packages to be installed. Each time you click the Add button, the selected package is added to the list in the Install dialog box. When you are finished selecting packages, click Close to get rid of the Add Packages dialog box. The selected packages appear in the Install dialog box.

To finish installing the selected packages, click the Install button in the Install dialog box. Gnome RPM installs the packages and displays any errors it encounters. For example, if the packages are already installed, Gnome RPM displays a message that says so.

Gnome RPM is a handy utility to install, remove, and upgrade various software packages for Red Hat Linux. If you want to learn more about Gnome RPM, read the online help text by selecting the appropriate item from Gnome RPM's Help menu.

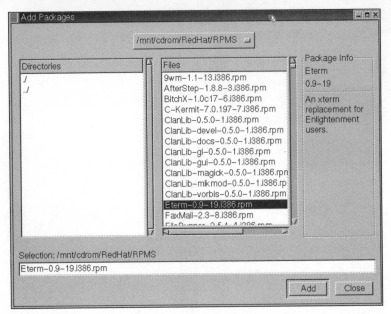

Figure 23-3   *Selecting a package to add to the package installation list*

Using the rpm Command to Install and Remove Packages

20 Min. To Go

When you install Red Hat Linux from the companion CD-ROM, the installation program uses the rpm command to unpack the RPM files and copy the contents to appropriate locations on the disk.

Although you do not need to understand the internal structure of an RPM file, you should know how to use the rpm command to work with RPM files. Specifically, you may want to perform one or more of the following tasks with RPMs:

- Query the RPM database to find out the version numbers and other information about RPMs installed on your system.
- Install a new software package from an RPM. For example, you have to install the source files for the Linux kernel before you can rebuild the kernel.
- Remove (uninstall) unneeded software that you previously installed from an RPM. You can uninstall a package to reclaim the disk space if you find that you never use the package. Another reason to uninstall RPMs is to remove buggy or defective software from your system.
- Upgrade an older version of an RPM with a newer one. You can upgrade after you download a new version of a package from Red Hat's FTP server.
- Verify that an RPM is in working order. You can verify a package to ensure that all of the files installed by the RPM are in their correct locations, have the proper permissions and ownerships, and whether or not they have been altered.

You can perform all of these tasks with the rpm command by using different options. The next few sections give you a brief introduction to the rpm command.

If you ever forget the rpm **options, type** the rpm --help | more **command to see a list of its command-line options. The number of options** rpm **has will amaze you!**

Understanding RPM filenames

An RPM is a kind of *archive* — a file that contains many other files. Even though an RPM contains multiple files, it appears as a single file on your Red Hat Linux system. RPM builders (the people who package software into RPMs) commonly follow a standard, or, more accurately, a convention that defines the structure of RPM filenames. To see the names of RPM files that come on the companion CD-ROM, follow these steps:

1. Place the CD-ROM in the CD-ROM drive and mount it with the following command (you must be logged in as root):

    ```
    mount /mnt/cdrom
    ```

    This mount command works because there is an entry for this mount point in the /etc/fstab file.

If the amd **and** nfs **daemons are running, the CD-ROM may automatically mount when you close the CD-ROM drive door and a dialog box will pop up asking you if you want to run** /mnt/cdrom/autorun. **Click No and then proceed with Step 2.**

2. Go to the directory in which the RPMs are located and view this listing (to conserve space, much of the listing was deleted):

    ```
    cd /mnt/cdrom/RedHat/RPMS
    ls *.rpm | more
    4Suite-0.10.1-1.i386.rpm
    a2ps-4.13b-13.i386.rpm
    alchemist-0.16-3.i386.rpm
    anacron-2.3-16.i386.rpm
    anonftp-4.0-4.i386.rpm
    apache-1.3.19-5.i386.rpm
    apacheconf-0.7-2.noarch.rpm
    (some lines deleted)
    xchat-1.6.3-4.i386.rpm
    Xconfigurator-4.9.27-1.i386.rpm
    XFree86-100dpi-fonts-4.0.3-5.i386.rpm
    XFree86-4.0.3-5.i386.rpm
    ```

```
XFree86-75dpi-fonts-4.0.3-5.i386.rpm
(rest of the listing deleted)
```

As you can guess from the listing, all RPM files end with an `.rpm` extension. To understand the various parts of the filename, consider the following RPM:

```
XFree86-4.0.3-5.i386.rpm
```

This filename has the following parts separated by dashes (-):

Package name   XFree86
Version number   4.0.3
Release number   0.5 (a Red Hat-assigned release number)
Architecture i386 (for Intel 80386-compatible processors)

Usually, the package name is descriptive enough for you to guess the contents of the RPM. The RPM's version number is almost always the same as the software package's current version number, even when it is distributed in some other form, such as a tar file. Red Hat assigns the release number to keep track of changes. In this case, the release number is 5, meaning that it is the fifth version of the RPM created for version 4.0.3 of the XFree86 package. The architecture should be i386, i486, i586, i686, or noarch for the RPMs you want to install on a PC with an Intel *x*86-compatible processor.

In Session 26, you'll learn how to use tar to back up and restore files.

Querying RPMs with the rpm command

As you install, upgrade, and remove RPMs, the rpm command updates a database of installed RPMs. You can use the rpm -q command to query this database in order to find out information about packages installed on your system. For example, to find out the version number of the Linux kernel installed on your system, type the following rpm -q command:

```
rpm -q kernel
kernel-2.4.2-2
```

The response is the name of the RPM for the kernel — the executable version of the kernel; not the source files. The name is the same as the RPM filename except that the last part, `.i386.rpm`, does not appear. In this case, the version part of the RPM tells you that the kernel is 2.2.16.

You can see a list of all installed RPMs by typing the following command:

```
rpm -qa | more
```

If you want to search for a specific package, feed the output of rpm -qa to the grep command. For example, to see all packages with kernel in their names, type:

```
rpm -qa | grep kernel
kernel-headers-2.4.2-2
kernel-2.4.2-2
kernel-source-2.4.2-2
kernel-doc-2.4.2-2
kernel-pcmcia-cs-3.1.24-2
```

You can query much more than a package's version number with the rpm -q command. By adding various single letter options, you can find out other useful information about a package. Combining l with -q lists all the files in a given RPM. For instance, try the following command to see the files in the kernel package:

```
rpm -ql kernel
/boot/System.map-2.4.2-2
/boot/module-info-2.4.2-2
/boot/vmlinux-2.4.2-2
/boot/vmlinuz-2.4.2-2
/dev/shm
/lib/modules
/lib/modules/2.4.2-2
/lib/modules/2.4.2-2/build
/lib/modules/2.4.2-2/kernel
/lib/modules/2.4.2-2/kernel/arch
(rest of the listing deleted)
```

Table 23-1 lists several useful forms of rpm -q commands to query information about a package. To use any of these rpm -q commands, type the command followed by the package name.

Table 23-1 *Common Forms of rpm –q Commands*

Command	Description
rpm -qa	Lists all installed RPMs.
rpm -qc	Lists all configuration files in a package.
rpm -qd	Lists all documentation files in a package. These are usually the online manual pages (also known as *man pages*), but may also include GNU text info pages, HTML pages, and documentation placed in /usr/share/doc.
rpm -qi	Displays detailed information about a package including version number, size, installation date, a brief description, and a summary of the package's functionality.
rpm -ql	Lists all the files in a package. For some packages, this can be a very long list.
rpm -qs	Lists the state of all files in a package.

Installing RPMs with the rpm command

To install an RPM, you have to use the rpm -i command. You must provide the name of the RPM file as the argument. A typical example is to install an RPM from this book's companion CD-ROM containing the Red Hat Linux RPMs. As usual, you have to first mount the CD-ROM and then change to the directory in which the RPMs are located. Then, use the rpm -i command to install the RPM followed by the name of the RPM.

For example, to install the kernel-source RPM (which contains the source files for the Linux operating system) from the CD-ROM, you'd type the following commands:

```
mount /mnt/cdrom
cd /mnt/cdrom/RedHat/RPMS
rpm -i kernel-source*
```

 You do not have to type the full RPM filename; you can use a few characters from the beginning of the name followed by an asterisk (*). Make sure that you type enough of the name to identify uniquely the RPM file or files you want to install.

If you try to install an already installed RPM, the rpm command displays an error message such as the following, which results after trying to install the Emacs editor on a sample system:

```
rpm -i emacs-20*

package emacs-20.7-34 is already installed
```

To force the rpm command to install a package even if there are errors, just add --force to the rpm -i command as follows:

```
rpm -i --force emacs-20*
```

If you combine the v option with -i, the rpm command will display a little more information about what rpm is doing while it is installing an RPM. If you use the h option, the rpm command will print hash marks (#) to show its progress while installing an RPM.

Here's how an RPM installation looks if you combine the v and h options with -i when installing the zsh RPM:

```
rpm -ivh zsh-3.0.8-8.i386.rpm
Preparing...               ###########################################
[100%]
   1:zsh                   ###########################################
[100%]
```

Removing RPMs with the rpm command

You can remove, or *uninstall*, a package if you realize that you don't really need the software, or if it is causing problems for your system. For example, if you install the X Window System development package, but are not interested in writing any X applications, you can remove the package easily by using the rpm -e command.

You need the name of the package before you can remove it. One good way to find the name is to use rpm -qa in conjunction with grep to search for the appropriate RPM file. For example, to locate the X Window System development RPM, you can try this:

```
rpm -qa | grep XFree
XFree86-75dpi-fonts-4.0.1-0.43
XFree86-twm-4.0.1-0.43
XFree86-libs-4.0.1-0.43
XFree86-xfs-4.0.1-0.43
XFree86-4.0.1-0.43
XFree86-devel-4.0.1-0.43
XFree86-tools-4.0.1-0.43
XFree86-xdm-4.0.1-0.43
XFree86-SVGA-3.3.6-32
```

In this case, XFree86-devel is the package name you need. To remove the package, type:

```
rpm -e XFree86-devel
```

You do not need the full RPM filename. All you need is the package name, which is the first part of the filename up to the dash (-) before the version number.

The rpm -e command does not remove a package that other packages need. For example, when you try to remove the kernel-headers package, you might get the following error message:

```
rpm -e kernel-headers
error: removing these packages would break dependencies:
        kernel-headers   is needed by glibc-devel-2.1.92-5
        kernel-headers >= 2.2.1 is needed by glibc-devel-2.1.92-5
```

As the output from the rpm -e command shows, the glibc-devel package needs the kernel-headers package in order to function properly. In RPM parlance, glibc-devel *depends* on kernel headers.

Upgrading RPMs with the rpm command

10 Min.
To Go

When you use the rpm -U command to upgrade an RPM, you must provide the name of the RPM file that contains the new software. For example, suppose you have version 4.74 of Netscape Communicator installed on you system, but you want to upgrade to version 4.76. You'd download the RPM file netscape-communicator-4.76-11.i386.rpm from Red Hat's FTP server (ftp://ftp.redhat.com/pub/redhat/updates/, or one of the mirror sites listed at http://www.redhat.com/mirrors.html), and then use the following command:

```
rpm -U netscape-communicator-4.76-11.i386.rpm
```

The rpm command performs the upgrade by first removing the old version of the Netscape Communicator package and then installing the new RPM.

Whenever possible, you should use `rpm -U` to upgrade software, rather than doing it manually yourself by removing the old package (`rpm -e`) and then installing the new version (using `rpm -i`). Why? Allowing RPM to perform the upgrade using `rpm -U` automatically saves the old configuration files, which saves you the hassle of configuring the software after a fresh installation. If you manually type `rpm -e` followed by `rpm -i` to erase an old RPM and install its replacement, the erase operation *also* deletes the old configuration files. The `rpm` upgrade command contains logic to save the old configuration files.

When you upgrade the kernel and the kernel module packages that contain a ready-to-run Linux kernel, do not use the `rpm -U` command. Instead, install it with the `rpm -i` command. Using `rpm -i` ensures that you don't overwrite files being used by the current kernel.

Verifying RPMs with the rpm command

You may not do this often, but if you suspect that a software package is not properly installed, use the `rpm -V` command to verify the package. For example, to verify the kernel package, type the following:

```
rpm -V kernel
```

This causes `rpm` to compare size and other attributes of each file in the package against the original files. If everything verifies correctly, the `rpm -V` command does not print anything. If it detects any discrepancies, `rpm` displays a report of the discrepancies. For example, suppose you modified the configuration files for the Apache Web server. Here is what you might see when you verified the Apache package:

```
rpm -V apache
S.5....T c /etc/httpd/conf/httpd.conf
```

In this case, the output from `rpm -V` shows that a configuration file has changed. Each line of this command's output consists of three parts:

- The line starts with eight characters; each character indicates the type of discrepancy found. For example, S means the size has changed since the file was originally installed. T means the last modification time has changed. A period (.) indicates that a specific attribute matches the original.

- For configuration files, an c appears next; otherwise, this field is blank. That's how you can tell whether a file is a configuration file. Typically, you don't have to worry if a configuration file has changed because you probably made the changes yourself.

- The last part of the line is the file's full pathname. From this part, you can tell the exact location of the file.

Troubleshooting

If you get error messages when using the rpm command to install, upgrade, or remove an RPM, make sure you are the root user. Any user can use the rpm command (or Gnome RPM) to query and verify RPMs, but only the root user can add, delete, or upgrade RPMs.

If you get an error message resembling "Package foo Is Already Installed" and want to reinstall the foo RPM again anyway, use the --force option with rpm -i. The reason that RPM does not reinstall already installed RPMs is to try and minimize the chance of overwriting configuration files or otherwise altering the configuration of a running system.

Similarly, if you are removing an RPM using rpm -e and encounter an error message resembling "Error: Removing These Packages Would Break Dependencies:" you can use the --nodeps option with rpm -e (rpm -e --nodeps) to tell RPM to ignore the dependencies and remove the package anyway. However, before using --nodeps, make sure you will not compromise your system's integrity and stability and be sure to have a way to boot the system and restore the original configuration.

Done!

REVIEW

This session introduced you to the Red Hat Package Manager (RPM) and its associated rpm commands. You learned to use the Gnome RPM graphical utility to install and uninstall RPMs. You also learned the syntax of a number of rpm commands to query, install, upgrade, remove, and verify RPMs.

QUIZ YOURSELF

1. What is an RPM? (See "Using Gnome RPM to Install and Remove Packages.")
2. What can you do with Gnome RPM and how do you run it? (See "Using Gnome RPM to Install and Remove Packages.")
3. What is the syntax of the rpm command to find out all of its command-line options? (See "Using the rpm Command to Install and Remove Packages.")
4. Which rpm command do you use to view a list of all installed RPMs? (See "Querying RPMs with the rpm command.")
5. How do you install a new RPM from this book's companion CD-ROM containing the Red Hat Linux RPMs? (See "Installing RPMs with the rpm command.")

Building a New Kernel

Session Checklist

✔ Installing the source files and rebuilding the kernel

✔ Configuring the kernel

✔ Building and installing the kernel and modules

✔ Rebooting the system with a rebuilt kernel

**30 Min.
To Go**

At some point, you may want or need to rebuild the kernel — the very core of the operating system — from scratch, that is, from the source code. For example, you may want to take advantage of a new driver not available in the kernel version shipped on the Red Hat Linux CD-ROMs. This session shows you how to install the kernel's source files; how to configure the kernel; and how to build and install the new kernel and modules. Finally, you will learn how to reboot the system using the newly built and installed kernel.

Rebuilding the Kernel

Rebuilding the kernel refers to creating new versions of the binary files constituting the heart of the Linux operating system. You may have to (or want to) rebuild the kernel for various reasons, including the following:

- You can recompile the kernel to support your specific CPU, especially features that improve performance. The default Red Hat Linux installation uses a kernel configured to run on the widest possible variety of Intel CPUs, all the way back to 386s and 486s. As a result, it does not take advantage of all the features and improvements available in the newest CPUs.

- You may want to create a new kernel that includes support for only the hardware actually installed on your system. The default kernel supports a wide variety of the most common hardware, but no single system needs all of that support.

- If you have a system with hardware not supported when you installed Red Hat Linux or for which only experimental support was available, you can rebuild the kernel to include that support once it becomes available.

Before you rebuild the kernel, make sure you have the emergency boot floppy that you prepared when installing Red Hat Linux (covered in Session 1). If the system does not boot after you rebuild the kernel, you can use that emergency boot floppy to start the system using a known good kernel.

Never rebuild and install a new kernel without first making sure that you have an emergency boot floppy. If you did not create the boot floppy during Red Hat Linux installation, use the /sbin/mkbootdisk **command to create the boot floppy. Type** man mkbootdisk **to learn the syntax of that command.**

Rebuilding the kernel involves the following steps:

1. Installing kernel source code.
2. Configuring the kernel.
3. Building the kernel.
4. Building and installing kernel modules (if any).
5. Installing the kernel and setting up LILO.

The rest of this session describes these steps in greater detail.

Installing the Kernel Source Code

To rebuild the Linux kernel, you need the kernel source code, which is usually not installed. So, follow these steps to install it on your system:

1. Log in as root and insert the Red Hat Linux CD-ROM (disk 2) into the CD-ROM drive.
2. Use the mount command to mount the CD-ROM drive on a directory in the file system, as shown here:

   mount /mnt/cdrom
3. Change the directory to the RedHat/RPMS directory on the CD-ROM and use the following commands to install the kernel source files:

   ```
   cd /mnt/cdrom/RedHat/RPMS
   rpm -ivh kernel-source*


   Preparing...
   ############################################# [100%]
        1: kernel-source
   ############################################# [100%]
   ```

The installation might appear to proceed slowly because the kernel source code RPM is over 20MB in size. After RPM finishes installing the kernel source package, the necessary source files appear in the /usr/src/linux-2.4 directory.

You have two options for the device drivers needed to support various hardware devices in Linux:

- *Link in support.* You can build the drivers for all hardware on your system into the kernel. As you can imagine, the size of the kernel grows as the device driver code is incorporated into the kernel. A kernel that includes all necessary support code is called a *monolithic kernel.*

- *Use modules.* You can create the necessary device drivers in the form of modules. A *module* is a block of code that the kernel can load after it starts running. You typically use modules to add support for a device without having to rebuild the kernel for each new device. Modules do not have to be device drivers; you can use them to add new functionality to the kernel. A kernel that uses modules is called a *modular kernel.*

You do not have to create a fully monolithic or fully modular kernel. In fact, it is common practice to link some support directly into the kernel. Conversely, you can build infrequently used device drivers in the form of modules. For a company such as Red Hat, it makes sense to distribute a modular kernel. Red Hat provides a generic kernel along with a large number of modules to support many different types of hardware. The installation program configures the system to load only those modules needed to support the hardware installed in a user's system.

Configuring the Kernel

The first phase in rebuilding a kernel is configuring the kernel. To configure the kernel, log in as root. Then change the directory to /usr/src/linux by using the cd command as follows:

```
cd /usr/src/linux-2.4
```

Red Hat Linux provides three ways for you to configure the kernel:

- Type make xconfig to use an X Window System-based configuration program to configure the kernel. You have to run X to use this tool.

- Type make menuconfig to enter the kernel configuration parameters through a text-based menu interface.

- Type make config to use a text-based program that prompts you for each configuration option one by one. When you use this option, you undergo a long question-and-answer process to specify the configuration parameters.

To configure the kernel, you select the features and device drivers that you want to include in your Red Hat Linux system. In essence, you build a copy of Linux that mixes and matches the features *you* want.

As you configure the kernel, you have to select how to include support for specific devices. For most configuration options, you must type one of the following choices:

- y to build support into the kernel
- m to use a module
- n to skip the support for that specific device
- ? to get help on that kernel configuration option

If a device does not have a modular device driver, you do not see the m option. For some configuration options, you may have to type a specific answer. For example, when responding to the processor type, you type Pentium to indicate that you have a Pentium PC.

The make menuconfig, make xconfig, and make config commands achieve the same end result — each stores your choices in a text file named .config located in the /usr/src/linux directory. Because the filename starts with a period (.), you don't see it when you use the ls command alone to list the directory. Instead, type ls -a to see the .config file in the directory listing.

All that the kernel configuration step does is capture your choices in the .config **file. The kernel file does not change until you actually compile it with the** make **command. That means you can go through the kernel configuration option as many times as you want.**

As noted in the preceding section, you can use any of the configuration tools (make xconfig, make menuconfig, or make config) to perform the kernel configuration. The easiest way is to type make xconfig. This builds an X Window System-based configuration tool and runs it. The initial window displays a set of buttons, each representing a category of kernel configuration options (as shown in Figure 24-1).

Linux Kernel Configuration		
Code maturity level options	SCSI support	File systems
Loadable module support	Fusion MPT device support	Console drivers
Processor type and features	IEEE 1394 (FireWire) support	Sound
General setup	I2O device support	USB support
Memory Technology Devices (MTD)	Network device support	Kernel hacking
Parallel port support	Amateur Radio support	
Plug and Play configuration	IrDA (infrared) support	
Block devices	ISDN subsystem	
Multi–device support (RAID and LVM)	Old CD–ROM drivers (not SCSI, not IDE)	Save and Exit
Networking options	Input core support	Quit Without Saving
Telephony Support	Character devices	Load Configuration from File
ATA/IDE/MFM/RLL support	Multimedia devices	Store Configuration to File

Figure 24-1 *Buttons in* xconfig *show categories of kernel configuration options.*

The four buttons, grouped together on the lower-right corner of the window, enable you to perform specific actions such as saving the configurations and exiting.

To change a configuration option, click a button. For example, if you click the button labeled Processor Type and Features on the upper-left corner, the configuration program displays another window with all the options you can set. From the new window, you can then set specific options. Next to each option in that window, there is a Help button. Whenever you have a question about an option, click the corresponding context-sensitive Help button to view help information for that option.

You can follow this approach — selecting a category button, locating the option, and clicking Help — to specify the options and complete the configuration step. When you are finished specifying the options, click the Save and Exit button in the main window (refer to Figure 24-1).

Building and Installing the Kernel and Modules

**20 Min.
To Go**

This section describes the next three key phases of rebuilding a kernel: building the kernel, building and installing the modules, and setting up LILO to load the new kernel when you reboot the system.

Building the kernel

You should initiate the next three tasks with a single command line by entering multiple semicolon-separated commands on the same line. That way, you can type the line, press Enter, and then take a break because building a kernel takes a while. Depending on your system, making a new kernel can take anywhere from a few minutes to over an hour.

Type the following on a single line to initiate the building process:

```
make dep; make clean; make bzImage
```

The `make dep` command identifies the files that have changed and must be recompiled. The `make clean` command deletes old, unneeded files, such as old copies of the kernel. Finally, `make bzImage` creates the new kernel in a compressed file and places it in a certain directory.

As the kernel is built, you see a lot of messages on the screen. When the process is complete, a new kernel in the form of a compressed file named `bzImage` appears in the `/usr/src/linux/arch/i386/boot` directory.

To use the new kernel, you have to copy it to the `/boot` directory under a specific name and edit the `/etc/lilo.conf` file to set up LILO (the Linux Loader). You learn these steps in the "Installing the New Kernel and setting up LILO" section later in this session. After successfully rebuilding the kernel, you have to build and install the modules.

Building and installing the modules

If you select any modules during the kernel configuration, you have to build the modules and install them. Follow these steps to perform these tasks:

1. The current set of modules in a directory is named after the version of Linux kernel your system is running. For example, if your system runs kernel version 2.4.2-2, the modules reside in the following directory:

    ```
    /lib/modules/2.4.2-2
    ```

Move the module directory to a new location as follows:

```
mv /lib/modules/2.4.2-2 /lib/modules/2.4.2-2-old
```

2. Type the following commands to build the modules:

```
cd /usr/src/linux

make modules
```

3. Install the new modules with the following command:

```
make modules_install
```

Now you can install the kernel and make it available for booting by LILO.

Installing the new kernel and setting up LILO

**10 Min.
To Go**

Red Hat Linux uses LILO to load the newly built Linux kernel from the disk. You must configure and install LILO to use the kernel. The configuration file /etc/lilo.conf lists the kernel binary that LILO runs. You can examine the contents of the LILO configuration file by typing the following command:

```
cat /etc/lilo.conf
```

Here is what appears on a sample system that has only IDE disks after issuing this command:

```
boot=/dev/hda
map=/boot/map
install=/boot/boot.b
prompt
timeout=50
message=/boot/message
default=linux

image=/boot/vmlinuz-2.4.2-2
        label=linux
        root=/dev/hda2
        initrd=/boot/initrd-2.4.2-2.img
        read-only

other=/dev/hda3
        label=win
        table=/dev/hda
```

The last three lines boot the Microsoft Windows installation on a VFAT partition. The five lines (referred to as a *stanza*) starting with image=/boot/vmlinuz-2.4.2-2 describe information LILO needs to know in order to boot the PC using a given kernel. In a moment, you will enable LILO to boot your new kernel by adding a new, similar section to the configuration file. The following list explains the meaning and purpose of each of these in the section that begins with image=, called a *stanza* in LILO terminology.

- The image=/boot/vmlinuz-2.4.2-2 line identifies the kernel that LILO loads. In this case, the kernel file, often called a *kernel image*, is vmlinuz-2.4.2-2, which you can locate in the /boot directory.

- The label=linux line gives a name to the kernel. This is the name you type (linux) at the boot: prompt to make LILO boot this particular kernel.

- The root=/dev/hda3 line specifies the disk partition where the root Linux file system is located. This may differ on your system.

- LILO passes the read-only statement to the kernel, which tells the kernel to mount the root file system in read-only mount.

- The initrd=/boot/initrd-2.4.2-2.img line specifies a file that contains an initial RAM disk image — a block of memory used as a disk — that contains a file system and key drivers the kernel needs to load before the disks are available.

Ordinarily, you see the initrd line only if your system has a Small Computer System Interface (SCSI) adapter and the kernel uses a modular SCSI driver. Why? When your system boots Red Hat Linux from a SCSI disk and uses a modular SCSI disk driver, the kernel faces a classic chicken-and-egg situation. In order to boot, the kernel has to read the SCSI modules from disk, but in order to read the disk, it has to load the SCSI modules. The RAM disk solves this conundrum. The SCSI drivers are stored in the RAM disk image, which is placed in a location the kernel can access without needing to load a driver. The kernel reads the RAM disk image, loads the drivers it contains, and then continues the boot process using the SCSI hard disk. You do not need the initrd line if you create a kernel with the SCSI adapter support built into the kernel.

 On systems that have an MS-DOS partition, the LILO configuration file can include another section with details for the operating system (perhaps Windows 95, 98, or 2000) on that partition.

To configure LILO to boot the kernel you just built, follow these steps:

1. Copy the new kernel binary to the /boot directory. The new compressed kernel file is in the /usr/src/linux/arch/i386/boot directory. You may simply copy the new kernel binary file to the /boot directory with the same name:

   cp /usr/src/linux/arch/i386/boot/bzImage /boot

   When you build the kernel, if you type the command make bzImage, the kernel filename is zImage. You can use any other filename you want as long as you use that same filename when referring to the kernel in the /etc/lilo.conf file of Step 3.

2. Rename the old System.map file in the /boot directory and copy the new map file. Assuming that you'll rebuild kernel version 2.4.2-2 after changing some configuration options, execute the following commands to rename the map file:

   mv /boot/System.map-2.4.2-2 /boot/System.map-2.4.2-2-old

   cp /usr/src/linux-2.4.2/System.map /boot/System.map-2.4.2-2

   cd /boot

   ln -sf System.map-2.2.16-21 System.map

3. Using your favorite text editor, edit /etc/lilo.conf and add the following lines
    just after the timeout line in the file:

    ```
    image=/boot/bzImage
            label=new
            root=/dev/hda2
            read-only
    ```

    On your system, you should make sure that the root line is correct; instead of
    /dev/hda2, list the correct disk partition where the Linux root directory (/) is
    located. Also, use the filename matching the kernel image file (for example,
    /boot/newkernel if the kernel file is so named).

> **The** initrd **line isn't displayed anymore based on the assumption that you
> are no longer using a modular SCSI driver, even if your system has a SCSI
> adapter.**

4. Save the lilo.conf file and exit the editor.
5. Install LILO again by issuing the following command:

    ```
    /sbin/lilo
    ```

    Now you are ready to reboot the system and try out the new kernel.

Rebooting the System

After you finish configuring and installing LILO, shut down and restart the system as you
learned to do in Session 3. When you see the LILO boot: prompt, type the name you
assigned to the new kernel in the /etc/lilo.conf file. You do not have to type anything if
you added the new kernel description as the first entry in the LILO configuration file.

After the system reboots, you should see the familiar graphical login screen. To see proof
that you are indeed running the new kernel, log in as a user, open a terminal window, and
type uname -srv. This command shows you the kernel version as well as the date and time
when this kernel was built. If you upgraded the kernel source, you should see the version
number for the new kernel. If you simply rebuilt the kernel for the same old kernel version,
the date and time should match the time when you rebuilt the kernel. That's your proof
that the system is running the new kernel.

Troubleshooting

While building the kernel, you may get an error such as the following:

```
System is too big. Try using bzImage or modules.
```

If you used make bzImage and encounter this error, redo the configuration process and configure the kernel to use modules, build as many device drivers as possible as modules, eliminate unnecessary features by answering No to those configuration questions, or use a combination of these three options.

The problem you have encountered is that the kernel file, which is initially compressed, is too big to fit into 640KB of memory after it is uncompressed during your PC's boot process. This 640KB limit exists because the Intel *x*86 processors start in what is known as *real mode* and can only access 1MB of memory; 640KB of this is available for programs. This limit is left over from the old MS-DOS days and applies only as the Linux kernel is initially loaded when the PC starts.

If the system appears to *hang*, meaning that there is no screen output and little or no disk activity, you may have skipped a step during the kernel rebuild. Cycle the power to reboot again, and this time, enter linux (the old working kernel's name) at the LILO boot: prompt.

If you cannot boot the older version of Red Hat Linux either, use the emergency boot disk (containing an earlier, but working, version of Linux) to start the system. Then you can repeat the kernel rebuild and installation process making sure that you follow all the steps correctly.

If LILO fails to load completely and you do not get to the boot: prompt, reboot using the emergency boot disk, add the word linear to /etc/lilo.conf immediately below the prompt line, execute /sbin/lilo, and then reboot.

If LILO only partially loads, the point at which it stops indicates a specific type of problem. Use the following list in Table 24-1 to select the solution.

Table 24-1 *LILO Boot Diagnostic Messages*

Message	Description
LIL-	Reboot using the emergency boot disk and rerun /sbin/lilo.
LIL?	Reboot using the emergency boot disk and rerun /sbin/lilo.
LIL	Make sure that your hard disk is properly configured in the system BIOS.
LI:	Confirm that the hard disk is properly configured in the system BIOS, and then reboot using the emergency boot disk and rerun /sbin/lilo.
L:	Make sure that your hard disk is properly configured in the system BIOS.
(nothing):	Make sure that your hard disk is properly configured in the system BIOS and that the partition on which LILO is installed is set as the active partition.

Done!

REVIEW

In this session, you learned how to install the kernel source files and configure the kernel using the make xconfig command. Then you learned the command to build a new kernel and new driver modules. You also learned the procedure for installing the new kernel so that you can boot the system and start using the newly built kernel.

QUIZ YOURSELF

1. What does "rebuilding the kernel" mean, and what are the key phases of performing this task? (See "Rebuilding the Kernel.")

2. What are the three ways you can configure the kernel? (See "Configuring the Kernel.")

3. What command line do you type to build the kernel? (See "Building and Installing the Kernel and Modules.")

4. How do you build and install the modules? (See "Building and installing the modules.")

5. How do you install the new kernel? (See "Installing the new kernel and setting up LILO.")

Scheduling Jobs in Red Hat Linux

Session Checklist

✔ Scheduling one-time jobs

✔ Scheduling recurring jobs

**30 Min.
To Go**

A s a system administrator, you may need to run some programs automatically at regular intervals or execute one or more commands at a specified time in the future. Your Red Hat Linux system includes the facilities so you can schedule jobs to run at any future date or time you want. You can set up the system to perform a task periodically or just once at any future date. Here are some typical tasks you can perform by scheduling jobs on your Red Hat Linux system:

- Backing up files in the middle of the night.
- Downloading large files in the early morning when the system is not busy.
- Sending yourself messages as reminders of meetings.
- Analyzing the system logs periodically and looking for any abnormal activities.

You can perform these tasks on a one-time basis with the at command or on a recurring basis using the Red Hat Linux crond daemon and the crontab command. This session introduces you to these job scheduling features of Red Hat Linux.

Scheduling One-time Jobs

To schedule programs that you want to run only once and at a later time, you can use the at command. The atd daemon executes the commands at the specified time and mails the output to you.

The following configuration files control which users can schedule tasks using the at command:

- `/etc/at.allow` contains the names of the users who may submit jobs using the at command.
- `/etc/at.deny` contains the names of users who are not allowed to submit jobs using the at command.

If these files are not present or there is an empty `/etc/at.deny` file, then any user can submit jobs using the at command. The default in Red Hat Linux is an empty `/etc/at.deny` file, so anyone can use the at command. If you do not want some users to use at, simply list those user names in the `/etc/at.deny` file.

Submitting a one-time job

To use at to schedule a one-time job for execution at a later date, follow these steps:

1. Run the at command with the date or time when you want your commands executed. When you press Enter, the at> prompt appears as follows:

   ```
   at 14:45
   warning: commands will be executed using (in order) a) $SHELL b) login
   shell c) /bin/sh
   at>
   ```

   This is the simplest way to indicate the time when you want to execute one or more commands; simply specify the time in a 24-hour format. In this case, you want to execute the commands at 9:30 p.m. tonight (or tomorrow, if it's already past 2:45 p.m.). However, you can specify the execution time in many different ways (see Table 25-1 for examples).

2. At the at> prompt, type the commands you want to execute just as you do at the shell prompt. After each command, press Enter and continue with the next command. When you are finished entering the commands you want to execute, press Ctrl+D to end this step. Here is an example showing a single command:

   ```
   at> ps
   at> <EOT>
   warning: commands will be executed using /bin/sh
   job 2 at 2001-07-08 14:45
   ```

   After you press Ctrl+D, the at command displays a job number and the date and time when the job will execute.

Table 25-1 *Specifying the Time of Execution with the at Command*

Command	When the Job Runs
at now	Immediately
at now + 15 minutes	15 minutes from the current time

Command	When the Job Runs
at now + 4 hours	4 hours from the current time
at now + 7 days	7 days from the current time
at noon	At noon today or tomorrow, if it's already past noon
at now next hour	Exactly 60 minutes from now
at now next day	At the same time tomorrow
at 17:00 tomorrow	At 5:00 p.m. tomorrow
at 4:45pm	At 4:45 p.m. today or tomorrow, if it's already past 4:45 p.m.
at 3:00 Aug 16, 00	At 3:00 a.m. on August 16, 2000

Verifying scheduled one-time jobs

After you enter one or more jobs, you can view the current list of scheduled jobs with the atq command as follows:

```
atq
1       2001-07-08 14:45 a kwall
2       2001-07-09 14:45 a kwall
3       2001-08-06 01:00 a kwall
4       2001-07-08 17:00 a kwall
6       2001-07-08 14:46 a kwall
```

The first field on each line shows the job number, which is the same number that the at command displays when you submit the job. The next field displays the year, month, day, and time of execution. The last two fields show that the jobs are pending in the a queue along with the user who submitted the jobs. The root user can see the at jobs submitted by all users, but normal users can only see their own.

Canceling one-time jobs and receiving the output

If you want to cancel a job, use the atrm command to remove that job from the queue. When removing a job with the atrm command, refer to the job by its number as follows:

```
atrm 3
```

This deletes job number 3 scheduled for 1:00 a.m. on August 6, 2001.

When a job executes, the output is mailed to you. You can type mail to read your mail and view the output from your jobs.

Scheduling Recurring Jobs

While the at command is good for running commands at a specific time, it's not useful for running a program automatically at repeated intervals. You have to use the crond daemon and the crontab command to schedule such recurring jobs. For example, you need to do this if you want to back up your files to tape at midnight every day.

You schedule recurring jobs with the crontab command in one of two ways. You can place job information in a file with a specific format and submit this file to crond, or you can use crontab in interactive mode. The results are the same. (This session uses a file to store the job information.) The cron daemon, crond, checks the job information every minute and executes the recurring jobs at the specified times. Because the cron daemon processes recurring jobs, such jobs are also referred to as *cron jobs*.

Any output from the job is mailed to the user who submits the job. In the submitted job information file, you may specify a different recipient for the mailed output.

As with the at command, two files control who can schedule cron jobs using crontab:

- /etc/cron.allow contains the names of the users who may submit jobs using the crontab command.
- /etc/cron.deny contains the names of users who are not allowed to submit jobs using the crontab command.

If the /etc/cron.allow file exists, only users listed in this file can schedule cron jobs. If only the /etc/cron.deny file exists, then users listed in this file cannot schedule cron jobs. If neither file exists, the default Red Hat Linux setup enables any user to submit cron jobs.

Submitting a cron job

To submit a cron job, perform the following steps:

1. Prepare a shell script (or an executable program in any programming language) that can perform the recurring task you want to perform. You can skip this step if you want to execute an existing program periodically.

2. Prepare a text file with information about the times when you want the shell script or program (from Step 1) to execute. This is the file you submit using crontab. You can submit several recurring jobs with a single file. Each line with timing information about a job has a standard format with at least six fields. The first five fields specify when the job runs and the sixth and subsequent fields constitute the actual command to be run. For example, this line executes the myjob shell script in a user's home directory at five minutes past midnight each day:

```
5 0 * * * $HOME/myjob
```

Table 25-2 shows the meaning of the first five fields. Also, an entry in any of the first five fields can be a single number, a comma-separated list of numbers, a pair of numbers separated by a dash (indicating a range of numbers), or an asterisk (*). An asterisk means all possible values for that field.

3. Submit the information to `crontab` with the following command:

```
crontab jobinfo
```

In this case, the text file `jobinfo` (in the current directory) contains the job information.

Table 25-2 *Specifying the Time of Execution in crontab Files*

Field Number	Meaning of Field	Acceptable Range of Values*
1	Minute	0-59
2	Hour of the day	0-23
3	Day of the month	0-31
4	Month	1-12 (1 means January, 2 means February, and so on) or the names of months using the first letters (Jan, Feb, Mar, Apr, May, Jun, Jul, Aug, Sep, Oct, Nov, Dec)
5	Day of the week	0-7 (0 and 7 both mean Sunday, 1 means Monday, and so on) or the three-letter abbreviations of the weekdays (Sun, Mon, Tue, Wed, Thu, Fri, Sat)

That's it! You're all set with the cron job. From now on, if there are no errors in the file you submitted, the cron job should run at regular intervals (as specified in the job information file) and you should receive mail messages with the output from the job.

Verifying the cron job is scheduled

To verify that the job is indeed scheduled, type the following command:

```
crontab -l
# DO NOT EDIT THIS FILE - edit the master and reinstall.
# (jobinfo installed on Tue May 16 20:44:23 2000)
# (Cron version -- $Id: crontab.c,v 2.13 1994/01/17 03:20:37 vixie Exp $)
SHELL=/bin/sh
5 0 * * * $HOME/myjob
```

The output of the `crontab -l` command shows the cron jobs currently installed in your name. To remove your cron jobs, type `crontab -r`.

Setting up cron jobs for any user

If you log in as root, you can also set up, examine, and remove cron jobs for any user. To set up cron jobs for a user, use this command:

```
crontab -u username filename
```

**10 Min.
To Go**

Here, *username* is the user for whom you are installing the cron jobs, and *filename* is the file that contains the information about the jobs.

Use the following `crontab` command to view the cron jobs for a user:

```
crontab -u username -l
```

To remove a user's cron jobs, use the following command:

```
crontab -u username -r
```

After root **creates a user's cron job, users are free to edit it using the command** crontab -e.

The cron daemon also executes the cron jobs listed in the system-wide cron job file /etc/crontab. Here's the default /etc/crontab file in Red Hat Linux (type `cat /etc/crontab` to view the file):

```
SHELL=/bin/bash
PATH=/sbin:/bin:/usr/sbin:/usr/bin
MAILTO=root
HOME=/

# run-parts
01 * * * * root run-parts /etc/cron.hourly
02 4 * * * root run-parts /etc/cron.daily
22 4 * * 0 root run-parts /etc/cron.weekly
42 4 1 * * root run-parts /etc/cron.monthly
```

The first four lines set up several environment variables for the jobs listed in this file. The MAILTO environment variable specifies the user who receives the mail message with the output from the cron jobs in this file.

The line that begins with a pound sign (#) is a comment line. The last four lines execute the run-parts shell script (located in the /usr/bin directory) at various times with the name of a specific directory as an argument. Each of the arguments to run-parts — etc/cron.hourly, /etc/cron.daily, /etc/cron.weekly, and /etc/cron.monthly — are directories. Essentially, run-parts executes all scripts located in the directory that you provide as an argument.

The /etc/crontab **file has a special format. Between the last time field and the command field you can place a user name. The** cron **daemon will run the commands or script using that user name.**

Table 25-3 lists what those directories contain.

Table 25-3 *System Crontab Directories*

Directory Name	Contents
/etc/cron.hourly	Scripts executed every hour
/etc/cron.daily	Scripts executed each day at 4:02 a.m.
/etc/cron.weekly	Scripts executed weekly on Sunday at 4:22 a.m.
/etc/cron.monthly	Scripts executed at 4:42 a.m. on the first day of each month

You have to look at the scripts in these directories to learn what gets executed at periodic intervals. For example, the /etc/cron.daily contains, among others, the scripts listed in Table 25-4.

Table 25-4 *System Cron Jobs*

Script Name	Description
logrotate	Automatically rotates, compresses, and mails out log files based on configuration information in the /etc/logrotate.conf file.
tmpwatch	Removes old files from temporary directories such as /tmp and /var/tmp.
tetex.cron	Removes old font files and other temporary files created used by a typesetting program called TeX.
slocate.cron	Updates the filename database that the locate command consults. For example, try typing locate slocate to show all files that contain slocate in their names.

Troubleshooting

If programs that you schedule with the at command or which use crontab do not execute, make sure that they are in your path. Alternatively, you can specify a command's complete pathname, such as /home/kwall/bin/myjob.sh, in order to make sure that the atd and crond daemons can find it.

A common problem, especially on stand-alone Red Hat Linux systems used at home, is that the crond or atd daemons are not running. To make sure they are running, log in as the root user and type the following commands:

```
/etc/rc.d/init.d/atd restart
/etc/rc.d/init.t/cron restart
```

If the command in a cron job contains embedded % signs (for example, the date command uses % signs to format its output), they must be escaped with a backslash (\). Otherwise, erond interprets the % as a new line, which can cause a command not to execute, or at least change its meaning.

Done!

REVIEW

This session showed you how to perform commands at a future time and submit recurring jobs. You learned how to use the at command to execute one or more commands on a one-time basis in the future and have the output mailed to you. Next, you used the crontab facility to set up periodic jobs, called *cron jobs,* to execute at recurring intervals and have the output mailed to you.

QUIZ YOURSELF

1. What are some of the tasks that you can perform by scheduling jobs? (See the introduction to the session.)

2. What command do you use to schedule one-time jobs? (See "Scheduling One-time Jobs.")

3. What feature of Red Hat do you use to set up recurring jobs? (See "Scheduling Recurring Jobs.")

4. How can you control which users are allowed to submit recurring jobs on your system? (See "Scheduling Recurring Jobs.")

5. How do you specify the time of execution for recurring jobs? (See "Scheduling Recurring Jobs.")

Backing Up and Restoring Files

Session Checklist

✔ Selecting a backup strategy and storage media

✔ Using `tar` to backup and restore files

✔ Backing up on tapes

30 Min.
To Go

B y now, you have learned a number of system administration tasks from configuring X to building a new kernel. This session introduces you to another important system administration task — backing up and restoring files from backup storage media. In this session, you'll learn how to back up and restore files using the tape archiver (tar) program that comes with Red Hat Linux. You'll also learn how to perform incremental and automatic backups on tapes.

Selecting a Backup Strategy and Storage Media

Your Red Hat Linux system's hard disk contains everything needed to keep the system running, as well as other files such as documents and databases that you need to keep your business running. You must back up these files so that you can recover data quickly and bring the system back to normal in case the hard disk crashes. You should adhere to a strict schedule of regular backups because you can never tell when the hard disk might fail or the file system might get corrupted. To implement such a schedule, decide what files to back up, how often to back them up, and what backup storage media to use. This involves selecting a backup strategy and backup media.

Your choice of backup strategy and backup media depend on your assessment of the risk of business disruption due to hard disk failure. Depending on how you use your Red Hat Linux system, a disk failure may or may not have much impact on you.

For example, if you use your Red Hat Linux system as a learning tool to learn about Linux or programming, all you may need are backup copies of some system files needed to configure Red Hat Linux. In this case, your backup strategy may be to save important system configuration files on one or more floppies every time you change any system configuration.

On the other hand, if you use your Red Hat Linux system as an office server that provides shared file storage for many users, the risk of business disruption and the associated cost due to disk failure is much higher. In this case, you have to back up all the files every week and back up any new or changed files every day. You should perform these backups in an automated manner (using the job-scheduling features that you learned in Session 25). Also, you probably need a backup storage medium that can store large amounts (multiple gigabytes) of data on a single tape. In other words, in high-risk or business critical situations, your backup strategy is more elaborate and thus requires additional equipment such as a tape drive.

Your choice of backup media depends on the amount of data you have to back up. For a small amount of data, such as system configuration files, you can use floppy disks as your backup media. If your PC has a Zip drive, you can use Zip disks as your backup media, which are especially well suited for backing up a single-user directory. To back up servers, you should use a tape drive — typically, a 4mm or 8mm tape drive that connects to a SCSI (Small Computer System Interface) controller. Such tape drives can store several gigabytes of data per tape, and you can use them to back up an entire file system on a single tape.

When using the tar command to back up files to these backup storage media, you have to refer to the backup device by name. Table 26-1 lists the device names for some common backup devices.

Table 26-1   *Device Names for Common Backup Devices*

Backup Device	Linux Device Name
Floppy disk	/dev/fd0
IDE Zip drive	/dev/hdc4 or /dev/hdd4
SCSI Zip drive	/dev/sda (assuming it's the first SCSI drive); otherwise, the device name depends on the SCSI ID
SCSI tape drive	/dev/st0 or /dev/nst0 (the n prefix means that the tape does not rewind after files are copied to the tape)

Although this session focuses on backing up and restoring files with the tape archiver (tar) program that comes with Red Hat Linux, there are other free software packages, such as Amanda, and also commercially available utilities for Red Hat Linux that perform backups. Refer to the upcoming sidebar for information about some well-known commercial utilities.

Backing Up and Restoring Files with the tar Program

**20 Min.
To Go**

You can use the tape archiver (tar) program to archive files to a device such as a floppy disk or tape. The tar program creates an archive file that contains other directories and files, and optionally compresses the archive for efficient storage. The archive is then written

Commercial Backup Utilities for Red Hat Linux

Although you can manage backups with `tar`, a number of commercial backup utilities come with graphical user interfaces (GUIs) and other features to simplify backups. Here are some well-known backup utilities for Red Hat Linux:

- **LONE-TAR**: tape backup software package from Lone Star Software Corporation (see `http://www.cactus.com/`)
- **Arkeia**: backup and recovery software for heterogeneous networks from Knox Software (see `http://www.knox-software.com/`)
- **CTAR**: backup and recovery software for UNIX systems from UniTrends Software Corporation (see `http://www.unitrends.com/`)

to a specified device or another file. In fact, many software packages are distributed in the form of a compressed `tar` file.

The command syntax of the `tar` program is as follows:

```
tar options destination source
```

The *options* are usually specified by a sequence of single letters, each specifying what `tar` should do. The *destination* entry identifies the name of the archive file, or, if backing up to a device, the backup device. The *source* entry is a list of file or directory names denoting the files to back up.

Backing up and restoring a single-volume archive

Suppose you want to back up the contents of the /etc/X11 directory on a single floppy disk. Log in as root, place a disk in the floppy drive, and then type the following command:

```
tar zcvf /dev/fd0 /etc/X11
```

The `tar` program displays a list of filenames as each file is copied to the compressed `tar` archive on the floppy disk. In this case, the options are zcvf, the destination is /dev/fd0 (the floppy disk), and the source is the /etc/X11 directory (which implies all its subdirectories and their contents). You can use a similar `tar` command to back up files to a tape. Simply replace /dev/fd0 with the tape device, such as /dev/st0 for a SCSI tape drive. Table 26-2 lists a few common `tar` options.

Table 26-2 *Common tar Options*

Option	Definition
z	Compresses the `tar` archive using `gzip`.
J	Compresses the `tar` archive using bzip2.

Continued

Table 26-2   *Continued*

Option	Definition
c	Creates an archive.
v	Displays verbose messages.
x	Extracts files from the archive.
t	Lists the contents of the archive.
M	Specifies a multi-volume archive (discussed in the next section).
f	Specifies the name of the archive file or device on the next field in the command line.

To view the contents of the tar archive you create on the floppy disk, type the following command:

```
tar ztf /dev/fd0
```

You should see a list of the filenames (each begins with /etc/X11) indicating the contents of the backup. In this tar command, the t option lists the contents of the tar archive.

To learn how to extract the files from a tar backup, try the following steps while logged in as root:

1. Change the directory to /tmp by typing the command:

   ```
   cd /tmp
   ```

   That is where you extract the files from the tar backup.

2. Type the following command:

   ```
   tar zxvf /dev/fd0
   ```

   This tar command uses the x option to extract the files from the archive stored on /dev/fd0 (the floppy disk).

If you check the contents of the /tmp directory, you notice that the tar command creates an etc/X11 directory tree in /tmp and restores all the files from the tar archive into that directory. The tar command strips off the leading / from the filenames in the archive and restores the files in the current directory. If you want to restore the /etc/X11 directory from the archive on the floppy, use the following command:

```
tar zxvf /dev/fd0 /
```

The / at the end of the command denotes the directory where you want to restore the backup files.

As you can see, the tar command enables you to create, view, and restore an archive. You can store the archive in a file or in any device that you specify with a device name.

Backing up and restoring a multi-volume archive

Sometimes, the capacity of a single storage medium is less than the total storage space needed to store the archive. In that case, you can use the M option for a multi-volume archive, meaning that the archive can span multiple tapes or floppies.

 You cannot create a compressed, multi-volume archive. That means you cannot use the z option.

To see how multi-volume archives work, log in as root, place one disk in the floppy drive, and type the following tar command:

```
tar cvMf /dev/fd0 /usr/doc/ghostscript*
```

Note the M option, which tells tar to create a multi-volume archive. The tar command prompts you for a second floppy when the first one fills to capacity. Take out the first floppy and insert another floppy when you see the following prompt:

```
Prepare volume #2 for `/dev/fd0' and hit return:
```

When you hit Enter, the tar program continues with the second floppy. In this example, you need only two floppies to store the archive. For larger archives, the tar program continues to prompt for floppies in case more floppies are needed.

To restore from this multi-volume archive, type cd /tmp to change the directory to /tmp and then type:

```
tar xvMf /dev/fd0
```

The tar program prompts you to feed the floppies as necessary.

Use the du -s command to determine the amount of storage you need to archive a directory. For example, here's how you can get the total size of the /etc directory in kilobytes:

```
du -s /etc
8040    /etc
```

The resulting output shows that the /etc directory contains 8,040 blocks (blocks are usually 1,024 bytes), requiring at least 8,040K of storage space to back up. If you plan to back up on multiple high-density floppies, you need about 8,040/1,200, or about 7 double-sided, high density, 3.5" floppy diskettes.

Backing Up on Tapes

**10 Min.
To Go**

Although backing up on tapes is as simple as using the right device name in the tar command, you do need to know some nuances of the tape device to use it well. When you use tar to back up to the device named /dev/st0 (the first SCSI tape drive), the tape device automatically rewinds the tape after the tar program finishes copying the archive to the tape. The /dev/st0 device is called a *rewinding tape device* because it rewinds tapes by default.

If your tape can hold several gigabytes of data, you may want to write several `tar` archives, one after another, to the same tape. Otherwise, much of the tape may be empty. However, you do not want the tape device to rewind the tape after the `tar` program finishes. To help you with this, some Red Hat Linux tape devices are non-rewinding devices. The non-rewinding SCSI tape device is called `/dev/nst0`. Use this device name if you want to write one archive after another on a tape.

After each archive, the non-rewinding tape device writes an end-of-file (EOF) marker to separate one archive from the next. You can use the `mt` command to control the tape. Essentially, it moves from one marker to the next or rewinds the tape. For example, after you finish writing several archives to a tape using the `/dev/nst0` device name, you can rewind the tape with the following command:

```
mt -f /dev/nst0 rewind
```

After rewinding the tape, you can use the following command to extract files from the first archive to the current disk directory:

```
tar xvf /dev/nst0
```

After that, you must move past the EOF marker to the next archive. To do this, use the following `mt` command:

```
mt -f /dev/nst0 fsf 1
```

This positions the tape at the beginning of the next archive. You can now use the `tar` `xvf` command again to read this archive.

 If you save multiple archives on a tape, you have to keep track of the archives yourself.

Performing incremental backups

Suppose you backed up your system's hard disk on a tape using the `tar` command. Because such a full backup can take quite some time, you do not want to repeat this task every night. Besides, only a small number of files may have changed during the day. You can use the `find` command to list those files that have changed in the past 24 hours, as follows:

```
find / -mtime -1 -type f -print
```

This command prints a list of files that have changed within the last day. The `-mtime -1` option means you want the files that were modified less than one day ago. You can now combine the `find` command with the `tar` command to back up only those files that have changed within the last day, as follows:

```
tar cvf /dev/st0 `find / -mtime -1 -type f -print`
```

When you place a command between single back quotes (`), the shell executes that command and places the output at that point in the command line. The net result is that the tar program saves only the changed files in the archive. Thus, you get an *incremental backup* that includes files that have changed since the previous day.

Automating backups

In Session 25, you learned how to use crontab to set up recurring jobs called cron jobs, which are tasks that the Linux system performs at regular intervals. Backing up your system is a good use of the cron facility. Suppose your backup strategy is as follows:

- Every Sunday morning at 1:15 a.m., you back up the entire disk to a new tape.
- On the other days of the week (Monday through Saturday), you perform an incremental backup at 3:10 a.m. by saving only those files that have changed during the past 24 hours. Incremental backups are stored on a separate tape than the full backup, but all incremental backups are appended to this tape in order to save tapes.

To set up this automated backup schedule, log in as root and type the following lines in a file named backups (this example assumes that you are using a SCSI tape drive):

```
15 1 * * 0 tar zcvf /dev/st0 /
10 3 * * 1-6 tar zcvf /dev/nst0 `find / -mtime -1 -type f -print`
```

Next, submit this job schedule with the following crontab command:

```
crontab backups
```

Now you should be set for an automated backup. All you need to do is place a new tape in the tape drive on Sunday for the full backup, and on Monday, to store that week's incremental backups. You should also label each tape appropriately.

Troubleshooting

If files restored from a backup tape are corrupted, try using tar's -W or --verify options to verify the tar archive as it is written.

Before using a brand new tape, it should be retensioned in order to equalize tension across the tape and to prevent stretching. The command to do this is
mt -f /dev/nst0 reten.

If you seem to be losing backups, make sure that your backup commands, such as the tar commands discussed in this session, are using the non-rewinding device (/dev/nst0, for example). Remember, after a tape operation completes, the rewinding devices *automatically* rewind to the beginning of the tape, so the result of a second backup operation will partially or completely overwrite the results of a previous one.

Done!

REVIEW

In this session, you learned the importance of backing up your files. This session highlighted the selection of a backup strategy and backup media based on your needs and your level of tolerance for the risk of business interruption from a hard disk failure. You also learned to use the tape archiver program, tar, to back up and restore files. Finally, this session showed you how to perform incremental tape backups and set up cron jobs for automated full and incremental tape backups.

QUIZ YOURSELF

1. How do you decide what to back up and how often? (See "Selecting a Backup Strategy and Storage Media.")

2. What are some commercial backup utilities for Red Hat Linux? (See the sidebar, "Commercial Backup Utilities for Red Hat Linux.")

3. How do you use the tar program to back up files if the total size of files exceeds the capacity of a single copy of the backup medium? (See "Backing up and restoring a multi-volume archive.")

4. What commands do you use to back up only those files that have changed in the previous day? (See "Performing incremental backups.")

5. How do you automate the job of backing up files to a tape? (See "Automating backups.")

PART

V

Sunday Morning

1. What does an X server do?

2. Name the file that configures the X server and identify a utility that you can use to create or modify it.

3. If X is not starting properly and you boot to run level 5, what steps can you take to solve the problem?

4. Provide a short explanation of the init process and name the file that controls its behavior.

5. How do you determine or change your system's default run level?

6. Where are the scripts that the init process executes when it runs?

7. What is RPM?

8. How do you determine if a specific RPM is installed on your Red Hat Linux system?

9. Show one way to install an RPM named fortune-mod-1.3.4-59.i386.rpm.

10. Name two ways to remove an installed RPM.

11. Why would you want to rebuild the Linux kernel?

12. Briefly describe the steps involved in rebuilding the kernel.

13. What command would you use to run the ls utility four hours from now?

14. Which Linux program allows you to run a program at regularly scheduled intervals?

15. Show a command line that schedules a job named $HOME/backup.sh to run every night of the week at 11:30 p.m.

16. Which file controls who may schedule jobs for regular, unattended execution?

17. What are some of the backup media you can use to create backups of your system?

18. Suppose you have a SCSI tape drive. What utility would you use to back up files to that device? Show a command line that will do so.

19. How can you copy or back up a single large file onto multiple floppy disks?

20. Explain how to store multiple backups on a single tape. Show the commands to rewind the tape and to skip over an archive.

PART

VI

Sunday Afternoon

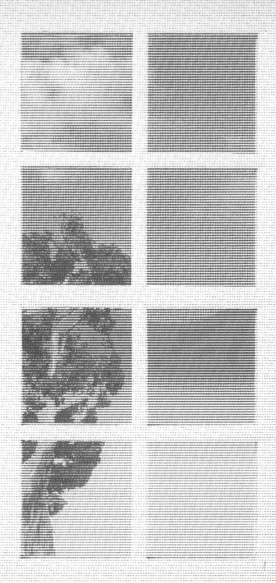

SESSION

Building Software Packages from Source Files

Session Checklist

✔ Downloading and unpacking software

✔ Building and installing software from source files

*30 Min.
To Go*

In Session 23, you learned how to install software packages distributed in the Red Hat Package Manager (RPM) format. RPM files bundle all the executable binary files and configuration files needed to install a software package. However, many open source software packages are distributed in source code form without any executable binaries. Before you can use such software, you have to build the executable binary files and then follow some instructions to install the package. This session shows you how to download and unpack the source files. It then shows you how to build software packages from source files and install them.

Downloading and Unpacking the Software

Open source files are typically distributed in compressed tar archives. As you learned in Session 26, the tar program creates these archives and then the gzip program compresses them. The distribution is in the form of a single large file with a .tar.gz or .tar.Z extension, which is often referred to as a *compressed* or *gzipped tarball*. If you want the software, you have to download the compressed tarball and unpack it.

You download the compressed tar file using anonymous File Transfer Protocol (FTP) or the Web browser. Typically, this action involves no more effort on your part than clicking a link and saving the file in an appropriate directory on your system.

To try your hand at downloading and building a software package, you can practice on the *X Multimedia System (XMMS)*, which is a graphical X application for playing MP3 files and other multimedia files. XMMS is bundled with Red Hat Linux and installed on your system when you select the Multimedia Support package group during Red Hat Linux installation. However, there is no harm in downloading and rebuilding the XMMS package again.

You can access the source files for XMMS from `http://www.xmms.org/download.html` in the form of a compressed `tar` archive. You can also download the files from the `xmms/1.0` directory of the anonymous FTP server (`ftp.xmms.org`).

Try downloading the XMMS source files from the anonymous FTP server so you know how to access files manually.

Before attempting to download a file from an FTP server, make sure that your Linux system is connected to the Internet. You should also change the directory to the location where you want to store the downloaded file (although you can always move the file after downloading). You may want to log in as `root` and change the directory to `/usr/local` before typing the `ftp` command. If you use the GNOME or KDE desktop, type these commands from a terminal window.

Downloading the software

20 Min. To Go

Here is a sample session that you can use as a guideline when you download the compressed `tar` file for XMMS from the anonymous FTP server. Typed lines appear in bold text.

```
ftp ftp.xmms.org
Connected to ftp.xmms.org.
220 ProFTPD 1.2.0pre10 Server (FTP server for awpti.org) [awpti.org]
Name (ftp.xmms.org:naba): anonymous
331 Anonymous login ok, send your complete e-mail address as password.
Password:   (Type your e-mail address and press Enter)
230 Anonymous access granted, restrictions apply.
Remote system type is UNIX.
Using binary mode to transfer files.
ftp> cd xmms/1.0
250 CWD command successful.
ftp> ls
200 PORT command successful.
150 Opening ASCII mode data connection for file list.
drwxr-xr-x   6 xmms      xmms         4096 Jan 30 15:20 rpm
-rw-r--r--   1 xmms      xmms       700909 Jan 30 15:22 xmms-1.0.0.tar.gz
-rw-r--r--   1 xmms      xmms       715574 Jan 30 15:15 xmms-1.0.1.tar.gz
226 Transfer complete.
ftp> binary
200 Type set to I.
ftp> get xmms-1.0.1.tar.gz
200 PORT command successful.
150 Opening BINARY mode data connection for xmms-1.0.1.tar.gz (715574 bytes).
226 Transfer complete.
715574 bytes received in 383 secs (1.8 Kbytes/sec)
ftp> bye
ftp ftp.xmms.org
Connected to ftp.xmms.org (194.236.124.44).
220 fs02 FTP server (Version 6.00+krb4-1.0.8) ready.
Name (ftp.xmms.org:kwall): anonymous
331 Guest login ok, type your name as password.
Password:   (Type your e-mail address and press Enter)
```

```
230 Guest login ok, access restrictions apply.
Remote system type is UNIX.
Using binary mode to transfer files.
ftp> cd xmms/1.2.x
250 CWD command successful.
ftp> ls
227 Entering Passive Mode (194,236,124,44,187,21)
150 Opening ASCII mode data connection for '.'.
-rw-r--r--  1 1136   xmms   1944572 May 11 01:16 xmms-1.2.4.tar.gz
-rw-r--r--  1 1136   xmms   1486604 Jun 19 21:39 xmms-1.2.5.tar.bz2
-rw-r--r--  1 1136   xmms   2414840 Jun 19 21:37 xmms-1.2.5.tar.gz
226 Transfer complete.
ftp> binary
200 Type set to I.
ftp> get xmms-1.2.5.tar.gz
local: xmms-1.2.5.tar.gz remote: xmms-1.2.5.tar.gz
227 Entering Passive Mode (194,236,124,44,187,61)
150 Opening BINARY mode data connection for 'xmms-1.2.5.tar.gz' (2414840 bytes).
226 Transfer complete.
2414840 bytes received in 634 secs (3.7 Kbytes/sec)
ftp> bye
221 Goodbye.
```

Notice that you have to log in with the user name anonymous, which is the standard login name for anonymous FTP. *Anonymous FTP* allows people who do not have a user account on a server to log in and retrieve files. However, the anonymous account is severely restricted and is only used to send and retrieve files from FTP servers. For the password, you should type your e-mail address and then press Enter. To change the directory, use the cd command. For a directory listing, use the ls command.

You need to type the binary command to make sure that the data transfer occurs in binary mode because the .tar.gz file is a binary file. Then you can use the get command to download the file, in this case, xmms-1.0.1.tar.gz. Recall that the .tar.gz extension tells you that this is a compressed tar archive. After the download is complete, type bye or quit to end the anonymous FTP session.

After downloading the compressed tar file, you should first examine the contents with this command (not all of the output is shown in order to conserve space):

```
tar ztf xmms*.gz | more
xmms-1.2.5/
xmms-1.2.5/Makefile.in
xmms-1.2.5/README
xmms-1.2.5/stamp-h1.in
xmms-1.2.5/ABOUT-NLS
xmms-1.2.5/AUTHORS
xmms-1.2.5/COPYING
xmms-1.2.5/ChangeLog
xmms-1.2.5/INSTALL
xmms-1.2.5/Makefile.am
xmms-1.2.5/NEWS
xmms-1.2.5/TODO
xmms-1.2.5/acconfig.h
xmms-1.2.5/acinclude.m4
xmms-1.2.5/aclocal.m4
```

```
xmms-1.2.5/config.guess
xmms-1.2.5/config.h.in
xmms-1.2.5/config.sub
xmms-1.2.5/configure
```

The output of this command shows you the contents of the archive and gives you an idea of the directories that are created once you unpack the archive. In this case, a directory named xmms-1.0.1 is created in the current directory, in this case, /usr/local). From the listing, you also learn the programming language used to write the package. If you see .c and .h files, that means the source files are in the C programming language, which is used to write many open source software packages.

Unpacking the software

To extract (or unpack) the contents of the tar archive, type the following tar command:

```
tar zxvf xmms*.gz
```

You again see the long list of files as they are extracted from the archive and copied to the appropriate directories on your hard disk.

If you download an archive with .bz2 at the end instead of .gz, it means the archive was compressed with the bzip2 utility. In order to unpack this kind of archive, replace z with j in the tar command. That is, type tar jxvf xmms*.bz2.

Now you are ready to build the software.

Building the Software from Source Files and Installing It

After you unpack the compressed tar archive, all source files are in a directory whose name is usually that of the software package with a version number suffix. For example, the XMMS version 1.2.5 source files are extracted in the xmms-1.2.5 directory. To start the process of building the software, change the directory with this command:

```
cd xmms*
```

You don't have to type the entire name. The shell can expand the directory name and change it to the xmms-1.0.1 directory.

Nearly all software packages come with one or more README or INSTALL files, or something similarly named. These files are text files containing instructions on what to do to build and install the packages. XMMS is no exception; it comes with a README file that you should read by typing more README. There is also an INSTALL file that contains instructions for building and installing XMMS.

Most open source software packages, including XMMS, also come with a file named COPYING. **This file contains the full text of the GNU** *General Public License (GPL)*, **which spells out the conditions under which you can use and redistribute the software. If you are not familiar with the GNU GPL, you should read this file and show the license to your legal counsel for a full interpretation and an assessment of applicability to your business. The file containing the license may have other names, too, such as** LICENSE.

For the XMMS package, the README file lists some of the prerequisites, such as libraries that you need, and then tells you what commands you should type to build and install the package. In the case of XMMS, the instructions direct you to use the following commands:

1. Type ./configure to run a shell script that checks your system configuration and creates a *Makefile*, which the make command uses to build and install the package. The configure shell script guesses system-dependent variables and creates a Makefile with commands needed to build and install the software.

2. Type make to build the software. This step compiles the source files in all the sub-directories.

3. Type make install to install the software. This step copies libraries and exe-cutable binary files to appropriate directories on your system.

Although these steps are specific to XMMS, most other packages follow this procedure: configure, make, and then install.

Usually, you do not have to do anything but type the commands to build the software; however, you must install the software development tools on your system. This means that you must install the Development package when you install Red Hat Linux. To build and run XMMS, you must also install the X Window System package because it's an X application.

Building the software

10 Min. To Go

To begin building XMMS, type the following command to run the configure script while in the xmms-1.2.5 directory:

```
./configure
```

The configure script starts running and prints lots of messages as it checks various fea-tures of your system, from the existence of the C compiler to various libraries that are needed to build XMMS. Finally, the configure script creates a Makefile that you can use to build the software.

If the configure **script displays error messages and fails, read the** INSTALL **and** README **files again to find any clues in solving the problem. You may be able to circumvent the problem by providing some information through command-line arguments to the** configure **script.**

After the `configure` script finishes, build the software by typing the following command:

```
make
```

This command runs the GNU `make` utility, which may take up to 10 or 15 minutes to complete, depending on the speed of your system. The `make` utility reads a Makefile, which contains information the compiler needs to create the XMMS program from the source code you downloaded. The `make` command goes through the source directories, compiles the source files, and creates the executable files and libraries needed to run XMMS. You see a lot of messages scroll by as each file is compiled. These messages show the command used to compile and link the files.

Installing the software

After the `make` command finishes, you can install the XMMS software with the following command:

```
make install
```

This command also runs GNU `make`, but the install argument instructs GNU `make` to perform a specific set of commands from the Makefile. These instructions essentially search the subdirectories and copy various files to their final locations. For example, the binary executable files `xmms`, `gnomexmms`, `wmxmms`, and `xmms-config` are copied to the `/usr/bin` directory.

Running the software

Now that you have installed XMMS, try running it by typing `xmms` in a terminal window from the GNOME or KDE desktop. From the XMMS window, you can open an MP3 file and try playing it. Note that your PC must have a sound card and you must have it configured correctly. (Session 18 discusses sound card configuration.) Figure 27-1 shows a typical view of XMMS playing an MP3 music clip.

Figure 27-1   *Playing MP3 music with XMMS*

Reviewing the basic building steps

Now you know how to download, unpack, build, and install a typical software package. Here's an overview of the steps you follow to complete these tasks:

1. Download the source code, usually in the form of a `.tar.gz` file, from the anonymous FTP site or Web site. Use the Web browser or download the source code manually from the anonymous FTP server.

2. Unpack the file with a `tar zxvf filename` command.

3. Change the directory to the new subdirectory where the software is unpacked with a command such as this one:

   `cd software_dir`

4. Read any README or INSTALL files to identify requirements that the software has and to learn any specific instructions you must follow to build and install the software.

5. The details of building the software may differ slightly from one software package to another, but typically, you type the following commands to build and install the software:

   `./configure`

   `make`

   `make install`

6. Read any other documentation that comes with the software to learn how to configure and use it.

Troubleshooting

If you use anonymous FTP to download a file such as a compressed `tar` archive, and it appears to be corrupted, make sure that you switched to binary mode before downloading the file. Downloading binary files in text mode (also known as ASCII mode) corrupts the downloaded file. The following two messages are symptoms of this:

```
$ tar zxvf mytarball.tar.gz

gzip: stdin: not in gzip format
tar: Child returned status 1
tar: Error exit delayed from previous errors
$ gunzip mytarball.tar.gz


gunzip: mytarball.tar.gz: not in gzip format
```

You might have problems building software, such as receiving an error message complaining about missing programs or, in particular, the message `installation or configuration problem: compiler cannot create executables`. The most likely explanation is that you do not have a complete development environment installed. To solve the problem, follow the instructions in Session 23 to install *at least* the RPMs in the following list from the Red Hat Linux installation CDs:

- `bzip2`
- `fileutils`
- `gcc`
- `gcc-c++`
- `glibc-devel`
- `gzip`
- `kernel-headers`
- `kernel-source`
- `make`
- `ncompress`
- `tar`

The particular package you are building might have additional requirements, but in many cases, the RPMs in this list are all you need.

Done!

REVIEW

This session showed you how to download and unpack open source software distributed in compressed `tar` archives. Using the X Multimedia System (XMMS) package as an example, you learned to build the software and install it.

QUIZ YOURSELF

1. What is a "compressed tarball"? (See "Downloading and Unpacking the Software.")
2. What command do you use to unpack a compressed tarball? (See "Downloading and Unpacking the Software.")
3. What are some typical files that provide information on building and installing the software package? (See "Building the Software from Source Files and Installing It.")
4. What is the name of the file that usually contains the full text of the GNU General Public License? (See "Building the Software from Source Files and Installing It.")
5. What are the three commands you have to type to build and install the XMMS package? (See "Building the Software from Source Files and Installing It.")

Monitoring System Performance

✔ Using the top utility

✔ Using the GNOME System Monitor

✔ Using the vmstat utility

✔ Checking disk performance and usage

✔ Exploring the /proc file system

30 Min. To Go

A key system administration task is keeping track of how well your Red Hat Linux system performs. You can monitor the overall performance of that system by gathering information such as central processing unit (CPU) usage, physical memory usage, virtual memory (swap space) usage, and hard disk usage. Red Hat Linux comes with a number of utilities that you can use to monitor one or more of these performance parameters. This session introduces you to a few of these utilities and explains the information presented by these utilities.

Using the top Utility

To view the *top*, or most frequently used CPU processes, you can use the top program. To start that program, type top in a terminal window or text console. The top program then displays a text screen listing the current processes, arranged in descending order of CPU usage. The program also shows other information such as memory and swap space usage. Figure 28-1 shows typical output from the top program.

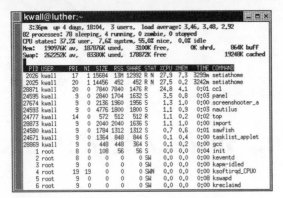

Figure 28-1   *Viewing top CPU processes*

The top utility updates the display every five seconds. You can keep top running in a window so that you can monitor the status of your Red Hat Linux system continuously. You quit top by pressing q or by closing the terminal window.

The first five lines of the output screen provide summary information about the system. Here is what these five lines show:

1. The first line shows the current time, how long the system has been up, how many users are logged in, and three *load averages* (the average number of processes ready to run during the last 1, 5, and 15 minutes).

2. The second line lists the total number of processes and the status of these processes.

3. The third line shows *CPU usage* — what percentage of CPU time user processes employ, what percentage system (kernel) processes use, and what percentage of time the CPU is idle.

4. The fourth line shows how the physical memory is being used. This includes the total amount of memory, how much is used, how much is free, how much is shared, and how much is allocated to buffers for reading from disk, for instance.

5. The fifth line shows how the virtual memory or swap space is being used. This includes the total amount of swap space, how much is used, how much is free, and how much is cached.

In top's output screen (refer to Figure 28-1), the table below the summary information lists information about the current processes, arranged in decreasing order of CPU time usage. Type man top in a terminal window to learn the meanings of the column headings in the table that top displays.

If the RSS field is drastically smaller than the SIZE field for a process, it means that the process employs too little physical memory compared with what it needs. This means that the process is doing a lot of swapping as it runs. You can use the vmstat utility (which you try later in this session) to find out how much your system is swapping.

Using the GNOME System Monitor

**20 Min.
To Go**

Like the text-mode top utility, the *GNOME System Monitor* tool also enables you to view the system load in terms of the number of processes that are currently running, their memory usage, and the free disk space on your system. To run the tool, select Main Menu ⇨ Programs ⇨ Systems ⇨ System Monitor. You can also start the tool by typing gtop in a terminal window. The tool starts and displays its output in the Processes tab of its main window, as shown in Figure 28-2.

```
┌─ GNOME System Monitor ──────────────────── _ □ x ┐
│  File   View   Settings   Windows   Help           │
│  ⊘   ⊘                                              │
│ ┌Processes (all)┐┌Memory Usage (resident)┐┌Filesystems (free)┐ │
│ ┌CPU─────┐    ┌MEM─┐      ┌SW─┐      ┌LA────┐ │
│ │PID   User   Pri  Size  Resident Stat  CPU   MEM   Time ▽        Cmd      │▲│
│  2026 kwall   16  15732   14140  R N  44.6  7.4    2d  ./setiathome       │
│  2025 kwall   17  14460    3640  R N  45.0  1.9    2d  ./setiathome       │
│   676 root     8    188       4  S     0.0  0.0  10.43s /usr/sbin/sshd    │
│     5 root     9      0       0  SW    0.0  0.0   8.26s kswapd            │
│    17 root     9      0       0  SW    0.0  0.0   5.47s kjournald         │
│ 32088 kwall   14   4396    4396  R     4.6  2.3   5.12s gtop              │
│ 24596 kwall    9   4108    3476  S     2.0  1.8   4.55s panel             │
│     1 root     8    108      56  S     0.0  0.0   4.09s init              │
│ 24593 kwall    9   4796    1872  S     0.0  0.9   4.00s nautilus          │
│ 24580 kwall    9   2580    2444  S     0.6  1.2   3.23s sawfish           │
│     8 root     9      0       0  SW    0.0  0.0   2.60s kupdated          │
│   814 root     9    496     292  S     0.0  0.1   1.90s nmbd              │
│   520 root     9     96       4  S     0.0  0.0   1.62s syslogd           │
│   881 gdm      9   1296     860  S     0.0  0.4   1.55s /usr/bin/gdmlogin │
│   874 root     9  54040     328  SW    0.0  0.0   1.53s /etc/X11/X        │
│ 24005 kwall    9   1740     736  S     0.0  0.3   1.17s gnome-session     │
│ 24671 kwall    9   2072    1576  S     0.0  0.8   0.86s tasklist_applet   │
│ 24673 kwall    9   1528     980  S     0.3  0.5   0.70s deskguide_applet  │
│  8909 root     9    636       4  S     0.0  0.0   0.61s smbd              │
│ 24468 kwall    9    552     328  S     0.0  0.1   0.58s gnome-smproxy     │
│ 27674 kwall    9   1420     928  S     0.3  0.4   0.58s screenshooter_applet │▼│
│ ┌CPU: 6.37% user,  6.37% system┐ ┌3:41pm, up 4 days┐ ┌loadavg: 2.17, 2.86, 2.84┐ │
└────────────────────────────────────────────────────┘
```

Figure 28-2 *Viewing current processes in the GNOME System Monitor window*

This output resembles what you see when you type top in a text-mode console or a terminal window. In fact, the column headings in the table match what the top utility uses in its output. As with the text-mode top utility, the display keeps updating to reflect the current state of the system. You see the current processes in descending order of CPU usage.

The GNOME System Monitor window has two more tabs that display the memory usage and the free space on the file system. To view this information, click the appropriate tab. For example, to see how various processes are using memory, click the Memory Usage tab.

The bottom of the window shows the CPU usage summary, system up time (how long the system has been up and running), and load averages (the average number of processes ready to run in the last 1, 5, and 15 minutes).

The load average gives you an indication of how busy the system is. In addition to the top and GNOME System Monitor programs, you can also get the load average with the uptime command, as follows:

```
uptime
 11:40am  up 2 days, 57 min,  3 users,  load average: 0.13, 0.23, 0.27
```

The output shows the current time, how long the system has been up, the number of users, and the three load averages. Load averages greater than 1 imply that multiple processes are competing for the CPU time simultaneously.

Using the vmstat Utility

You can get summary information about the overall system usage with the vmstat utility. To view system usage information averaged over five-second intervals, type the following command (the second argument indicates the total number of lines of output vmstat should display):

```
vmstat 5 8
   procs                     memory      swap        io    system      cpu
 r  b  w  swpd  free  buff  cache  si  so   bi  bo   in   cs  us  sy  id
 1  0  0  4724  1620  3420  18244   0   0    2   0  129  736  27   5  68
 3  0  0  4724  2068  3420  18244   0   0    0   2  124  179   3   8  89
 0  0  0  4724  2052  3420  18244   0   0    0   2  125  301  57  13  30
 0  0  0  4724  2124  3420  18232   0   0    0   3  134  213   6   8  86
 0  0  0  4724  1980  3416  18064   0   0    4   4  182  363  54  15  31
 2  0  0  4724  1960  3416  18064   0   0    0   4  142  126  13   7  80
 0  0  0  4724  1960  3416  18064   0   0    0   3  132  183   7   9  84
 0  0  0  4724  1948  3416  18076   0   0    0   1  112   90   7   8  86
```

The tabular output is grouped into six categories of information, as indicated by the fields in the first line of output. The second line shows categories for each of the six major fields. Table 28-1 interprets the six fields and their categories.

Table 28-1   *Fields Displayed in vmstat*

Field Name	Description
procs	Number of processes and their types: r = processes waiting to run; b = processes in uninterruptible sleep; w = processes swapped out, but ready to run.
memory	Information about physical memory and swap space usage (all numbers in kilobytes): swpd = virtual memory used; free = free physical memory; buff = memory used as buffers; cache = cached virtual memory.
swap	Amount of swapping (all numbers in kilobytes per second): si = amount of memory swapped in from disk; so = amount of memory swapped to disk.
io	Information about input and output (all numbers in blocks per second in which the block size depends on the disk device): bi = rate of blocks sent to disk; bo = rate of blocks received from disk.
system	Information about the system: in = number of interrupts per second (including clock interrupts); cs = number of context switches per second — the number of times the kernel changes the running process.
cpu	Percentages of CPU time used: us = percentage of CPU time used by user processes; sy = percentage of CPU time used by system processes; id = percentage of time CPU is idle.

The first line of output following the two header lines shows the averages since the last reboot. After that, vmstat displays the five-second average data seven more times over the next 35 seconds. In the vmstat utility's output, high values in the si and so fields indicate too much swapping. High numbers in the bi and bo fields indicate too much disk activity.

**All of the system performance monitoring tools you have looked at so far —
top, gtop, and** vmstat **— impose a performance penalty when running, which
means that actual performance is slightly better than the values these utilities report.**

Checking Disk Performance and Disk Usage

Red Hat Linux comes with the /sbin/hdparm program that you can use to check disk performance and usage. It controls the Integrated Drive Electronics (IDE) or Advanced Technology Attachment Package Interface (ATAPI) hard disks that are common on most PCs. One feature of the hdparm program is that the -t option enables you to determine the rate at which data can be read from the disk into a buffer in memory. For example, here's the result of this command on a sample system:

```
/sbin/hdparm -t /dev/hda

/dev/hda:
 Timing buffered disk reads:  64 MB in 15.18 seconds =  4.22 MB/sec
```

As you can see, the command requires the IDE drive's device name (/dev/hda) as an argument. If you have an IDE hard disk, you can try this command to see how fast data can be read from your system's disk drive.

To display the space available in the currently mounted file systems, use the df command. If you want a more human-readable output from df, type the following command:

```
df -h
Filesystem          Size  Used Avail Use% Mounted on
/dev/hda2           1.9G  1.1G  765M  59% /
/dev/hda1           2.0G  1.8G  256M  88% /dosc
```

As this example shows, the -h option causes the df command to show the sizes in gigabytes (G) and megabytes (M).

To check the disk space a specific directory uses, employ the du command. You can specify the -h option to view the output in kilobytes (K) and megabytes (M), as shown in the following example:

```
du -h /var/log
12k     /var/log/httpd
4.0k    /var/log/news/OLD
8.0k    /var/log/news
4.0k    /var/log/vbox
20k     /var/log/samba
4.0k    /var/log/sa
576k    /var/log
```

The du command displays the disk space used by each directory and the last line shows the total disk space used by that directory. If you want to see only the total space used by a directory, type the -s option like this:

```
du -sh /home
16M     /home
```

Exploring the /proc File System

10 Min.
To Go

You can find out a great deal about your Red Hat Linux system by consulting the contents of a special file system known as the /proc (also called the *process file system*) file system. It can help you monitor a wide variety of information about your system. In fact, you can even change kernel parameters through the /proc file system and thereby modify the system's behavior.

The /proc file system is not a real directory on the disk, but a collection of data structures in memory managed by the Linux kernel and stored in memory. The /proc file system is considered a *virtual file system* because it does not really exist on disk, only in memory, and simply appears to the user as a set of directories and files.

You can access the /proc file system and navigate it just as you do any other directory, but you have to know the meaning of various files to interpret the information. Typically, you can use the cat or more command to view the contents of a file in /proc; the file's contents provide information about some aspect of the system.

As with any directory, you may want to start by looking at a detailed directory listing of /proc. To do so, type ls -l /proc. In the output, the first set of directories (indicated by the letter d at the beginning of the line) represents the processes that are currently running on your system. Each directory that corresponds to a process has the process ID number as its name.

You should also notice a very large file in the listing named /proc/kcore, which represents the entire physical memory of your system. There is no physical file occupying that much space on your hard disk, so do not try to remove the file to reclaim disk space.

The /proc/cpuinfo file in /proc lists the key characteristics of your system's CPU, such as its type, speed, and (on Intel CPUs) whether or not it suffers from one of several known CPU bugs. You can view the processor information by typing cat /proc/cpuinfo. For example, here is what results after typing this command on a sample system:

```
cat /proc/cpuinfo
processor       : 0
vendor_id       : GenuineIntel
cpu family      : 5
model           : 4
model name      : Pentium MMX
stepping        : 3
cpu MHz         : 199.616468
fdiv_bug        : no
hlt_bug         : no
```

```
sep_bug         : no
f00f_bug        : yes
fpu             : yes
fpu_exception   : yes
cpuid level     : 1
wp              : yes
flags           : fpu vme de pse tsc msr mce cx8 mmx
bogomips        : 398.13
```

This output is from a 200MHz Pentium MMX system. The listing shows many interesting characteristics of the processor. Notice the line that starts with fdiv_bug. Remember Intel's infamous Pentium floating-point division bug? The bug is in an instruction called fdiv (for floating-point division). Thus, the fdiv_bug line indicates whether this particular Pentium has the bug. Fortunately, it does not.

The last line in the /proc/cpuinfo file shows the BogoMips for the processor, as computed by the Linux kernel when it boots. The BogoMips value is a measure of CPU speed that Linux uses internally to calibrate time delay loops but that has no real meaning in terms of comparisons between CPUs of different speeds or between different systems.

Table 28-2 summarizes some of the files in the /proc file system from which you can get information about your Red Hat Linux system. You can view some of these files on your system to see what they contain.

 Not all the files shown in Table 28-2 are present on your system. The contents of the /proc file system depends on the kernel configuration and the loaded driver modules (which, in turn, depend on your PC's hardware configuration).

Table 28-2   *Some Files and Directories in /proc*

Filename	Contents
/proc/apm	Information about advanced power management (APM).
/proc/bus	Directory with bus-specific information for each bus type, such as PCI.
/proc/cmdline	The command line used to start the Linux kernel (for example, auto BOOT_IMAGE=linux ro root=303).
/proc/cpuinfo	Information about the CPU (the microprocessor).
/proc/devices	Available block and character devices in your system.
/proc/dma	Information about DMA (direct memory access) channels in use.
/proc/filesystems	List of supported file systems.
/proc/ide	Directory containing information about IDE devices.

(continued)

Table 28-2 *Continued*

Filename	Contents
/proc/interrupts	Information about interrupt request (IRQ) numbers and how they are used.
/proc/ioports	Information about input/output (I/O) port addresses and how they are used.
/proc/kcore	Image of the physical memory.
/proc/kmsg	Kernel messages.
/proc/ksyms	Kernel symbol table.
/proc/loadavg	Load average (average number of processes waiting to run in the last 1, 5, and 15 minutes).
/proc/locks	Current kernel locks, which are used to ensure that multiple processes do not write to a file at the same time.
/proc/meminfo	Information about physical memory and swap space usage.
/proc/misc	Miscellaneous information.
/proc/modules	List of loaded driver modules.
/proc/mounts	List of mounted file systems.
/proc/net	Directory with many subdirectories that contain information about networking.
/proc/partitions	List of partitions known to the Linux kernel.
/proc/pci	Information about Peripheral Component Interconnect (PCI) devices found on the system.
/proc/rtc	Information about the PC's real-time clock (RTC).
/proc/scsi	Directory with information about Small Computer System Interface (SCSI) devices found on the system.
/proc/sound	Information about the sound driver module, if any.
/proc/stat	Overall statistics about the system.
/proc/swaps	Information about the swap space and how much is used.
/proc/sys	Directory with information about the system. You can change kernel parameters by writing to files in this directory. This is one way to tune the system's performance, but one that requires expertise to do it properly.

Filename	Contents
/proc/uptime	Information about how long the system has been up.
/proc/version	Kernel version number.

Troubleshooting

In rare cases, top, gtop, or vmstat may not work. This usually happens when the /proc file system is not mounted because all three utilities use some of the files in /proc to display their reports. If this happens, reboot your system after shutting it down properly, of course.

If you are having trouble viewing a file in /proc, it may be because you do not have read permissions on the file. Not all files in the /proc file system are world-readable, so use su to become the root user before looking at the file.

Similarly, disk usage statistics from the du command require read access to files and execute permissions for directories. If you try to use du on directories or files to which you do not have access, you will get an error message and the report it displays will not be accurate. Again, become the root user using the su command to solve the problem.

Finally, if hdparm does not seem to be working, keep in mind that it requires root access because it accesses hardware directly.

Done!

REVIEW

This session showed you how to keep an eye on your Red Hat Linux system's performance. You learned how to use and interpret the displays produced by top, the GNOME System Monitor, vmstat, and the uptime command. You also learned some commands to check the available disk space as well as your hard disk's performance. Finally, you explored the /proc file system that contains an extensive amount of information about the system.

QUIZ YOURSELF

1. What does the top utility do? (See "Using the top Utility.")
2. How do you start the GNOME System Monitor? (See "Using the GNOME System Monitor.")
3. What information does the vmstat utility provide? (See "Using the vmstat Utility.")
4. Which program can you run to check the speed at which data can be read from your IDE hard disk? (See "Checking Disk Performance and Disk Usage.")
5. What command do you use to view information about interrupt requests (IRQs) from the /proc file system? (See "Exploring the /proc File System.")

Maintaining System Security

Session Checklist

✔ Establishing a security policy

✔ Securing your system

✔ Monitoring system security

**30 Min.
To Go**

As a system administrator, you have to worry about your Linux system's security. For a stand-alone system or a system used in an isolated local area network (LAN), you must ensure that a user does not intentionally or inadvertently modify, delete, or destroy system files. If your Linux system is connected to the Internet, you must also secure the system from unwanted accesses. Intruders, also known as *crackers*, typically impersonate a user, steal or destroy information, and even deny you access to your own system (known as *denial of service*). This session only briefly covers some key aspects of securing your Linux system. As you'll see, Red Hat Linux already includes the tools you need to maintain system security.

To learn more about Linux security, consult the *Linux Security HOWTO* at http://metalab.unc.edu/pub/Linux/docs/HOWTO/Security-HOWTO. **Another good resource is the *Linux Administrator's Security Guide*, which you can read online at** http://www.securityportal.com/lasg/.

Establishing a Security Policy

The first step in securing your Linux system is to set up a security policy. A *security policy* establishes the principles and rules that determine what you enable users (as well as visitors over the Internet) to do on the Linux system. The level of security depends on how you use the Linux system and how much is at risk if someone gains unauthorized access to your system.

If you are a system administrator for Linux systems at an organization of any sort, you probably want to involve the management as well as the users in setting up the security policy. Obviously, you cannot create such an imposing policy that no one can do any work on the system. On the other hand, if the users are creating or using data that's valuable to the organization, you have to set up a policy that aims to protect the data from disclosure to outsiders. In other words, the security policy should strike a balance between the users' needs and the necessity of protecting the system.

For a stand-alone Linux system or a home system that you occasionally connect to the Internet, the security policy can be just a listing of the Internet services that you want to run on the system and the user accounts you plan to set up on the system. For any larger organization, you probably have one or more Linux systems on a LAN connected to the Internet, preferably through a *firewall*, which is a device that controls the flow of Internet Protocol (IP) packets between the LAN and the Internet. These days, with the widening availability of broadband Internet access for home users (typically through DSL or cable service), home users should also consider using a firewall. In these cases, the security policy typically addresses the following areas:

- *Authentication*: Who gets access to the system? What is the minimum length and complexity of passwords? How often must you change passwords? How long can a user be idle before that user is logged out automatically?

- *Authorization*: What can different classes of users do on the system? Who can have the root password?

- *Data Protection*: What data has to be protected? Who has access to the data?

- *Internet Access*: What are the restrictions on users (from the LAN) accessing the Internet? What Internet services (such as access to the Web, Internet Relay Chat (IRC), and so on) can the users access? Are incoming e-mails and attachments scanned for viruses? Is there a network firewall?

- *Internet Services*: What Internet services are allowed on each Linux system? Are there any file servers? Mail servers? Web servers? What services run on each type of server? What services, if any, run on Linux systems used as desktop workstations?

- *Responsibilities*: Who is responsible for maintaining security? Who monitors log files and any audit trails for signs of unauthorized access? If any security breach occurs, who must be informed?

- *Security Audits*: Who tests whether the security is adequate? How often is the security tested? How are problems found during security testing handled?

The remainder of this session shows you some of the ways in which you can enhance and maintain the security of your Red Hat Linux system.

Securing the System

Once you have a security policy defined, you can proceed to secure the system according to the policy. The exact steps depend on what you want to do with the system, whether it is a server or a workstation, and how many users must access the system. The general steps for securing the system and maintaining the security are as follows:

- Select only those package groups that you need for your system when installing Red Had Linux. Do not install any unnecessary software. For example, if your system is a workstation, you do not need to install most of the server packages, such as the Web server, news server, e-mail server, and so on.

- Create initial user accounts and make sure that all passwords are strong ones that password-cracking programs cannot guess. As you will learn in the next section, "Securing Passwords," Red Hat Linux includes the tools to enforce strong passwords.

- Enable only those Internet services that you need on a system. In particular, do not enable services that are not properly configured. Later in this session, in the section titled "Securing Internet Services," you learn about enabling and disabling Internet services.

- Check various log files periodically for signs of any break-ins or attempted break-ins. These log files are in the /var/log directory of your system.

- Check security news by regularly visiting and installing updates from Red Hat once a fix becomes available.

Securing passwords

Historically, UNIX passwords were stored in the /etc/passwd file, which any user could read. For example, a typical old-style /etc/passwd file entry for the root user looks like this:

```
root:t6Z7NWDK1K8sU:0:0:root:/root:/bin/bash
```

The fields are separated by colons (:) and the second field contains the password in encrypted form. To check if a password is valid, the login program encrypts the plain-text password entered by the user and compares it with the contents of the /etc/passwd file. If there is a match, the user is allowed to log in.

Password-cracking programs work just like the login program except that these programs pick one word at a time from a dictionary, encrypt the word, and compare the encrypted word with the encrypted passwords in the /etc/passwd file for a match. To crack the passwords, the intruder needs the /etc/passwd file. Often, crackers use weaknesses of various Internet servers (such as mail and FTP) to get a copy of the /etc/passwd file.

Recently, several improvements have been made to UNIX passwords to make them more secure. These include shadow passwords and pluggable authentication modules, described in the next two sections.

 Red Hat Linux includes password security enhancements that you can use by selecting them during installation. In Session 1, as you completed the Red Hat Linux installation, one step involved selecting authentication options. If you accepted the default selections, Enable MD5 passwords **and** Enable shadow passwords, **you automatically enabled more secure passwords in Red Hat Linux.**

Shadow passwords

Instead of storing the passwords in the /etc/passwd file, which any user can read, passwords are now stored in a shadow password file. On Red Hat Linux, the shadow passwords are in the /etc/shadow file. Only the super user (root) can read this file. For example, here is the entry for root in the new-style /etc/passwd file:

```
root:x:0:0:root:/root:/bin/bash
```

As you can see, the second field contains an x instead of an encrypted password. The encrypted password is now stored in the /etc/shadow file where the entry for root is like this:

```
root:$1$AAAni/yN$uESHbzUpy9Cgfoo1Bf0tSO:11077:0:99999:7:-1:-1:134540356
```

The format of the /etc/shadow entries with colon-separated fields resembles the entries in the /etc/passwd file, but the meanings of many fields differ. The first field is still the user name and the second one is the encrypted password.

The remaining fields in each /etc/shadow entry control when the password expires. You do not need to interpret or change these entries in the /etc/shadow file. Instead, you should use the chage command to change the password expiration information. For starters, you can check a user's password expiration information by using the chage command with the -l option as follows (in this case, you have to be logged in as root):

```
chage -l root
Minimum:              0
Maximum:              99999
Warning:              7
Inactive:             -1
Last Change:                   June 18, 2001
Password Expires:              Never
Password Inactive:             Never
Account Expires:               Never
```

In this case, the output shows various expiration information: you can change the root password any time — that's what zero minimum time means. The root password lasts for 99,999 days, and the root user gets a warning seven days before the password expires.

If you want to ensure that the password changes every 90 days, you can use chage's -M option to set the maximum number of days the password stays valid. For example, to make sure that user kwall is prompted to change the password in 90 days, you would log in as root and type the following command:

```
chage -M 90 kwall
```

You can do this for each user account to ensure that all passwords expire and all users must pick new passwords.

Pluggable Authentication Modules

In addition to improving the password file's security by using the shadow passwords, Red Hat Linux also enhances the actual encryption of the passwords stored in the /etc/shadow file. Password encryption is now done using the MD5 message-digest algorithm to convert the plain-text password into a 128-bit *fingerprint* or *digest*. The MD5 algorithm, described in RFC1321 (http://www.faqs.org/rfcs/rfc1321.html), compresses a large file in a secure manner so that you can sign in digitally through encryption with a private key. It works quite effectively for password encryption as well.

Another advantage of MD5 over the older-style password encryption is that the older passwords were limited to a maximum of eight characters in length; new passwords (encrypted with MD5) can be much longer, currently up to 255 characters.. Longer passwords are harder to guess even if the /etc/shadow file falls into the wrong hands.

A clue to the use of MD5 encryption in the /etc/shadow file is the increased length of the encrypted password and the 1 prefix, as in the second field of the following sample entry:

```
root:$1$AAAni/yN$uESHbzUpy9Cgfoo1BfOtSO:11077:0:99999:7:-1:-1:134540356
```

A Pluggable Authentication Module (PAM) performs the actual MD5 encryption. PAM provides a flexible method for authenticating users on Linux systems. Through settings in configuration files, you can change the authentication method on the fly without having to modify programs such as login and passwd, which verify a user's identity.

Red Hat Linux uses PAM extensively, and the configuration files are located in the /etc/pam.d directory of your system. Check out the contents of this directory on your system.

Securing Internet services

For an Internet-connected Linux system (or even one on a TCP/IP LAN), a significant threat is the possibility that someone will use one of many Internet services to gain access to your system. Each service — such as mail, access to the Web, or FTP — requires running a server program that responds to client requests arriving over the TCP/IP network. Some of these server programs have weaknesses that can allow an outsider to log into your system — maybe with root privileges. Luckily, Red Hat Linux comes with some facilities that you can use to make these Internet services more secure.

Potential intruders often employ port scanners to identify potential weaknesses. A *port scanner* is a tool that attempts to establish a TCP/IP connection on a specific port and look for a response. A response on a given port indicates that an Internet server is running on your system. Then the intruder can attempt to attack any known weaknesses of that server in order to gain access to your system.

Disabling Internet services

To avoid opening up unnecessary entry points into your system and to close existing ones, make sure that you run only those Internet services that you need. You can enable and disable the services directly by changing the permissions of the files in the /etc/rc.d/init.d directory.

To disable a service, first make sure it is not currently running and then remove the execute permissions from the script. For example, suppose that you want to disable the Web server, which is controlled by the /etc/rc.d/init.d/httpd script. First, make /etc/rc.d/init.d your current directory by typing cd /etc/rc.d/init.d and pressing

Enter. Next, stop the service by invoking the script with an argument of stop. To shut down the httpd service, then, execute the following command:

```
./httpd stop
```

Finally, use the chmod command to remove the execute permissions. This step will prevent the script from executing when the system is booted. To disable the Web server, execute the following command:

```
chmod a-x httpd
```

You can perform a similar procedure for other unnecessary services.

xinetd server

In addition to the stand-alone servers such as Web server (httpd), mail (sendmail), and Domain Name Server, or DNS (named), you have to configure another server separately. That other server, xinetd, called the Internet super server, starts a number of other Internet services such as FTP, Telnet, and so on. Here, you briefly look at the security aspects of the xinetd server.

The xinetd server reads a configuration file named /etc/xinetd.conf at startup. This file, in turn, refers to configuration files stored in the /etc/xinetd.d directory. The configuration files in /etc/xinetd.d tell xinetd which ports to listen and which server to start for each port. You can browse through the files in /etc/xinetd.d directory on your system to find out the kinds of services that xinetd is set up to start. Some of these services provide information that intruders may use to break into your system. You should turn off these services by placing a diasble = yes line in that service's configuration file.

 To learn more about the xinetd **configuration files, type** man xinetd.conf **at the shell prompt in a terminal window.**

Depending on what you need on your system, you may want to disable everything but the ftp and telnet services. After making any changes to the xinetd configuration files, you must restart the xinetd server by typing the following command:

```
/etc/rc.d/init.d/xinetd restart
Stopping xinetd: [  OK  ]
Starting xinetd: [  OK  ]
```

Another security feature of xinetd is its use of the TCP wrapper facility to start various services. The TCP wrapper provides an access control facility for Internet services. The TCP wrapper can start other services such as FTP and Telnet; but before starting the service, it consults the /etc/hosts.allow file to see if the host requesting service is allowed access. If nothing appears in /etc/hosts.allow about that host, the TCP wrapper checks the /etc/hosts.deny file to see if it should deny the service. If both files are empty, the TCP wrapper allows the host to access the requested service.

The ftp **and** telnet **services are potential security holes. They transmit passwords as clear, unencrypted text, so someone using the right tool can intercept passwords transmitted over the network. For this reason, never use** ftp **or** telnet **to log into a system as the** root **user.**

You can place the line ALL:ALL in the /etc/hosts.deny file to deny all hosts access to any Internet services on your system. Then you can add to /etc/hosts.allow the names of those hosts that can access services on your system. For example, to allow only hosts from the 192.168.1.0 network to access services on your system, place the following line in the /etc/hosts.allow file:

ALL: 192.168.1.0/255.255.255.0

If you want to permit access to a specific Internet service to a specific remote host, you can do so using the following syntax for a line:

server_program_name: hosts

Here *server_program_name* is the name of the server program (for example, in.telnetd for Telnet and in.ftpd for FTP), and *hosts* is a comma-separated list of hosts allowed to access the service. The *hosts* list can also take the form of a network address or an entire domain name such as .mycompany.com. For example, here's how you can allow Telnet access to all systems in the mycompany.com domain:

in.telnetd: .mycompany.com

Monitoring System Security

10 Min.
To Go

After you set up your system's security, you have to monitor the log files periodically for any signs of intrusion. You should also periodically check security news to learn about recently discovered weaknesses in any of your system components (such as mail server or Web server). If Red Hat provides an upgrade to fix a security problem, download the new RPM files and install them on your system.

Follow the steps covered in Session 23 to download the new RPM files and install them. If you chose to use the Red Hat Network, discussed in Session 20, you will automatically be notified when security and system updates become available.

Log files

Many Linux system applications, including some servers, write log information using the logging capabilities of syslogd. On Red Hat Linux systems, the log files written by syslogd reside in the /var/log directory. Make sure that only the root user can read and write these files.

You should routinely monitor the following log files:

- /var/log/messages contains a wide variety of logging messages from user logins to messages from services started by the TCP wrapper.
- /var/log/secure contains reports from services such as in.telnetd and in.ftpd that the TCP wrapper starts.
- /var/log/maillog contains reports from sendmail.
- /var/log/xferlog contains a log of all FTP file transfers.

Unfortunately, there is no easy-to-use tool for viewing these log files. The best approach is to browse them routinely using a text file viewer such as less or more to prevent accidentally overwriting one of the log files. Using less or more, you can search for a date of interest and begin browsing from that point in the file.

Because many potential intruders use port-scanning tools that attempt to establish TCP/IP connections to well-known ports on your system, you should look for messages that indicate attempted connections from unknown hosts (indicated by names or IP addresses). For such attempted network accesses, you should browse through the /var/log/secure file. For example, here's what a line in the /var/log/secure file shows when connecting to a sample Linux system from one of the PCs on a LAN:

```
Aug 16 20:18:19 lnbp200 xinetd[511]: START: ftp pid=23824 from=192.168.1.40
```

Notice the text pid=23824, which appears next to the word ftp. That's the process ID of the FTP server program started by xinetd. You can use this number to look at corresponding messages in the /var/log/messages file to see whether this attempt did or did not succeed. Here is a sample of how you could check this:

```
grep "\[23824\]" messages
Aug 16 20:30:01 lnbp200 ftpd[23824]: FTP LOGIN FROM lnbp400 [192.168.1.40], naba
Aug 16 20:30:22 lnbp200 ftpd[23824]: FTP session closed
```

The resulting output tells you that the user naba successfully logged in and sometime later closed the FTP session.

To identify the host name associated with an address, use the command dig -x *ipaddress*, **where** *ipaddress* **is the IP address in which you are interested.**

In a similar manner, you should analyze any suspicious messages you find in these log files. You may be surprised by the number of attempts curious outsiders make to gain access to your system.

Security news and updates

To keep up with the latest security alerts, you may want to visit one or more of the following sites on a daily basis:

- CERT Coordination Center at http://www.cert.org/
- Computer Incident Advisory Capability (CIAC) at http://www.ciac.org/

- National Infrastructure Protection Center at http://www.nipc.gov/

If you have access to Internet newsgroups, you can periodically browse the following ones:

- news://comp.security.announce is a moderated newsgroup that includes announcements from CERT about security.
- news://comp.security.unix includes discussions of UNIX security issues, including items related to Red Hat Linux.

If you prefer to receive regular security updates through e-mail, you can also sign up on, or subscribe to, various mailing lists:

- redhat-watch-list@redhat.com: Send an e-mail message to redhat-watch-list-req@redhat.com with the word *subscribe* in the Subject line.
- linux-security@redhat.com: Send an e-mail message to linux-security-sub@redhat.com with the word subscribe in the Subject line.
- FOCUS-LINUX: Fill out the form at http://www.securityfocus.com/focus/linux/list/subscribe.html to subscribe to this mailing list focused on Linux security issues.
- Cert Advisory mailing list: Send an e-mail message to cert-advisory-request@cert.org with SUBSCRIBE *myname@myisp.com* in the Subject line. Replace *myname@myisp.com* with your e-mail address.

Finally, you should check Red Hat's Web site at http://www.redhat.com/support/errata/ for updates that might fix any known security problems with Red Hat Linux.

Troubleshooting

If a service controlled by xinetd does not stop after you have disabled it, try using the command /etc/rc.d/init.d/xinetd reload to force xinetd to reread its configuration files and detect any changes.

If you directly edit the password file, /etc/passwd, to add a new user account, the shadow password system will not detect the change. To update the shadow password file with the new account, execute the commands pwconv and pwck. pwconv converts the /etc/passwd file to /etc/shadow, and pwck makes sure that all of the accounts in /etc/passwd have corresponding entries in /etc/shadow.

If, heaven forbid, you discover that someone has obtained unauthorized access to your system by cracking it, immediately disconnect it from the Internet or the LAN, as the case may be, by disconnecting the network cabling. Then use the information at the Web sites listed in the previous section to identify the extent of the compromise and to repair any damage done. Do not reconnect to the network until you are confident that you have solved the problem.

Done!

REVIEW

This session introduced you to the subject of security for your Red Hat Linux system. You learned the importance of establishing a security policy for a medium to large organization. Next, this session showed you how to secure two key elements — the passwords and the network services — on your Linux system. Finally, this session included a discussion of how to review log files for signs of intrusion attempts and how to keep up with any late-breaking security news. Because this session could not cover many security topics, it provided you with some additional online resources from which you can learn more about securing your Red Hat Linux system.

QUIZ YOURSELF

1. Why should you set up a security policy? (See "Establishing a Security Policy.")
2. What are shadow passwords? (See "Shadow passwords.")
3. What does MD5 refer to? (See "Pluggable Authentication Modules.")
4. Why should you secure Internet services? (See "Securing Internet services.")
5. Which log files should you review periodically for signs of intrusion attempts? (See "Monitoring System Security.")

Getting Help from Available Resources

Session Checklist

✔ Using the help viewers

✔ Using the commands

✔ Looking up online HOWTO files

✔ Accessing other Linux resources

**30 Min.
To Go**

By now you have learned a lot about Red Hat Linux, but there is much more that this book cannot cover because of time constraints. To make sure that you can find help when you need it, this final session of the weekend introduces you to a wide variety of Linux resources that provide more information if you are experiencing a problem with a particular topic or with Red Hat Linux in general. Some of the help is available right on your system, but you can find many more resources on the Internet.

Using the Help Viewers

Both GNOME and KDE desktops come with help viewers — the GNOME Help Browser and KDE Help — that enable you to view online help information.

GNOME Help Browser

From the GNOME desktop, select Main Menu ⇨ Programs ⇨ Help System or click the question mark icon on the GNOME Panel to launch the GNOME Help Browser. The *GNOME Help Browser* provides a Web browser-like graphical interface. It allows you to access various forms of documentation available on your Red Hat Linux system and on the Internet. The initial screen of the GNOME Help Browser organizes the help information into several categories:

- *GNOME User's Guide* is a hyperlink to help information on how to use the GNOME desktop.
- *GNOME Documents* is a link that provides access to documentation on some GNOME applications and games.
- *Man Pages link* refers to the online manual pages (called *man pages* for short).
- *Info Pages link* refers to online documentation for the GNU utilities (mostly software development tools).

Typically, you look for help in the man pages. To view a table of contents of the available man pages, click the Man Pages link. The table of contents is organized by categories and alphabetically within each category. You can jump to a category by clicking a link in the category list at the beginning of the page. For example, clicking Administration takes you to the system administration commands. You can then scroll down in that category and click a command for which you want more help. You should explore the table of contents of the man pages and view other man pages that interest you.

You can also access Red Hat's Web site by clicking on the Red Hat icon on the GNOME desktop. The icon is labeled www.redhat.com. That probably gives you a clue that this is a link to Red Hat's Web site. Clicking on that icon causes Netscape Communicator to start and go to the URL http://www.redhat.com.

KDE Help

From the KDE desktop, you can start KDE Help by selecting K ⇨ KDE Help or by clicking the icon that shows a light bulb on a book. The KDE Help application uses Konqueror, a Web browser, as the user interface through which you can view online help information. When it starts, KDE Help shows a number of links organized into a number of categories. There are links to learn about KDE and obtain information about the KDE Project. Another set of links provides information that teaches you how to use and get the most out of KDE. A third set of links provide access to the man pages and GNU info pages, just as the GNOME Help Browser does. One of the links in the third set enables you to search for online help using one or more keywords.

To look for a man page, click the link labeled System Man Page contents. This brings up the online man pages' table of contents, organized by sections such as User Commands, File Formats, and System Administration. Click on a section head to view the list of items in that section. You can then click on a specific item to read the man page for that item. For example, to learn more about the xinetd configuration files, select the section labeled File Formats. Then click on the link labeled xinetd.conf. KDE Help that displays the man page with information about the xinetd configuration file.

You can also access Red Hat's Web sites directly from the KDE desktop by clicking on one of three Red Hat icons labeled: www.redhat.com, Red Hat Errata, and Red Hat Support. Each of these icons is a link to a specific Red Hat Web site. For example, clicking on Red Hat Support takes you to the support.redhat.com Web site.

**20 Min.
To Go**

Using the Linux Commands to Get Help

Although it's convenient to browse help information through graphical help browsers, you often need help while typing Linux commands in a terminal window.

Another trick you should know is that most Linux commands have a help option. Typically, if you invoke the command with the --help option, the command prints some help information. At a minimum, this information includes the command-line options that the command accepts. Often the help information can span more than one screen, so you should pipe the output through more, as shown in the following example:

```
ls --help | more
```

You may vaguely recall a command's name, but you cannot remember the exact syntax of what you are supposed to type. This is a situation in which the man command can come to your rescue. With the man command, you can view the man page on a Linux command and then use that command correctly.

You do have to remember to use the man command to look up online help. For example, to view the man page for the modprobe command, type the following command in a terminal window:

```
man modprobe
```

The man command then displays the help information page by page. Press the spacebar to move to the next page. Press b to move backward by a page. To look for a specific word in the man page, press the forward slash (/), type the word, and press Enter. For example, to search for the word *debug*, type /debug and press Enter. When you finish reading the man page, press q to return to the Linux command prompt.

If you do not want to read the full man page, you can use whatis to read a one-line summary of a command. To use whatis, type whatis *command*, where *command* is the command you want to summarize. For example, here's how you use whatis to see a brief description of the modprobe command:

```
whatis modprobe
modprobe              (8)  - high level handling of loadable module
```

The parenthesized number (8) indicates the man page section where the modprobe command is listed. You should try the whatis command to view one-line descriptions of a few other commands.

You can use the shell's wildcard feature and the whatis command to explore the files in various system directories such as /bin, /sbin, /usr/sbin, /usr/bin, and so on. Simply change the directory to one of interest and type whatis * to view one-line descriptions of the programs in that directory. (The whatis command displays information for those programs for which such information is available.) For example, here is how you can explore the /sbin directory (the listing is shortened to save space):

```
cd /sbin; whatis * | more
arp                   (7)  - Linux ARP kernel module
arp                   (8)  - manipulate the system ARP cache
askrunlevel: nothing appropriate
badblocks             (8)  - search a device for bad blocks
```

```
cardctl              (8)  - PCMCIA card control utility
cardmgr              (8)  - PCMCIA device manager
```

As you can see, the output is an alphabetical list of all programs in the current directory, along with the one-line descriptions where available. The whatis command displays a message saying nothing appropriate if there is no information available for a program.

apropos command

The man and whatis commands are useful when you know the name of a command. If you do not know the exact name of a command, you can use the apropos command to search for a command by a keyword (even a part of a word). For example, if you remember the command contains the word probe, type the following apropos command to perform a search:

```
apropos probe
```

```
modprobe             (8)  - high level handling of loadable modules
pnpprobe             (8)  - scan ISA bus for PnP sound cards
SuperProbe          (1x)  - probe for and identify installed video hardware
```

In this case, the search result shows three candidate commands, each with a brief description. You can then select the command that does what you want it to do.

 If apropos **displays a long list of commands that scroll by too fast for you to read, you can type** apropos *keyword* | more **to view the output one screen at a time.**

Looking Up Online HOWTO Files

Another form of online documentation that you can refer to is the HOWTO file listing that you access by opening the URL http://www.redhat.com/mirrors/LDP/ in Netscape Communicator. The *LDP* in that URL refers to the *Linux Documentation Project* and on that Web page, you can find links to Frequently Asked Questions (FAQs) and HOWTOs. You can click the HOWTOs link and download (or read) HOWTO documents in several formats, including text and HTML format. For example, if you click to view text-format HOWTOs, the Web browser shows a list of over 170 HOWTO files (see Figure 30-1).

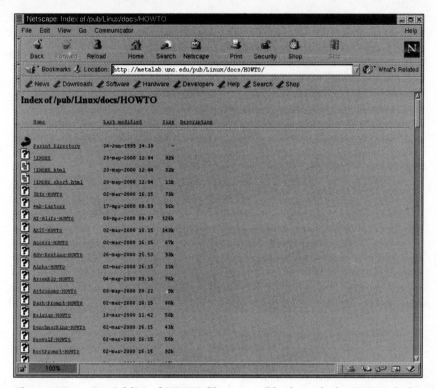

Figure 30-1 *Partial list of HOWTO files accessible through the GNOME desktop's LDP icon*

Each HOWTO file contains information about some area of Linux, such as how to configure hardware in Linux or how to create a boot disk. To view any of these HOWTO files, click the name and the Web browser loads the full text file. For example, Figure 30-2 shows the result of clicking the CD-Writing HOWTO, which explains how to record a CD using a CD-ROM recordable (CD-R) device installed in a Linux system.

You should browse through the list of HOWTO files (see Figure 30-1) and view one or more that interest you.

At the very end of the list of HOWTO files, you see a folder named mini. Click that link to view the list of mini-HOWTOs, which cover many more narrowly focused topics.

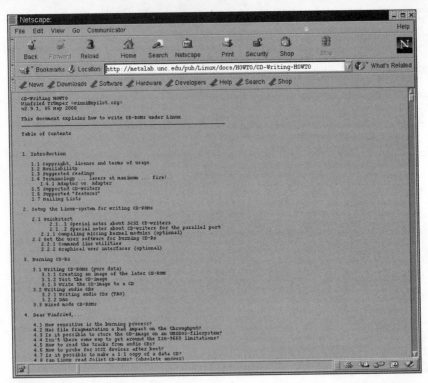

Figure 30-2 *Browsing the plain-text version of the CD-Writing HOWTO file*

Accessing Other Linux Resources

**10 Min.
To Go**

In addition to the online help just described, several other resources can provide more information on specific topics. Most of the resources are on the Internet because that's where you can get the latest information on Red Hat Linux and Linux in general. The rest of this session introduces you to some of these Linux resources. Instead of providing a long listing of URLs, the remaining sections include a few key Web sites that you can use as starting points for your search.

Web pages

If you browse the Internet, you may notice that there are quite a few Web pages with Linux-related information. A good starting point is the following Linux page at http://www.linux.org/. This page provides a starting point for locating information about Linux. You can click the buttons to access more information on the topic identified by that button's label. At this page, you'll also find an organized collection of links to Linux-related Web sites.

To browse recent news about Linux, visit the Linux Resources page at http://www.linuxresources.com/. Specialized Systems Consultants (SSC), Inc., the publisher of the *Linux Journal*, maintains this page. You can scan the articles in the latest issue of *Linux Journal* and find out other information such as the latest version of the kernel and links to other Linux resources.

Another popular and definitive source of Linux information is the home page of the Linux Documentation Project (LDP) at the following URL: http://www.linuxdoc.org/. On this Web site, you can find many more pointers to other Linux resources on the Internet. In particular, you can browse and download the latest HOWTO documents from http://metalab.unc.edu/pub/Linux/docs/HOWTO/.

For Red Hat Linux-specific questions, you can visit Red Hat's Support Web site at http://www.redhat.com/apps/support/. This Web site provides links such as Product Updates and Errata, Hardware Compatibility List, and Installation Guides and Manuals. In particular, you can find the manuals and FAQs at http://www.redhat.com/support/docs/howto/.

Internet newsgroups

To keep up with Linux developments, you need access to the Internet and especially to the newsgroups. You can find discussions on specific Linux-related topics in the newsgroups listed in Table 30-1.

Table 30-1 *Linux Newsgroups on the Internet*

Newsgroups	Topics
comp.os.linux.admin	Information about Linux system administration.
comp.os.linux.advocacy	Discussions about promoting Linux.
comp.os.linux.announce	Important announcements about Linux. This is a *moderated* newsgroup, which means you must mail the article to the moderator who then posts it to the newsgroup.
comp.os.linux.answers	Questions and answers about Linux. All the Linux HOWTOs are posted in this moderated newsgroup.
comp.os.linux.development	Current Linux development work.
comp.os.linux.development.apps	Linux application development.
comp.os.linux.development.system	Linux operating system development.
comp.os.linux.hardware	Discussions about Linux and various hardware.
comp.os.linux.help	Help with various aspects of Linux.
comp.os.linux.misc	Miscellaneous topics about Linux.
comp.os.linux.networking	Networking under Linux.
comp.os.linux.setup	Linux setup and installation.
comp.os.linux.x	Discussions about setting up and running the X Window System under Linux.

You can use Netscape Communicator to read the newsgroups. For a newsgroup, use a URL of the form news://*newsserver*/*newsgroup* in which *newsserver* is the fully qualified domain name (FQDN) of your news server (your Internet Service Provider should give you this name) and *newsgroup* is the name of the newsgroup you want to read. For example, assuming that your news server is *news.myisp.net*, you can browse the comp.os.linux.setup newsgroup by typing the following URL in the Location field of the Netscape Web browser:

    news://*news.myisp.net*/comp.os.linux.setup

FTP archive sites

You can download Red Hat Linux and other Linux distributions from one of several FTP sites around the world. In addition to the Linux distribution itself, these sites also contain many other software packages that run under Linux.

For the latest list of Red Hat Linux FTP sites worldwide, visit the Web page maintained by Red Hat at http://www.redhat.com/mirrors.html. This page displays a table of URLs of sites that maintain the Red Hat distribution for downloading. In that table, the Updates column lists the URLs for downloading specific Red Hat Package Manager (RPM) files for the latest Red Hat Linux version (for Intel-based PCs).

Red Hat provides many fixes and improvements as updates in the form of Red Hat Packages distributed from Red Hat's FTP server. Try ftp://ftp.redhat.com/pub/redhat/updates/; if it's busy, consult http://www.redhat.com/mirrors.html for a mirror site near you. To install these packages, you have to use the Red Hat Package Manager (RPM).

See Session 20 to learn how to use the Red Hat Network to keep your Red Hat Linux system current with the latest updates and security patches.

Magazines

Linux Journal is a monthly magazine devoted entirely to Linux. On the Web, the magazine home page is at http://www.linuxjournal.com/. There, you can find information on how to subscribe to this magazine.

Linux Magazine is another monthly magazine that covers everything Linux. Visit their home page at http://www.linux-mag.com/ to learn more about *Linux Magazine* and to subscribe to it.

Done!

REVIEW

This session showed you how to get help on various aspects of Red Hat Linux. You learned how to use the GNOME Help Browser and also how to use several helpful commands such as man, whatis, and apropos. Finally, you familiarized yourself with a number of Internet-based Linux resources from Web pages, to FTP archives, to two popular Linux magazines.

QUIZ YOURSELF

1. What types of help information can you view with the GNOME Help Browser? (See "Using the Help Viewers.")

2. What is man and what can you do with it? (See "Using the Help Viewers.")

3. How can you view a brief description of a command? (See "Using the Linux Commands to Get Help.")

4. How do you access the HOWTO files? (See "Looking Up Online HOWTO Files.")

5. What are some of the Linux newsgroups? (See "Internet newsgroups.")

PART

VI

Sunday Afternoon

1. Why should you learn how to build software from source code?

2. What is the most common format for source code distributed on the Internet? How do you download and unpack it?

3. After downloading a source code package from the Internet, what should you do next?

4. Briefly outline the steps to take, without giving specific command lines, to unpack, configure, build, and install a typical source code package.

5. What is the XMMS package? How would you build and install it after downloading and unpacking it?

6. Name some of the factors to which you should pay attention when monitoring your system's performance.

7. Name two tools that you can use to monitor system performance.

8. Give a short definition of "system load average."

9. Show the `vmstat` command line that displays its output 10 times in 60-second intervals.

10. What is the purpose of the `/proc` file system?

11. What is the purpose of a security policy and what are some of the areas that a security policy should address?

12. Briefly describe the procedure for securing your system.

13. Identify two ways Red Hat Linux helps you make your system more secure.

14. What command line forces the user named `marys` to change her password every 30 days?

15. What is `xinetd` and what purpose does it serve?

16. What package makes `xinetd` more secure?

17. Name the help-system viewers for the GNOME and KDE desktops and explain how to start them.

18. How do you view a one-line description of what the `tr` command does? How would you view the complete online help for the `tr` command?

19. What command can you use to search for commands that match a keyword?

20. What are `HOWTO` files and how can you access them from the GNOME desktop?

APPENDIX

Answers to Part Reviews

This appendix contains the answers to the part review questions at the end of each part in this Weekend Crash Course. Think of these reviews as mini-tests that are designed to help you prepare for the final — the Skills Assessment Test on the CD.

Friday Evening Review Answers

1. It is important to review the Red Hat Linux compatibility lists in order to make sure that your PC's hardware will work with it. At a bare minimum, you must have a Linux-compatible CPU, bus type, disk drive, video adapter, monitor, keyboard, mouse, and CD-ROM drive to install Red Hat Linux from the companion CD-ROMs. If you want to run the X Window System and graphical desktops such as GNOME or KDE, you also must ensure that XFree86 (the X Window System for Linux) supports the mouse, the video card, and the monitor.

2. It is not necessary to create a Red Hat boot floppy if your system is capable of booting from a CD-ROM because the installation CD-ROM has a bootable file system on it.

3. Usually a PC's hard disk has a single partition that is used by Windows 95/98. If you decide to keep Windows on your PC, you have to repartition the hard disk to create room for the Linux file system. It's possible to repartition in two ways: by backing up everything and destructively repartitioning the disk with the FDISK command or by using the FIPS program to non-destructively create room for a new partition. You probably want to use the FIPS program because it is easier than destructive repartitioning. You could also use tools such as PartitionMagic to create a new partition non-destructively for Linux.

4. The Linux fdisk utility is a text-mode disk partitioning utility that enables you to partition or repartition your hard disk during and after the Red Hat Linux installation program.

5. Linux uses the swap partition, or space, as virtual memory where disk storage is used as an extension of physical memory (RAM). When the Linux kernel runs out of physical memory to run a program, it can move (or swap out) the contents of currently unneeded parts of RAM to make room for a program that needs more

memory. As soon as the time comes to access anything in the swapped-out data, the Linux kernel has to find something else to swap out and then it swaps in the required data from disk into physical memory. You should set aside at least twice the amount of RAM in your PC, if possible.

6. You can add one or more normal users during Red Hat Linux installation. To add a user account, enter the user information in the Account Configuration screen and click the Add button to add the user.

7. A *package group* is a collection of several Red Hat packages. You can select individual packages from a package group by selecting the item labeled Select individual packages, that appears below the list of package groups in the Package Group Selection screen.

8. The Red Hat Linux installation program supports NFS installations and a Kickstart installation. NFS installation is ideal for allowing machines on a network to install Red Hat Linux without needing the CD-ROMs. The Kickstart installation makes it easy to install the same configuration on multiple machines without needing to intervene or monitor the installation.

9. The X Window configuration tool described in Session 2 is named Xconfigurator.

10. A monitor's vertical and horizontal refresh rates, or *synchronization frequencies*, are important because they define the maximum performance capabilities of the monitor. The *horizontal refresh rate* is the number of times per second that the monitor can display a horizontal raster line, usually expressed in kilohertz (kHz). The *vertical refresh rate* specifies how many times a second the monitor can display the entire screen. You can find the value of these parameters in your monitor's manual.

11. You could type the dmesg | grep par and look for any indication of parallel port information in the output.

12. Installation help is available in *The Official Red Hat Linux x86 Installation Guide*, *The Official Red Hat Linux Getting Started Guide*, the Red Hat Knowledge Base (http://www.redhat.com/apps/support/), and the Red Hat mailing list archives (http://www.redhat.com/apps/support/updates.html).

13. X Window handles the mechanics of drawing windows and communicating between an X client and the X server or another X client. It does nothing to decorate a window with pretty title bars, scrollbars, interpret mouse movement, keystrokes, and the like. However, X Window does provide a *protocol*, the rules or the general framework, that window managers must follow. *Window manager* creates title bars, scrollbars, menus, and so on, on the unadorned windows that X creates.

14. To log out of a GNOME session, select Main Menu (Foot) ⇨ Log Out. To log out of a KDE session, select K ⇨ Logout and then click the Logout button in the resulting dialog box.

15. If you forget the root password, reboot the system and then, at the LILO boot: prompt, type linux single and press Enter. Then, at the # prompt, type passwd root, and follow the prompts to reset root's password. Finally, type shutdown -r now and the system will reboot and recognize the new password.

16. The capplet that switches your desktop from GNOME to KDE and back is called Desktop Switcher or switchdesk.

17. To undo a change in the GNOME Control Center, click the Revert or Cancel button.

18. A *desktop theme* is a collection of user interface components, including the background, screensaver, mouse cursors, sounds, buttons, checkboxes, scrollbars, and so on, that are similar in both look and feel.

19. The KDE Control Center allows you to customize the background wallpaper, window colors, layout and number of virtual desktops, icon appearance, key bindings, panel behavior, screensaver, window styles, system notifications, change themes, and the taskbar.

20. The GNOME Control Center allows you to customize the desktop wallpaper, panel behavior, screensaver, theme; select the window manager you want to use, to define and redefine MIME type; and configure the properties of the audio CD player, keyboard, mouse, and the behavior of the Sawfish window manager itself.

Saturday Morning Review Answers

1. The Linux file system provides a unified model of all storage in the system. The file system has a single root directory, indicated by a forward slash (/). Then there is a hierarchy of files and directories. Parts of the file system can reside in different hard drives or different partitions of a hard disk.

2. To change to your home directory, you can type cd, cd ~, or cd/home/kwall.

3. The ls -lt command gives a detailed listing of the files in the current directory in order of last modification.

4. The command cd - switches the most recent working directory.

5. You can use the find and locate commands to find a file in the file system. To use the find command to locate a file named book.txt, you could type the command find / -name book.txt -print.

6. Separate multiple commands on the same line using semicolons (;), for example, cd /usr/doc; ls -la. To continue a command on multiple lines, type a backslash (\), and then press Enter after each line.

7. The ls -l /usr/doc | more command uses the output of one command as the input to another.

8. The *I/O redirection* feature of the shell allows you to redirect the standard output, standard input, or standard error of a command or program.

9. The ps ax | grep gnome command line finds all processes with gnome in their names.

10. First, type ps ax | grep gpm to find the process ID of the gpm process. Then, type kill -9 *N* where *N* is the process ID.

11. If the input file is books.txt, use the command sort +3 -u < books.txt.

12. The df -h / shell function displays the amount of used disk space in an easily understood format, such as in megabytes or gigabytes.

13. Type vi /etc/inittab to begin editing the file. Then, type :16 to go to line number 16, press i, and begin typing the line. To save and exit the file, press Esc, and then type :wq to save the file and exit.

14. The `tr -s ' ' <swapme.txt | tr [:lower:] [:upper:]`. swaps the case of letters and converts any sequence of two or more spaces to a single space. The source file is named `swapme.txt`.

15. These are three ways to unpack a file named `unpackme.gz`:

    ```
    gunzip unpackme.gz
    gunzip < unpackme.gz
    gzip -d unpackme.gz
    ```

    Recall that `gunzip` and `gzip` are the same command.

16. The files `zcat`, `zless`, `zgrep`, `zmore`, and `zdiff` let you work with the contents of compressed files without first needing to uncompress the files.

17. You can use the `mount` command to mount file systems. The `rpm` command installs new software packages. You can use the `tar` command to create backups.

18. You can use `netstat` to view information about active network connections, `ifconfig` to check the status of various network interfaces, and `ping` to make sure that a connection is working.

19. You have to enter the login name, the user's home directory, and a password. Linuxconf checks the password for words that can be easily guessed.

20. Edit the `/etc/passwd` file using a text editor like vi. Change the second field (fields are delimited by :) to `*` or change the last field, the login shell, to `/bin/false`.

Saturday Afternoon Review Answers

1. The Linux device name for COM1 is `/dev/ttyS0` and that for COM2 is `/dev/ttyS1`. COM1 uses IRQ 4 and I/O port 0x3f8 whereas COM2 uses IRQ 3 and I/O port 0x2f8.

2. Type `minicom` in a terminal window to start the program. Then type the modem dialing command ATDT followed by the phone number to dial out using Minicom.

3. To be able to run Minicom as an ordinary user, log in as root and, assuming the modem is on COM1, type `chmod o+rw /dev/ttyS0` to give everyone write permission for that device.

4. Type `dmesg | grep ttyS*` or `grep ttyS /var/log/messages` to look for the serial device names ttyS0 or ttyS1 in the output of the commands.

5. You need an Ethernet card and a cable to connect a PC to an Ethernet LAN. 10Base2 refers to Ethernet that uses thin, flexible coaxial cables as the data transmission media. 10BaseT is Ethernet over unshielded twisted-pair (UTP) cables that look like ordinary phone wires.

6. The common TCP/IP diagnostic commands are `/sbin/ifconfig`, `/sbin/route`, `ping`, and `netstat`. Use the `/sbin/ifconfig` command to see if the network interfaces are running and `ping` to see if your Linux system has a network path to another host.

7. A PPP connection puts your PC on the Internet, enabling any application on the PC such as a Web browser or an e-mail program to communicate over the dial-up connection. A regular serial communication program, such as Minicom, exclusively uses dial-up connection. You may not be able to run another copy of Minicom and use the same modem connection, for example.

8. To set up a PPP connection, you need a phone number, a user name and password, and the IP addresses for the Domain Name Server (DNS) from your ISP.

9. On your Linux system, you can run pppd, if up, if down, or the PPP Dialer to set up a PPP connection.

10. You must use the Linux IP masquerading feature to share a single Internet connection with other systems on the LAN. Use the IPCHAINS software (/sbin/ipchains) to set up IP masquerading. The other computers must use the IP address of the Linux system's Ethernet card as their gateway device and the name server addresses listed in the /etc/resolv.conf file on the Linux system.

11. Telnet, FTP, e-mail, and the World Wide Web are some of the common Internet services. A *port* is a number between 1 and 65,535 that uniquely identifies each end point of a TCP/IP communication link between two processes. The /etc/services file contains information about Internet services and the corresponding port numbers.

12. To provide or use an e-mail service, you need a mail transport agent (MTA) and a mail user agent (MUA). Simple Mail Transfer Protocol (SMTP) is the TCP/IP protocol for transporting e-mail between systems.

13. The Apache Web server configuration files are located in the /etc/httpd/conf directory. The /var/log/httpd directory is where the Apache Web server's access logs and error logs are located.

14. The /etc/rc.d/init.d/httpd script starts and stops the httpd process, which controls the Apache Web server.

15. To use anonymous FTP to transfer files to or from a remote system, log in using the user name anonymous. Anyone can use this user name with FTP to transfer files from a system, and provide your e-mail address as the password.

16. To set up a file server with Network File System (NFS), first export one or more directories by listing them in the /etc/exports file. Then, start the NFS server using Linuxconf.

17. To use an NFS exported directory on a client system, mount the directories exported by the server using the mount command.

18. Samba is software that allows your Red Hat Linux system to function as a Windows file and print server. To configure the Samba software to make your Linux system work as a Windows server, edit the Samba configuration file, /etc/smb.conf, and then restart the Samba software using the following command:

    ```
    /etc/rc.d/init.d/smb restart
    ```

19. The following command mounts the /dev/hda2 file system at the mount point /mnt/dos:

    ```
    mount -t vfat /dev/hda4 /mnt/dosc
    ```
    To make sure that Linux automatically mounts /dev/hda2 whenever the system boots, you add the following line to the /etc/fstab file:

    ```
    /dev/hda2  /mnt/dos  vfat    defaults    0 0
    ```

20. The following command copies all files with the .doc extension from a DOS floppy to the current directory on the hard disk:

    mcopy "a:*.doc".

Saturday Evening Review Answers

1. You can customize the look and feel of the GNOME desktop by using the GNOME Control Center.

2. Sawfish is a window manager. It is the default window manager in GNOME. To configure Sawfsh, select Desktop ⇨ Window Manager from the GNOME Control Center menu.

3. To change the default desktop from GNOME to KDE, select the Main menu ⇨ System ⇨ Desktop Switching Tool, and then select KDE as the desktop. To change the default desktop back to GNOME from KDE, use the same desktop switching tool.

4. Use the KDE Control Center to customize various aspects of the KDE desktop. You can customize the background, the window manager, or select a theme for the user interface (UI).

5. To select and try out a screensaver from the GNOME desktop, start the GNOME Control Center by clicking on the toolbox icon on the GNOME Panel, and then select Desktop ⇨ Screensaver from the tree menu in the Control Center.

6. Select K ⇨ KDE Control Center. Then select Desktop ⇨ Screensaver from the tree menu in the KDE Control Center. From there you can select and configure a screen saver.

7. To play the GNOME games, select Main Menu ⇨ Programs ⇨ Games while using the GNOME desktop. AisleRiot, Gnome-Stones, and GNOME Mahjongg are some games in GNOME. AisleRiot is a card-playing program that can play 30 different card games, including well-known ones, such as Freecell and Klondike.

8. Minesweeper, Patience, and Shisen-Sho are some games in KDE. To use them, select K ⇨ Games while using the KDE desktop.

9. Select Main Menu ⇨ KDE Menus ⇨ Games.

10. Use /usr/sbin/sndconfig to start the sound card configuration program, and then follow the program's prompts to configure the sound card.

11. To play audio CDs in Red Hat Linux, you can use xplaycd or the GNOME or KDE CD players.

12. To allow a normal user to play audio CDs, log in as root and type chmod 666 /dev/cdrom.

13. CDDB is a CD database on the Internet. The GNOME CD player gets the song titles from CDDB if your Red Hat Linux system has an active Internet connection.

14. The GIMP and Xpaint are two image manipulation programs that come with Red Hat Linux. The GIMP is a program for viewing images and performing tasks such as photo retouching, image composition, and image creation. Xpaint is a bitmap painting program patterned after MacPaint.

15. Ghostscript is a nearly complete implementation of the PostScript language that enables you to print PostScript documents on many non-PostScript devices.

16. The name of the spreadsheet application is Gnumeric. Gnumeric's default file format is XML (eXtensible Markup Language). Gnumeric can exchange files with Microsoft Excel.

17. You would use the command `aspell check report.txt` to check the spelling of a text file named `report.txt`.

18. The Red Hat Network is a system management tool consisting of Software Manager. Software Manager provides several services, including a software update subscription service, automatic RPM updates, and e-mail notification of bugs and security alerts.

19. First, you must create a system profile, and then register it with the Red Hat Network by sending the file to Red Hat. Next, you have to log in to the Red Hat Network and activate your Software Manager subscription.

20. Log in as `root`, and select Main Menu ⇨ Programs ⇨ System ⇨ Update Agent from the GNOME desktop. Then select the updates, if any are available, that you wish to install on your system. Start the download and installation process by following Update Agent's prompts.

Sunday Morning Review Answers

1. The *X server* is a process that manages a bitmapped display, a keyboard, and a mouse. The X server controls the monitor, the keyboard, and the mouse on behalf of X clients requesting some sort of input or output activity using those devices, such as a request to open a window or draw in a window.

2. The X configuration file is `/etc/X11/XF86Config-4`. You can use `xf86config`, `xf86cfg`, or `Xconfigurator` to create a new X configuration file.

3. If the X graphical screen is partially working, press Ctrl+Alt+F1 to switch to the text console and log in as root at the text login prompt. Then type `telinit 3` to kill the running X server. Next, create a new X configuration file, and type `telinit 5` to restart the graphical display manager. Finally, type Alt+F7 to switch back to the graphical login screen, and press Ctrl+Alt+Backspace to kill the X server and force it to restart with the new configuration file.

4. The `init` runs all other processes on the system. It starts at boot time and is primarily responsible for starting system daemons that provide essential services, and mounting file systems. The contents of the `/etc/inittab` file control `init`'s behavior.

5. Look for the line with the keyword `initdefault` in the third field of the `/etc/inittab` file; the fields are separated by colons (:). The second field of this line specifies the default run level.

6. The `init` process runs the `/etc/rc.d/rc.sysinit` script. This script, in turn, runs many other scripts from the subdirectories in `/etc/rc.d`, especially `/etc/rc.d/init.d`.

7. *RPM* refers to the Red Hat Package Manager, a system for packaging all the necessary files for a software product into a single file known as an *RPM file*, or simply an *RPM*. Red Hat Linux and the bundled applications are distributed in the form of a large number of RPMs.

8. To see if a specific RPM is installed on your system, type the command `rpm -q` *package_name* where *package_name* is the name of the RPM. For example, to see if the `samba` RPM is installed, type `rpm -q samba`.

9. Assuming that the RPM is in the current working directory, type the command `rpm -ivh fortune-mod-1.3.4-59.i386.rpm`.

10. Use the `rpm -e <package>` command or GnoRPM, the GNOME graphical RPM tool, to remove an installed RPM.

11. A few reasons to rebuild the Linux kernel are to bring the compiled version up to date after patching the kernel sources, to add SCSI support directly into the kernel, and to add support for hardware that was unsupported when you originally installed Red Hat Linux.

12. First, install the kernel source code. Next, configure the kernel, compile the kernel, compile the modules, and install the modules and kernel and a few other files.

13. Use the `at` command to submit commands to be executed at a future time. In some cases, the `crontab` facility can be used to run programs automatically at regular intervals.

14. Use cron and the `crontab` command to schedule jobs to run at regular intervals.

15. The 30 23 * * * $HOME/backup.sh command schedules a job named $HOME/backup.sh to run every night of the week at 11:30 p.m.

16. The /etc/cron.allow file lists the names of the users who are allowed to use cron. /etc/cron.deny lists users forbidden to use cron.

17. You can back up files to floppy disks, Zip disks, and SCSI tape drives.

18. To use the `tar` utility to back up the /home file system to a SCSI tape drive, you can type:

    `tar cvf /dev/st0 /home`

19. To back up several large files in the /home/share directory onto multiple floppies, use `tar`'s -M option, which creates multi-volume archives, as shown in the following command:

    `tar -cvMf /dev/fd0 /home/share`

20. To store multiple backup archives on a single tape, use a non-rewinding tape device with a command such as `tar cvf /dev/nst0 /home` and use similar `tar` commands to create one archive after another. Rewind the tape with the following command:

    `mt -f /dev/nst0 rewind`
    Skip over an archive with the following command:

    `mt -f /dev/nst0 fsf 1`

Sunday Afternoon Review Answers

1. Many open source software packages are distributed in source code form without any executable binaries. Before you can use such software, you have to build the executable binary files. That's why it's important to learn how to build software from source files.

2. Open source software is typically distributed in compressed `tar` archives, also known as compressed tarballs. You can download the file using anonymous FTP or through a Web browser. To unpack it, use a command of the form `tar zxvf` *tarball_name* where *tarball_name* is the name of the file you downloaded.

3. After downloading and unpacking the source files, look for files with the names resembling README or INSTALL for instructions on how to build and install the software.

4. First download the file using anonymous FTP. Then use the `tar zxf` command to unpack the file. Next, check the README or INSTALL files, in any, for instructions. In most cases, type `./configure` to configure the software; `make` to build the software; and `make install` to install it.

5. The XMMS package is the X Multimedia System, a graphical X application for playing MP3 and other multimedia files. Build and install XMMS with the command `./configure; make; make install`.

6. Look for information such as CPU usage, physical memory and swap space usage, and hard disk usage to monitor your system's performance.

7. Red Hat Linux includes tools such as the GNOME System Monitor, and the `top`, and `vmstat` commands to monitor system performance.

8. The *system load average* is the average number of processes that were ready to run in the last 1, 5, and 15 minutes.

9. The `vmstat 60 10` command line displays 60-second averages and prints a total of 10 lines of output. The first line of output from `vmstat` shows the averages since the last reboot.

10. The purpose of /proc is to allow users to access information about the Linux kernel and the processes that are currently running on the system.

11. The *security policy* provides the rules you use when setting up your Red Hat Linux system's security. The security policy should address areas such as how users are authenticated, what various users can do, what data must be protected, which Internet services are allowed to run, and who is responsible for maintaining and auditing security.

12. The general steps are to install only those packages that you need, create user accounts with strong passwords, enable only the necessary Internet services, and periodically check log files for signs of break-in attempts. You should also keep up with security news and install upgrades from Red Hat.

13. Shadow passwords and the use of MD5 encryption are two ways in which passwords are made more secure in Red Hat Linux.

14. The `chage -M 30 marys` command line forces the user named `marys` to change her password every 30 days.

15. The `xinetd` server starts Internet services using the TCP wrapper program. As specified in the `/etc/xinetd.conf` file, the `/usr/sbin/tcpd` program starts other services such as FTP and Telnet.

16. The TCP wrapper program provides an access control facility for Internet services started by `xinetd`. Before starting a service using `xinetd`, the TCP wrapper consults the `/etc/hosts.allow` file to see if the host requesting service is allowed that service. If there is nothing in `/etc/hosts.allow` about that host, the TCP wrapper checks the `/etc/hosts.deny` file to see if the service should be denied. If both files are empty, the TCP wrapper allows the host access to the requested service.

17. GNOME Help Browser and KDE Help are two help viewers that you can use to view online help information from the graphical desktops in Red Hat Linux.

18. Type `whatis tr` to read a one-line description of the `tr` command. To view the manual page for the `tr` command, use the command `man tr`.

19. Use the `apropos` command to search for other commands using a keyword.

20. Each `HOWTO` file contains information about some area of Linux, such as how to configure hardware in Linux or how to create a boot disk. If your system is connected to the Internet, you can access the `HOWTO` files by clicking on the LDP icon on the GNOME desktop, and then clicking the link to `HOWTO` documents.

APPENDIX

What's on the CD-ROM?

This appendix provides you with information on the contents of the CD-ROM that accompanies this book.

Two components are included on the CD:

- Red Hat Linux 7.2
- The Red Hat Linux 7.2 Weekend Crash Course Assessment Test

Also included is an electronic, searchable version of the book that can be viewed with Adobe Acrobat Reader.

System Requirements

Make sure that your computer meets the minimum system requirements listed in this section. If your computer doesn't match up to most of these requirements, you may have a problem using the contents of the CD.

- PC with a Pentium processor running at 90 Mhz or faster
- At least 32MB of RAM, 64MB or more if you will use the X Window system
- Between 300MB and 2.4GB of free disk space, depending on installation options (1.2GB or more recommended)
- Ethernet network interface card (NIC) or modem with a speed of at least 28,800 bps
- A CD-ROM drive — double-speed (2x) or faster
- A 3.5" floppy disk drive for creating a boot floppy (optional)

You will need at least 2.4GB of hard drive space to install all the software from this CD.

What's on the CD

The CD-ROM contains source-code examples, applications, and an electronic version of the book. Following is a summary of the contents of the CD-ROM arranged by category.

Red Hat Linux 7.2

The CD-ROMs contain all Red Hat Linux 7.2 binary files with the Linux 2.4.7 kernel, which is the latest version of the Linux kernel available as of this writing (September 2001). In addition to the Linux kernel, Red Hat Linux includes a large selection of Linux applications. Here are some significant software packages on the Red Hat Linux 7.2 CD-ROMs:

- Linux kernel 2.4.7 with driver modules for all major PC hardware configurations, including IDE/EIDE, ATA, and SCSI drives, PCMCIA devices, many USB devices, and CD-ROM drives.
- Complete set of installation and configuration tools for setting up hardware devices (such as disk drives, video hardware, keyboards, and mice) and services.
- Graphical user interface (GUI) based on the XFree86 package with GNOME and KDE desktops.
- Full TCP/IP networking for Internet, LANs, and intranets.
- Tools for connecting your PC to your Internet Service Provider using dedicated connections (such as xDSL), PPP, and dial-up serial communications programs.
- Complete suite of Internet applications, including electronic mail (sendmail, mutt, pine, elm, mail), news (inn, tin, slrn, trn), Internet Relay Chat (ircii), Telnet, FTP, and NFS.
- Apache Web server 1.3.19 (to turn your PC into a Web server), Netscape Communicator 4.77, and Mozilla 0.9 (to surf the Net).
- Samba 2.0.7 LAN Manager software for Microsoft Windows connectivity.
- Several text editors (GNU Emacs 20.7, vim).
- Graphics and image manipulation software, such as The GIMP, XPaint, Ghostscript, Ghostview, and ImageMagick.
- Multimedia applications for playing audio CDs, MP3s, and other sound formats (xplaycd, XMMS 1.2, KSCD 1.3, GTCD 1.2), mixers, sound recorders, and audio meters.
- Programming languages (GNU C and C++ 2.96, Perl 5.6.0, Tcl/Tk 8.3.1, Python 1.5.2, GNU AWK 3.0.6) and software development tools (GNU Debugger 5.0, CVS 1.11, RCS 5.7, GNU Bison 1.28, flex 2.5.4a, TIFF, and JPEG libraries).
- Complete suite of standard UNIX utilities.
- Tools to access and use DOS files and applications (mtools 3.9.7).
- Games such as GNU Chess, Mahjongg, Reversi, Minesweeper, FreeCell, Gnobots, AisleRiot.

Red Hat Linux 7.2 Weekend Crash Course Assessment Test

The CD-ROM contains 60 multiple-choice questions with answers. These test questions serve two purposes. You can use them to assess how much you already know about Red Hat Linux and thereby determine what sessions you can skip. You can also go through the questions after reading individual sessions of this book to assess how much you have learned. The questions are organized by session; therefore they follow the order of topics discussed in this book. The session that each question corresponds with is noted next to each question

Electronic version of Red Hat Linux 7.2 Weekend Crash Course

The complete (and searchable) text of this book is on the CD-ROM in Adobe's Portable Document Format (PDF), readable with the Adobe Acrobat Reader (also included).

Adobe Acrobat Reader 5.0

The CD-ROM contains the latest version of Adobe Systems' Acrobat Reader, which enables you to read the documents in the popular Adobe Portable Document Format (PDF). For more information on Adobe Acrobat Reader, go to http://www.adobe.com/.

Installing Red Hat Linux

We do not have enough space in this short appendix to explain how to install Red Hat Linux from the CD. Please follow the instructions in Sessions 1 through 3 of the book to install Red Hat Linux on your system.

Troubleshooting

If you have difficulty installing or using the CD-ROM programs, try the following solutions:

- **Make sure that your PC's BIOS is correctly configured.** The companion CD-ROM is bootable, but the PC must have booting from a CD-ROM enabled in the BIOS in order for it to work.
- **Create a bootable floppy to install the software.** If you cannot boot from the CD-ROM, use the instructions in Session 1 to create a bootable floppy in order to install the software.

If you still have trouble with the CD, please call the Hungry Minds Customer Service phone number: (800) 762-2974. Outside the United States, call (317) 572-3993. Hungry Minds will provide technical support only for installation and other general quality control items; for technical support on the applications themselves, consult the program's vendor or author.

Index

Continued

Continued

Continued

Continued

redhat®

www.redhat.com

Hungry Minds, Inc.
End-User License Agreement

READ THIS. You should carefully read these terms and conditions before opening the software packet(s) included with this book ("Book"). This is a license agreement ("Agreement") between you and Hungry Minds, Inc. ("HMI"). By opening the accompanying software packet(s), you acknowledge that you have read and accept the following terms and conditions. If you do not agree and do not want to be bound by such terms and conditions, promptly return the Book and the unopened software packet(s) to the place you obtained them for a full refund.

1. **License Grant.** HMI grants to you (either an individual or entity) a nonexclusive license to use one copy of the enclosed software program(s) (collectively, the "Software") solely for your own personal or business purposes on a single computer (whether a standard computer or a workstation component of a multi-user network). The Software is in use on a computer when it is loaded into temporary memory (RAM) or installed into permanent memory (hard disk, CD-ROM, or other storage device). HMI reserves all rights not expressly granted herein.

2. **Ownership.** HMI is the owner of all right, title, and interest, including copyright, in and to the compilation of the Software recorded on the disk(s) or CD-ROM ("Software Media"). Copyright to the individual programs recorded on the Software Media is owned by the author or other authorized copyright owner of each program. Ownership of the Software and all proprietary rights relating thereto remain with HMI and its licensers.

3. **Restrictions on Use and Transfer.**

   (a) You may only (i) make one copy of the Software for backup or archival purposes, or (ii) transfer the Software to a single hard disk, provided that you keep the original for backup or archival purposes. You may not (i) rent or lease the Software, (ii) copy or reproduce the Software through a LAN or other network system or through any computer subscriber system or bulletin-board system, or (iii) modify, adapt, or create derivative works based on the Software.

   (b) You may not reverse engineer, decompile, or disassemble the Software. You may transfer the Software and user documentation on a permanent basis, provided that the transferee agrees to accept the terms and conditions of this Agreement and you retain no copies. If the Software is an update or has been updated, any transfer must include the most recent update and all prior versions.

4. **Restrictions on Use of Individual Programs.** You must follow the individual requirements and restrictions detailed for each individual program in Appendix B of this Book. These limitations are also contained in the individual license agreements recorded on the Software Media. These limitations may include a requirement that after using the program for a specified period of time, the user must pay a registration fee or discontinue use. By opening the Software packet(s), you will be agreeing to abide by the licenses and restrictions for these individual programs that are detailed in Appendix B and on the Software Media. None of the material on this Software Media or listed in this Book may ever be redistributed, in original or modified form, for commercial purposes.

5. **Limited Warranty.**

   (a) HMI warrants that the Software and Software Media are free from defects in materials and workmanship under normal use for a period of sixty (60) days from the date of purchase of this Book. If HMI receives notification within the warranty period of defects in materials or workmanship, HMI will replace the defective Software Media.

(b) HMI AND THE AUTHOR OF THE BOOK DISCLAIM ALL OTHER WARRANTIES, EXPRESS OR IMPLIED, INCLUDING WITHOUT LIMITATION IMPLIED WARRANTIES OF MERCHANTABILITY AND FITNESS FOR A PARTICULAR PURPOSE, WITH RESPECT TO THE SOFTWARE, THE PROGRAMS, THE SOURCE CODE CONTAINED THEREIN, AND/OR THE TECHNIQUES DESCRIBED IN THIS BOOK. HMI DOES NOT WARRANT THAT THE FUNCTIONS CONTAINED IN THE SOFTWARE WILL MEET YOUR REQUIREMENTS OR THAT THE OPERATION OF THE SOFTWARE WILL BE ERROR FREE.

(c) This limited warranty gives you specific legal rights, and you may have other rights that vary from jurisdiction to jurisdiction.

6. **Remedies.**

(a) HMI's entire liability and your exclusive remedy for defects in materials and workmanship shall be limited to replacement of the Software Media, which may be returned to HMI with a copy of your receipt at the following address: Software Media Fulfillment Department, Attn.: *Red Hat Linux 7.2 Weekend Crash Course*, Hungry Minds, Inc., 10475 Crosspoint Blvd., Indianapolis, IN 46256, or call 1-800-762-2974. Please allow four to six weeks for delivery. This Limited Warranty is void if failure of the Software Media has resulted from accident, abuse, or misapplication. Any replacement Software Media will be warranted for the remainder of the original warranty period or thirty (30) days, whichever is longer.

(b) In no event shall HMI or the author be liable for any damages whatsoever (including without limitation damages for loss of business profits, business interruption, loss of business information, or any other pecuniary loss) arising from the use of or inability to use the Book or the Software, even if HMI has been advised of the possibility of such damages.

(c) Because some jurisdictions do not allow the exclusion or limitation of liability for consequential or incidental damages, the above limitation or exclusion may not apply to you.

7. **U.S. Government Restricted Rights.** Use, duplication, or disclosure of the Software for or on behalf of the United States of America, its agencies and/or instrumentalities (the "U.S. Government") is subject to restrictions as stated in paragraph (c)(1)(ii) of the Rights in Technical Data and Computer Software clause of DFARS 252.227-7013, or subparagraphs (c)(1) and (2) of the Commercial Computer Software - Restricted Rights clause at FAR 52.227-19, and in similar clauses in the NASA FAR supplement, as applicable.

8. **General.** This Agreement constitutes the entire understanding of the parties and revokes and supersedes all prior agreements, oral or written, between them and may not be modified or amended except in a writing signed by both parties hereto that specifically refers to this Agreement. This Agreement shall take precedence over any other documents that may be in conflict herewith. If any one or more provisions contained in this Agreement are held by any court or tribunal to be invalid, illegal, or otherwise unenforceable, each and every other provision shall remain in full force and effect.

GNU General Public License

Version 2, June 1991

Copyright © 1989, 1991 Free Software Foundation, Inc.

59 Temple Place, Suite 330, Boston, MA 02111-1307, USA

Preamble

The licenses for most software are designed to take away your freedom to share and change it. By contrast, the GNU General Public License is intended to guarantee your freedom to share and change free software — to make sure the software is free for all its users. This General Public License applies to most of the Free Software Foundation's software and to any other program whose authors commit to using it. (Some other Free Software Foundation software is covered by the GNU Library General Public License instead.) You can apply it to your programs, too.

When we speak of free software, we are referring to freedom, not price. Our General Public Licenses are designed to make sure that you have the freedom to distribute copies of free software (and charge for this service if you wish), that you receive source code or can get it if you want it, that you can change the software or use pieces of it in new free programs; and that you know you can do these things.

To protect your rights, we need to make restrictions that forbid anyone to deny you these rights or to ask you to surrender the rights. These restrictions translate to certain responsibilities for you if you distribute copies of the software, or if you modify it.

For example, if you distribute copies of such a program, whether gratis or for a fee, you must give the recipients all the rights that you have. You must make sure that they, too, receive or can get the source code. And you must show them these terms so they know their rights.

We protect your rights with two steps: (1) copyright the software, and (2) offer you this license which gives you legal permission to copy, distribute and/or modify the software.

Also, for each author's protection and ours, we want to make certain that everyone understands that there is no warranty for this free software. If the software is modified by someone else and passed on, we want its recipients to know that what they have is not the original, so that any problems introduced by others will not reflect on the original authors' reputations.

Finally, any free program is threatened constantly by software patents. We wish to avoid the danger that redistributors of a free program will individually obtain patent licenses, in effect making the program proprietary. To prevent this, we have made it clear that any patent must be licensed for everyone's free use or not licensed at all.

The precise terms and conditions for copying, distribution and modification follow.

Terms and Conditions for Copying, Distribution, and Modification

0. This License applies to any program or other work which contains a notice placed by the copyright holder saying it may be distributed under the terms of this General Public License. The "Program", below, refers to any such program or work, and a "work based on the Program" means either the Program or any derivative work under copyright law: that is to say, a work containing the Program or a portion of it, either verbatim or with modifications and/or translated into another language. (Hereinafter, translation is included without limitation in the term "modification".) Each licensee is addressed as "you".

   Activities other than copying, distribution and modification are not covered by this License; they are outside its scope. The act of running the Program is not restricted, and the output from the Program is covered only if its contents constitute a work based on the Program (independent of having been made by running the Program). Whether that is true depends on what the Program does.

1. You may copy and distribute verbatim copies of the Program's source code as you receive it, in any medium, provided that you conspicuously and appropriately publish on each copy an appropriate copyright notice and disclaimer of warranty; keep intact all the notices that refer to this License and to the absence of any warranty; and give any other recipients of the Program a copy of this License along with the Program.

   You may charge a fee for the physical act of transferring a copy, and you may at your option offer warranty protection in exchange for a fee.

2. You may modify your copy or copies of the Program or any portion of it, thus forming a work based on the Program, and copy and distribute such modifications or work under the terms of Section 1 above, provided that you also meet all of these conditions:

   a) You must cause the modified files to carry prominent notices stating that you changed the files and the date of any change.

   b) You must cause any work that you distribute or publish, that in whole or in part contains or is derived from the Program or any part thereof, to be licensed as a whole at no charge to all third parties under the terms of this License.

   c) If the modified program normally reads commands interactively when run, you must cause it, when started running for such interactive use in the most ordinary way, to print or display an announcement including an appropriate copyright notice and a notice that there is no warranty (or else, saying that you provide a warranty) and that users may redistribute the program under these conditions, and telling the user how to view a copy of this License. (Exception: if the Program itself is interactive but does not normally print such an announcement, your work based on the Program is not required to print an announcement.)

   These requirements apply to the modified work as a whole. If identifiable sections of that work are not derived from the Program, and can be reasonably considered independent and separate works in themselves, then this License, and its terms, do not apply to those sections when you distribute them as separate works. But when you distribute the same sections as part of a whole which is a work based on the Program, the distribution of the whole must be on the terms of this License, whose permissions for other licensees extend to the entire whole, and thus to each and every part regardless of who wrote it.

Thus, it is not the intent of this section to claim rights or contest your rights to work written entirely by you; rather, the intent is to exercise the right to control the distribution of derivative or collective works based on the Program.

In addition, mere aggregation of another work not based on the Program with the Program (or with a work based on the Program) on a volume of a storage or distribution medium does not bring the other work under the scope of this License.

3. You may copy and distribute the Program (or a work based on it, under Section 2) in object code or executable form under the terms of Sections 1 and 2 above provided that you also do one of the following:

   a) Accompany it with the complete corresponding machine-readable source code, which must be distributed under the terms of Sections 1 and 2 above on a medium customarily used for software interchange; or,

   b) Accompany it with a written offer, valid for at least three years, to give any third party, for a charge no more than your cost of physically performing source distribution, a complete machine-readable copy of the corresponding source code, to be distributed under the terms of Sections 1 and 2 above on a medium customarily used for software interchange; or,

   c) Accompany it with the information you received as to the offer to distribute corresponding source code. (This alternative is allowed only for noncommercial distribution and only if you received the program in object code or executable form with such an offer, in accord with Subsection b above.)

The source code for a work means the preferred form of the work for making modifications to it. For an executable work, complete source code means all the source code for all modules it contains, plus any associated interface definition files, plus the scripts used to control compilation and installation of the executable. However, as a special exception, the source code distributed need not include anything that is normally distributed (in either source or binary form) with the major components (compiler, kernel, and so on) of the operating system on which the executable runs, unless that component itself accompanies the executable.

If distribution of executable or object code is made by offering access to copy from a designated place, then offering equivalent access to copy the source code from the same place counts as distribution of the source code, even though third parties are not compelled to copy the source along with the object code.

4. You may not copy, modify, sublicense, or distribute the Program except as expressly provided under this License. Any attempt otherwise to copy, modify, sublicense or distribute the Program is void, and will automatically terminate your rights under this License. However, parties who have received copies, or rights, from you under this License will not have their licenses terminated so long as such parties remain in full compliance.

5. You are not required to accept this License, since you have not signed it. However, nothing else grants you permission to modify or distribute the Program or its derivative works. These actions are prohibited by law if you do not accept this License. Therefore, by modifying or distributing the Program (or any work based on the Program), you indicate your acceptance of this License to do so, and all its terms and conditions for copying, distributing or modifying the Program or works based on it.

6. Each time you redistribute the Program (or any work based on the Program), the recipient automatically receives a license from the original licensor to copy, distribute or modify the Program subject to these terms and conditions. You may not impose any further restrictions on the recipients' exercise of the rights granted herein. You are not responsible for enforcing compliance by third parties to this License.

7. If, as a consequence of a court judgment or allegation of patent infringement or for any other reason (not limited to patent issues), conditions are imposed on you (whether by court order, agreement or otherwise) that contradict the conditions of this License, they do not excuse you from the conditions of this License. If you cannot distribute so as to satisfy simultaneously your obligations under this License and any other pertinent obligations, then as a consequence you may not distribute the Program at all. For example, if a patent license would not permit royalty-free redistribution of the Program by all those who receive copies directly or indirectly through you, then the only way you could satisfy both it and this License would be to refrain entirely from distribution of the Program.

    If any portion of this section is held invalid or unenforceable under any particular circumstance, the balance of the section is intended to apply and the section as a whole is intended to apply in other circumstances.

    It is not the purpose of this section to induce you to infringe any patents or other property right claims or to contest validity of any such claims; this section has the sole purpose of protecting the integrity of the free software distribution system, which is implemented by public license practices. Many people have made generous contributions to the wide range of software distributed through that system in reliance on consistent application of that system; it is up to the author/donor to decide if he or she is willing to distribute software through any other system and a licensee cannot impose that choice.

    This section is intended to make thoroughly clear what is believed to be a consequence of the rest of this License.

8. If the distribution and/or use of the Program is restricted in certain countries either by patents or by copyrighted interfaces, the original copyright holder who places the Program under this License may add an explicit geographical distribution limitation excluding those countries, so that distribution is permitted only in or among countries not thus excluded. In such case, this License incorporates the limitation as if written in the body of this License.

9. The Free Software Foundation may publish revised and/or new versions of the General Public License from time to time. Such new versions will be similar in spirit to the present version, but may differ in detail to address new problems or concerns.

    Each version is given a distinguishing version number. If the Program specifies a version number of this License which applies to it and "any later version", you have the option of following the terms and conditions either of that version or of any later version published by the Free Software Foundation. If the Program does not specify a version number of this License, you may choose any version ever published by the Free Software Foundation.

10. If you wish to incorporate parts of the Program into other free programs whose distribution conditions are different, write to the author to ask for permission. For software which is copyrighted by the Free Software Foundation, write to the Free Software Foundation; we sometimes make exceptions for this. Our decision will be guided by the two goals of preserving the free status of all derivatives of our free software and of promoting the sharing and reuse of software generally.

No Warranty

11. BECAUSE THE PROGRAM IS LICENSED FREE OF CHARGE, THERE IS NO WARRANTY FOR THE PROGRAM, TO THE EXTENT PERMITTED BY APPLICABLE LAW. EXCEPT WHEN OTHERWISE STATED IN WRITING THE COPYRIGHT HOLDERS AND/OR OTHER PARTIES PROVIDE THE PROGRAM "AS IS" WITHOUT WARRANTY OF ANY KIND, EITHER EXPRESSED OR IMPLIED, INCLUDING, BUT NOT LIMITED TO, THE IMPLIED WARRANTIES OF MERCHANTABILITY AND FITNESS FOR A PARTICULAR PURPOSE. THE ENTIRE RISK AS TO THE QUALITY AND PERFORMANCE OF THE PROGRAM IS WITH YOU. SHOULD THE PROGRAM PROVE DEFECTIVE, YOU ASSUME THE COST OF ALL NECESSARY SERVICING, REPAIR OR CORRECTION.

12. IN NO EVENT UNLESS REQUIRED BY APPLICABLE LAW OR AGREED TO IN WRITING WILL ANY COPYRIGHT HOLDER, OR ANY OTHER PARTY WHO MAY MODIFY AND/OR REDISTRIBUTE THE PROGRAM AS PERMITTED ABOVE, BE LIABLE TO YOU FOR DAMAGES, INCLUDING ANY GENERAL, SPECIAL, INCIDENTAL OR CONSEQUENTIAL DAMAGES ARISING OUT OF THE USE OR INABILITY TO USE THE PROGRAM (INCLUDING BUT NOT LIMITED TO LOSS OF DATA OR DATA BEING RENDERED INACCURATE OR LOSSES SUSTAINED BY YOU OR THIRD PARTIES OR A FAILURE OF THE PROGRAM TO OPERATE WITH ANY OTHER PROGRAMS), EVEN IF SUCH HOLDER OR OTHER PARTY HAS BEEN ADVISED OF THE POSSIBILITY OF SUCH DAMAGES.

End Of Terms And Conditions

CD-ROM Installation Instructions

The CD-ROM that comes with this book contains a copy of Red Hat Linux 8.0 Publisher's Edition.

The most common installation method is to insert the installation CD-ROM into your CD-ROM drive and restart your computer. When the computer restarts, the CD-ROM will start the installation procedure.

Follow the instructions to install Red Hat Linux 8.0.

Enjoy!